Pete Dunne
on Bird Watching

BOOKS BY PETE DUNNE

Pete Dunne
on Bird Watching

The How-to, Where-to, and When-to of Birding

PETE DUNNE

Houghton Mifflin Company
BOSTON   NEW YORK   2003

Library of Congress Cataloging-in-Publication Data

Dunne, Pete, date.
    Pete Dunne on bird watching : the how-to, where-to,
and when-to of birding / Pete Dunne.
      p. cm.
    Includes bibliographical references (p.).
    ISBN 0-395-90686-5
    1. Bird attracting. 2. Bird watching. I. Title.

QL676.2 .D85   2003
598'.07'234—dc21   2002027558

Book design by Anne Chalmers
Typefaces: Minion, Nueva, and Scala Sans

Printed in the United States of America

QUM 10 9 8 7 6 5 4 3 2 1

THIS BOOK IS DEDICATED TO
THE BOY WHO CLIMBED SWEDE HILL

Acknowledgments

Were honesty to be served, the names of those found here would be as deserving as mine to appear on the cover of this book. As in the spirit of birding itself, *Pete Dunne on Bird Watching* was very much a community effort. Accordingly, I extend to all who gave generously of their time and expertise my sincere thanks, and I ask, in the name of courtesy, that you offer them yours as well. "They" being...

Scott Edwards, Victor Emanuel, Don Freiday, Daphne Gemmill, Eldon Greij, Michael Hannisian, Tom Hince, Paul Kerlinger, Dan Klem, Paul Lehman, Judy Toups, Dick Walton, Peggy Wang, Karen Williams, and Sheri Williamson, for writing one (or more) sidebars on subjects that command their expertise;

Tom Barnes, Alicia Craig, Bucky Dennerlein, Pat Hayward, Lynn Kaufman, Susan Lenard, Greg Oskay, Chuck Otte, Reese Partridge, Wayne Petersen, Carol Pollard, Patty Van Vlack, and Karen Williams, for offering readers their region-tailored selections for natural plantings, and Pat Hayward, who orchestrated their efforts;

And Cindy Lippincott and Bob Berman, who exercised both cerebral and microchip magic to provide me with the updated American Birding Association bird checklist and the list of name changes that appear in appendix 2; Matt Pelikan, also of ABA, who provided the ABA code of ethics and compiled a list of hotline numbers; and Greg Butcher, former executive director of ABA, who granted the requisite permission.

It should surprise no one who understands writers and writing that elements of this book have previously surfaced as articles or essays in assorted other publications. Many of the thoughts and words that were the basis for columns in *Birding*'s "Tools of the Trade" and

"Building Birding Skills," as well as "Pete Dunne's Birding Tip of the Month" (written for *WildBird*), are born again here. Columns from *New Jersey Audubon* magazine and the New Jersey Sunday section of the *New York Times* also figure in the text.

Special thanks are extended to Swarovski Optik of North America, which allowed me to incorporate into chapter 2 elements of a brochure first written for it, on choosing optics; and to Nikon Sports Optics, for like graciousness and like-mindedness with regard to much of the text and organization of chapter 3.

Thanks also to Jane Crowley of Wild Bird Centers for assistance in preparing table 1.1, linking birds and seed, in chapter 1, and to Robin Clark of Robin's Wood Ltd. for compiling size specs for nest holes (table 1.2). Speaking of chapter 1, much credit and thanks go to Scott Edwards, proprietor of the Wild Bird Center in Aston, Pennsylvania, who offered primary insight, reflective review, and most of all, his expertise.

The photos that enliven this book were provided by a select and talented host. Recognized with thanks, they are Linda Dunne, Kevin Karlson, Brian O'Doherty, Noble Proctor, Frank Schleicher, Clay and Pat Sutton, Ted Swem, and Mark Wilson. Product photos were provided by Coveside, Droll Yankees, Inc., Leica Sports Optics, Swarovski Optik of North America, Inc., Woodlink, and the New Jersey Audubon Society. This acknowledgment also gives me leave to offer special recognition to the members and staff of the New Jersey Audubon Society, the organization that it has been my privilege to be part of for over twenty-five years. If there is a finer conservation organization on this planet, its existence escapes me.

No acknowledgment would be complete without my sincere expression of thanks to Judy Toups and Dorothy Clair, who have so often been called upon to serve as editors and friends, to Paul J. Baicich, whose review of the final draft made this a much better book (and saved me considerable embarrassment), and to Linda, my wife, who of course and with no need for explanation figures in everything.

Contents

Introduction

EVERY MONDAY, 7:30 A.M., SOUTH CAPE MAY

The parking lot had ten cars in it—about average for a Monday in early July. Come September, when bird migration runs full bore and birders are packing Cape May motels, the lot is full.

I parked in a spot that promised shade. Reached for the binoculars that live under the driver's seat. Extracted myself from the car, exhumed my spotting scope from the trunk, then paused, filtering the world through senses refined by more than forty years of birding.

The silhouette on the utility line belonged to the local mockingbird. My ears told me he was running through his standard repertoire (which even by mockingbird standards was considerable).

Audio reconnaissance also detected the spiraling yodel of a descending yellowlegs, a migrating shorebird, and the silver-toned call notes of Bobolinks migrating high overhead.

All the signs suggested a good day's birding, maybe even a great day's birding. Every morning I wake up carries this potential.

"Good morning," I said to the semicircle of faces. "I'm director of New Jersey Audubon Society's Cape May Bird Observatory. *You* have very cleverly positioned yourself at the crossroads of migration at the junction of three seasons."

I paused, allowing time for this disclosure to sink in. When most people think of bird migration, they focus upon the peak congestion periods in the spring and fall. The fact is that over much of North America birds are shifting constantly — from north to south, south to north, interior to coast, higher elevation to lower; from places with exhausted resources to places offering birds greater opportunity.

What this means for people who watch birds is that *every* trip afield is a treasure hunt with endless possibilities. Making the most of these opportunities is a matter of getting the right equipment, putting yourself in fortune's path, and learning how and where to look.

Topics which are, not coincidentally, central to this book.

Assisting me on my morning walk were two of Cape May Bird Observatory's associate naturalists. Tom Parsons, a retired professor of vertebrate biology, has been a birder all his life. Bill Glaser, a former engraver, took up birding after retirement. Together they make a wonderfully balanced team and a good point: *shared interest,* not experience, is the common denominator in birding. It truly doesn't matter if you started birding yesterday, last year, or before field guides were invented. All birders, no matter what their skill level, are drawn to the same thing: the excitement, the challenge, and the pleasure that comes from watching birds. And all birders are eager to share their knowledge with others, an ethic that is fundamental to field trips and, as you will discover, this book.

I resumed my litany, explaining to regulars and newcomers alike what we were about to do, how long we would be about it, and what

The author among a group of fellow birders at Ding Darling National Wildlife Refuge in Florida. *Linda Dunne.*

special birds of the season we were likely to encounter. As I spoke, I tried to gauge the skill levels of my listeners, to discern who might need extra attention or guidance. It seemed a pretty eclectic group.

Several individuals armed with high-quality, well-used binoculars were evidently serious birders who knew Cape May's fame and had probably come with a shopping list of species they hoped to see.

Most of the members of the group, however, looked more casually interested in birds. Several were carrying bird guides that might have been useful for back-yard bird watching but whose deficiencies made them more hindrance than help in the field. Even people who are casual about birding shouldn't be frustrated by it. I made a mental note to engage them during the walk and recommend a more field-worthy guide.

Far too many individuals were armed with binoculars that wouldn't pass muster—gimmick-ridden instruments that were too large, too small, or too poorly designed to be useful in the birding arena. We'd replace these with instruments from our arsenal of well-chosen loaners.

There were also a number of people, including a family of four, who were clearly beginners. The birds, the names, the skills, the etiquette, the very process of seeing a bird critically, noting distinguishing characteristics, and finding its likeness in a book, would be new to them.

This process, which binds a bird with its name, is replicated in this book. While the information in this book is intended to serve birders of all interests and skill levels, it has been organized to follow the developmental stages that birders go through as their interest develops and their horizons expand.

Must you read this book just to go out and look at birds? No. You can do what I did at the age of seven. Grab binoculars. Run out the back door. Start peering into the trees.

But you will discover (if you have not already) that there is a vast difference between looking for birds and finding them. While looking is fun, finding is *more* fun. And being able to identify what you find is the most fun of all. If forty years ago I had had this book, I would have

1
Back-yard Birding, Front-seat Adventure

Stefancik's Corollary

Mr. Stefancik was standing at the blackboard, expounding upon the wonders of decimal points and fractions. I was watching the clock, sweating out the closing seconds of math class.

Why (I demanded of an unsympathetic universe) did two plus two *always* have to equal four? It rigged the universe. It stifled creativity. It made everything so predictably *boring.*

And *why* (I wailed in my mind) would anyone want to take a perfectly good number like one and divide it by a nice number like three, to get a product that was less than either? It made about as much sense as taking good sunflower seed and diluting it with a cheap mix to attract fewer birds at a feeder.

Which is what I lived for. The time spent with nose pressed to the window watching birds coming to my feeders. All I knew (or cared) about fractions was that fifty cents on the dollar would buy one whole bag of seed, which equaled hours of in-your-face looks at . . .

Nuthatches, Mourning Doves, and tree sparrows! White-throated Sparrows, goldfinches, and Song Sparrows!

Blue Jays! (of the haughty stance). *Titmice!* (of the baleful eyes). *Chickadees!* (of the quicksilver reflexes). And every once in a while (hold your breath, don't move a muscle), an adult, male . . .

Cardinal! Wow!

What (I demanded of Mr. Stefancik's back) was some stupid, universal, mathematical principle next to something as incredible as a cardinal?

That's what *I* wanted to know.

The second hand met the two other hands already joined at the twelve. Halfway to the door I was stopped by the voice of Mr. Stefancik.

"Mr. Dunne. Can I see you for a moment, please?"

I approached the instructor's desk for the usual admonishment. Mr. Stefancik produced a corner-thumbed notebook with "Bird Sightings" written across the front. My notebook.

"I'm only guessing this is yours," he said. "There's no name in it. But I found it under your desk."

I didn't know what to do. It wasn't cool to admit that you were a bird watcher — not in seventh grade, not in 1964. Still, I wanted that book. All my sightings were in it. All my observations. Notes about the kind of seed Blue Jays prefer and pencil sketches of all my feeder regulars.

"That's top-secret stuff," I said.

"I understand," he said, lowering his voice but not his eyes. "I like birds too."

"Oh," I said, startled by the disclosure. Then, taking my book, mumbling my thanks, I headed for the door, marveling that an adult (and a math teacher!) could have the same interest I did. It made me wonder whether bird watching was maybe more popular than I'd imagined.

Just three of North America's estimated 63 million (or so) bird watchers. *Linda Dunne.*

America's Fastest-Growing Outdoor Activity

If you enjoy watching birds, you stand in good company. There are, in the estimate of the National Survey on Recreation and the Environment (U.S. Forest Service), 70 million bird watchers in the United States (and an equally representative number in Canada) — people who in the course of their lives make time to see and enjoy birds.

Some are very dedicated, traveling widely and frequently to view new species or gain greater bird-finding or identification skills. These are the people commonly called **birders.**

Most people who enjoy birds are more temperate in scope, if not enthusiasm. They are most fascinated by the birds they find in their own yards. These people are frequently referred to as **bird watchers.**

But there is no sharp distinction between a birder and a bird watcher — since all birders are bird watchers, and bird watchers differ in terms of how much, or little, birds mean to them. In a 1994 survey of members of the **American Birding Association** (the organization that caters to North America's most avid and travel-minded birders), 82 percent said that they feed birds in their yard — for no other reason than the pleasure this brings.

The Four Pillars of a Bird-filled Yard

There are *many* things that homeowners can do to attract birds to their yards. The trick is to offer birds what they need — and their needs are fundamentally simple: food, water, shelter, and a place to rear their young.

Setting the Table for Birds

THE MYTH OF SEED AND NEED

One of my earliest memories is of a paralyzing snowfall and my mom throwing bread into the snow to feed the hungry birds. It was a generous gesture, but it didn't do much for the birds. First, bread isn't particularly good for birds. It provides calories but little nutrition. Second, birds do not *need* handouts to survive. A bird-feeding station provides, at best, a supplement to the nutritional needs of birds. Birds will take advantage of your generosity. They will rely more heavily on your offerings when snow or ice covers natural food stocks or when temperatures fall and their energy requirements rise. But wild birds are far from dependent upon your offerings of food — even if you are offering the right food items. That's why they are called *wild* birds.

WHAT THEY NEED . . .

. . . differs from species to species. Most birds are not seed-eaters. Even many species that feed primarily upon seeds, berries, or fruit during the winter are **insectivorous.** But in winter, when cold temperatures enfold much of North America and most insect-*dependent* species have withdrawn to warmer climates, seed-eating and berry-eating species dominate the North American landscape. Seed is key to attracting birds to your yard in winter.

NOT JUST ANY OLD SEED WILL DO

A bag of **mixed birdseed** from the average local supermarket may or may not provide the types and amount of seed that birds favor. The primary ingredient of any birdseed mix should be **black-oil sunflower**

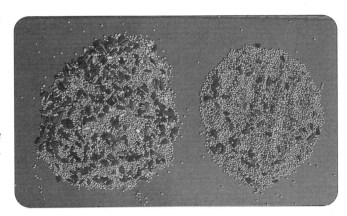

High-quality seed (left), poor-quality seed (right). The proof is in the amount of black-oil sunflower seed—a favorite seed type for many species. *Kevin Karlson.*

seed. Smaller and darker than **striped sunflower** (the grosbeak's delight), black-oil is a favorite of chickadees, Purple Finches, and Northern Cardinals. It also rates high with House Finches and Mourning Doves.

Other favored seeds include **peanut kernels** (a perennial favorite of jays and titmice) and **white proso millet** (top-rated by Mourning Doves and ranked high by assorted sparrow species). Any seed mix that offers a high percentage of these seed types will attract a variety of species.

Milo, flax, rapeseed, cracked corn, and canary seed are all **filler seed** and are considerably less attractive to birds. They are less expensive to buy, but birds vote with their beaks. The seed they don't want they **bill-sweep** aside to get to the quality items. All the seed piled beneath the bird feeder (now providing nutritional support for rats and mice) is the cheap "filler" you paid for.

TABLE 1.1: Preferred Foods of Some Common, Seed-Eating Back-yard Birds

BIRD SPECIES	PREFERRED SEED
Flickers	Hulled sunflower, peanut kernels
Jays	Peanut kernels, sunflower seed of all types
Black-billed Magpie	Peanuts in the shell, peanut kernels
Titmice	Peanut kernels, black-striped and black-oil sunflower

BIRD SPECIES	PREFERRED SEED
Chickadees	Black-oil and striped sunflower, peanut kernels
White-breasted Nuthatch	Striped sunflower, peanuts
Red-breasted Nuthatch	Striped sunflower, black-oil sunflower
Brown Thrasher	Hulled and striped sunflower
European Starling	Peanut hearts, hulled oats, cracked corn
Northern Cardinal	Sunflower seed of all types
Towhees	White proso millet
Song, Tree, Field, Chipping, and Fox Sparrows	White proso millet
Juncos	White proso millet
White-crowned and Golden-crowned Sparrows	Black-oil and hulled sunflower, white proso millet, peanuts, niger
Red-winged Blackbird	White proso millet
Brown-headed Cowbird	White proso millet
Common Grackle	Striped sunflower, hulled sunflower, cracked corn
House Sparrow	White proso millet, canary seed
Pine Siskin	Sunflower seed of all types, thistle
Goldfinches	Hulled sunflower, thistle, black-oil sunflower
Crossbills	Black-oil and striped sunflower
Redpolls	Thistle, hulled sunflower bits
Rosy Finch	Hulled and black-oil sunflower, white proso millet, cracked corn
Purple Finch	Sunflower seed of all types
Cassin's Finch	Hulled and black-oil sunflower
House Finch	Sunflower seed of all types, thistle
Grosbeaks	Sunflower seed of all types

Selections courtesy of Wild Bird Centers of America, Inc., and Scott Edwards.

Bird-feeding Myths

Bird watching, like most avocations, has its share of myths. Here are a few of the most common misconceptions.

❧ You shouldn't feed birds during warmer weather. There are no sound scientific data to support this notion. In fact, breeding season is a time of great stress for birds, and during this time feeders become the avian equivalent of fast-food restaurants — a quick bite to eat for overworked parents. Also, if you feed birds only in the winter, you miss the migratory visitors passing through your area as well as young birds that would otherwise learn that your yard is a good place to visit.

∾ BIRDS WON'T MIGRATE WHEN THEY ARE SUPPOSED TO IF THERE IS FOOD AVAILABLE. Some species shift their populations in response to the absence or presence of food, but most birds do not. Many migratory birds begin their migrations while there are still ample food supplies on their breeding grounds. A few pounds of sunflower seed is not going to derail thousands of years of evolution. Besides, many of the birds that visit feeders are year-round residents.

∾ HUMMINGBIRD "JUICE" MUST BE RED TO BE EFFECTIVE. This is one that just won't go away. If you were to milk a flower that a hummingbird was visiting, you would find nectar that is quite clear. A mixture of four or five parts water to one part ordinary table sugar, boiled well and cooled, is the appropriate recipe. Hummingbirds *are* very attracted to the color red, but any hummingbird feeder worth using will be more than red enough to serve that purpose.

∾ BIRDS' FEET WILL FREEZE TO METAL PERCHES. Birds' feet are dry and scaly, more like bone than skin. They are not inherently moist and therefore will not freeze on contact with cold metal. Imagine how long you would have to leave a chicken bone on a piece of metal to get it to freeze there.

— **Scott Edwards**

Scott Edwards is the owner-proprietor of the successful Wild Bird Center store in Aston, Pennsylvania.

BIRD FEEDER?

While some bird species, like juncos, towhees, and assorted sparrows, readily forage on the ground, others prefer an elevated platform or feeder.

Different types of **bird feeders** offer different advantages and cater to different species. The basic feeder types are the **platform feeder,** the **hopper feeder,** and the **tube feeder.**

The most basic feeder is a platform feeder (lower). A hopper feeder (upper) offers birds more protection and a reservoir for seed. *Woodlink.*

Platform Feeder

The simplest feeder is a platform feeder — an elevated surface, usually square or rectangular, with a raised lip to keep the seed on board. Platform feeders are usually attached to a pole or a window sill; less often they are suspended from a branch, hook, or wire. They can also be set very close (four to eight inches) to the ground, where they will appeal to ground-feeding species.

ADVANTAGES: Platform feeders offer free and open access to all bird species, particularly larger species like magpies and other jays. They also offer optimum viewing opportunity, because there is nothing to block your view. They can hold all manner of attractive (and difficult to dispense) food offerings, such as assorted large seeds, fruit, or mealworms.

DISADVANTAGES: One large species can dominate the entire feeder, preventing other birds from feeding. Seed is unprotected and, when wet, turns into birdseed mush. Since there is no seed reservoir, the feeder must also be refilled often and cleaned frequently.

FEATURES TO LOOK FOR: Strong wire-mesh bottom to let water drain off and facilitate cleaning or, with wooden-based feeders, drainage ports.

Hopper Feeder

A modified platform feeder, commonly made of wood, offers a seed-dispensing reservoir with a roof to protect the seed. Hoppers can be

A variation on the hopper feeder theme—this one, manufactured by Woodlink, features dual seed compartments along with obviously sturdy construction. *Woodlink.*

mounted on a pole or suspended from a wire. Their large capacity — reservoirs can hold from two to twenty-five pounds of seed — makes them maintenance-friendly. Well-designed hoppers, offering large landing platforms (not perches, which are shunned by some species) and ample room for birds to dip and feed (without bumping their heads against the food reservoir), are almost as bird-friendly as open platform feeders.

ADVANTAGES: Less maintenance than platform feeders. Attractive to a large number of species.

DISADVANTAGES: Depending upon position, hopper may block your view of the birds. Dispenses seed only. Is more expensive than a simple platform.

FEATURES TO LOOK FOR: Sturdy construction. Large landing area. Generous seed-dispensing slot. Metal-screen feeding surfaces or drainage openings at the corners.

Tube Feeder

A long, cylindrical feeder, most often plastic, affixed with two to ten perches that allow birds to draw seed through openings in the tube. This is an **exclusionary feeder,** designed to dispense specific types of seed and cater to smaller and more acrobatic species (although large tube feeders can be fitted with base trays that collect seed so as to accommodate larger birds).

The tube feeder is an exclusionary feeder. Smaller, more acrobatic species can use it; larger species can't. *Woodlink.*

ADVANTAGES: Attractive to smaller, easily displaced bird species. Easy to hang, maintain, fill.

DISADVANTAGES: Not attractive to many larger species. Poor designs sometimes cause birds to strangle in the seed ports, or unused seed and hulls can jam lower ports. Fairly expensive.

FEATURES TO LOOK FOR: Openings that offer unencumbered access to seed. Interior baffles that funnel seed to the lower ports and prevent it from collecting at the bottom of the tube (tempting birds to reach too deep, get their heads caught, and strangle).

SPECIALTY FEEDERS

Thistle Feeders

Thistle feeders are modified tube feeders that dispense **niger** (pronounced "ny-jur") seed — a tiny, caraway-shaped seed that goldfinches, siskins, and redpolls treat like opium (and vendors price like platinum). Perches are sometimes placed *above* the tiny openings — a refinement that favors smaller acrobatic species and discourages House Finches (which in some places, by dint of sheer numbers, crowd out other species). **Thistle socks,** nylon mesh dis-

Thistle feeders are a specialty feeder designed to dispense a specific food type—like tiny niger (thistle) seed, a food that goldfinches and Pine Siskins treat like an addictive substance. *Droll Yankees Inc.*

pensers, are inexpensive and effective but vulnerable to the maraudings of squirrels and starlings, which, caught in the grips of thistle lust, will rip a sock to shreds.

Peanut Feeders

Many bird species love peanuts — among them jays (including magpies), nuthatches, starlings, and grackles. Peanuts may be placed on platform feeders or large hoppers to accommodate larger species or served up in special **peanut feeders** that feature a coarse wire mesh fashioned in a tube-shape design that caters to smaller, clinging species.

Suet Feeders

Rubber or plastic-coated wire-mesh feeders, **suet feeders** hold beef **suet** — the energy-rich fat that surrounds beef kidneys. Woodpeckers, in particular, as well as chickadees, nuthatches, magpies, and other species, *love* suet. The feeders are most effective affixed to the trunk of a hardwood tree. Barring this, they can be fastened to a post or the support ends of a hopper feeder. Suet feeders can also be free-hanging, but models that offer a wooden "tail prop" board will be most favored by woodpeckers, who plant their specially designed tails for stability when feeding.

NOTE: Suet is not synonymous with ordinary beef fat, which has a high water content and usually contains pieces of meat. Beef fat freezes in cold temperatures and goes quickly rancid when warm. Suet, which has had all impurities boiled out, doesn't freeze and has a shelf life of two years. While beef fat works, suet works better.

Hummingbird Feeders

Highly specialized, **hummingbird feeders** hold a sugar-water solution that hummingbirds draw through openings surrounding the feeder's base. A solution of four or five parts water to one part white, granulated (ordinary table) sugar (one cup of water and a quarter-cup of sugar) is ideal. *Do not use honey.* The birds cannot metabolize it. *Do not use artificial sweeteners.* Any bird whose heart rate can reach 1,200 beats per minute and whose wings move at 50 beats per second doesn't need to diet. *Do not add red dye* as a hummingbird attractant. Most feeders come in hummingbird-attractive red, and this is sufficient. Whether food coloring is or is not harmful to hummingbirds is debatable, but it is also unnecessary. Be safe. Don't add food coloring to your sugar-water.

Do clean hummingbird feeders frequently: sugar-water ferments

Hummingbird feeders come in a variety of styles. This obviously popular model by Droll Yankees Inc. is easy to fill and maintain.
Droll Yankees Inc.

quickly, forming alcohol. Feeders should be emptied and cleaned at least *every other day* in very warm temperatures, every three to four days otherwise. Fill feeders with only as much sugar-water as you know birds will consume. Clean in a warm fifty-fifty solution of water and white wine vinegar, then refill. (Rather than mix a sugar solution for every refilling, a premixed batch can be refrigerated and drawn from as needed.) *Be responsible. If you are not willing to go to the necessary effort to maintain a hummingbird feeder properly, don't put one up in the first place.*

Incidentally, hummingbirds are not the only species attracted to sugar-water. Orioles in particular will come in for a drink, especially in hot desert climates. Since hummingbird feeders are specialized for birds that hover, a shallow saucer filled with sugar-water and placed where birds can perch and drink will serve for other species.

Specialty Foods

Seed is widely but not universally accepted among bird species. Other food items, besides suet and sugar-water, can help subsidize a bird's diet and make your feeding station attractive to non-seed-eating species.

Fruit is avidly sought by some species and easy to come by. In winter, grapes, raisins, or pieces of banana, orange, or apple, placed on a tray feeder, will gain favor with robins and mockingbirds, and where temperatures are more moderate other **half-hardy** species will also be attracted. In summer or year-round in extreme southern reaches of the United States, orange halves affixed to trees or set on trays will attract jays, woodpeckers, and orioles.

Even more attractive than fruit to some winter birds are **mealworms** — the larval form of the yellow mealworm beetle, *Tenebrio molitar*. These small, amber-colored protein packages not only will make seed-shunning birds (like wrens or bluebirds) swear allegiance to your feeder but will also benefit other birds by augmenting their diet with the protein they need.

Mealworms are not as easy to come by as birdseed. They can be found in pet stores, bird-watching specialty stores, and sporting goods stores that cater to the ice-fishing crowd. Mealworms can also be raised at home — an avocation that will certainly be a conversation-stopper at the next social event you host.

⌘ 𝕳 Distribution (Why Birds Are Where They Are)

Wherever you live, you know that bird life changes throughout the year. The power of flight allows birds to move freely over great distances, and migration allows them to move north, where food is abundant and competition low, to raise their young, and then return to regions that provide food and cover for winter.

To better appreciate why the birds at your feeders vary during the year, you need to understand bird **distribution** and relate it to where you live. Think of your back yard as a reference point. Birds observed in your part of the country can be classified in the following ways. Some birds, called **permanent residents,** live in your area year-round. As winter winds down, waves of spring migrants wing their way north. Those that stop off to breed in your area are called **summer residents.** The migrants that stop for a while but then continue north are called **transients.** As summer comes to an end, birds gather in flocks and begin their fall migration. Once again, the transients may stop for a while to rest but will continue on to wintering sites farther south. The migrants that stop in your area to spend the winter are appropriately called **winter residents.** The term **vagrant** refers to birds that appear far away from their normal range. They are sometimes storm-driven and can be of any age, but many are immatures which have a tendency to wander. Vagrancy usually involves either a single bird or a small number of birds.

For the most part, the birds that come to your back yard fit one of these categories. But occasionally birds that normally winter in Canada and the extreme northern United States come south in tremendous numbers, sometimes reaching southern states. Common examples include Evening and Pine Grosbeaks, Common Redpolls, Pine Siskins, and White-winged and Red Crossbills. These flights, called **irruptions,** are actually irregular migrations that typically occur every few years and are associated with the failure of the seed crops on which the birds depend. A number of predators, including Northern Goshawks, Snowy and Great Gray Owls, and Northern Shrikes, are also **irruptive species** that fly south in great numbers during some winters when populations of their regular prey species are low.

— **Eldon Greij**

Eldon Greij began his adventure with birds as a college professor and then became the founding editor of Birder's World *magazine.*

So Where Do You Get All This Stuff?

Bird-feeding equipment is widely available. One of the advantages of being part of a bloc with 70 million other consumers is that people are eager to sell you things. Commercial bird feeders and seed are seasonally available at most large retail outlets, shopping centers, and many general or hardware stores. Unfortunately, and unwittingly, many (but not all) of the products sold in such locations are poor in quality and performance. Garden centers and feed stores often offer better-quality products. For the most part, the best information and the best bird-feeding products are available from stores that cater specifically to the needs of bird watchers — privately owned shops and owner-operated stores in chains like Wild Bird Centers (call 1-301-229-9585 or visit www.wildbirdcenter.com) and Wild Birds Unlimited (1-800-326-4928, www.wbu.com); nature centers; and Audubon Society sanctuaries and stores that specialize in equipment and seed.

In the yellow pages of your phone book, look under "Bird Feeders and Houses."

Want Diversity? Mix Feeders, Not Seed

Mixed seed has one advantage. It caters to the greatest number of species simply and easily. If you have just one feeder, a mix of black-oil sunflower seed, peanut pieces, and white proso millet will serve best throughout most of North America. However, if you want to increase the number and diversity of birds coming to your back yard, add feeders that cater to the feeding habits of different birds and fill them with the specific seed favored by those species. By reducing competition for perch space and increasing feeding opportunities, you will get more visitors, more often — and *that* is what feeding birds is all about.

WHEN TO FEED

Most people feed birds during the winter months, primarily because that is when birds, particularly seed-eating birds, are most easily attracted by artificial feeding. Over most of North America, seed-eating birds begin migrating south in October. Having full feeders then will encourage migrant birds to remain in your area; keeping them filled will hold them until March and April when most depart.

Do feeding stations tempt birds to remain farther north than is good for them? There is no evidence supporting this possibility, and for those who anguish over it, take this wisdom to heart:

These are professional wild birds. They know what they are doing.

Similar concern has been expressed regarding hummingbird feeders: Does the presence of such feeders encourage hummingbirds to linger as cold weather approaches? Again, these are professional birds, every one the product of a long line of survivors. Hummingbirds that turn up at feeders above the year-round blossom belt (Florida, the Gulf Coast states, the extreme Southwest, southern and coastal California) are pioneers. Some exploratory twist in their genetic blueprint has prompted them to fly a road less traveled — and this is the cornerstone of evolution. Feeders that are maintained in marginally temperate places (like Massachusetts) are sometimes visited by hummingbird species thousands of miles outside of their normal range. The feeders don't draw these pioneers, but they may sustain, at least for a time, what would probably be an evolutionary dead end.

Since bird feeding is rooted in entertainment, not biological necessity, there is no reason not to continue to feed birds during warm weather months if you so desire. You'll probably want to change your mix to suit the nutritional interests of the summer crowd; for instance, the departure of northern breeding sparrows and juncos will reduce the demand for millet. But other offerings, like fruit, will continue to draw minions who stop in now and again to grab a quick bite during a busy day of defending their territory, sporting with the neighbor's mate, and feeding their young.

All the things wild birds do.

WHERE TO FEED BIRDS

Two key considerations must be balanced when placing feeders — *convenience* and *cover*. The optimally placed feeder is one that can be seen easily — from the kitchen window . . . from the office . . . from the porch . . . wherever you spend the most time and want to be enchanted by the mosaic of color and movement you will have created. Feeders should be close enough so that you can easily identify the birds and observe all the nuances of their behavior — the spatial defensiveness of juncos, the snatch-and-grab style of nuthatches, the alert assertiveness of cardinals.

You'll also want feeders placed so that keeping them filled, particularly when the weather is bad, isn't a daunting chore. Empty feeders don't attract birds, and harsh weather is precisely when your regulars will be counting on you.

The second major consideration when choosing the location of your feeders relates to cover. Birds need shelter — from the elements and from predators. Feeders should be located so that birds can feed

This winter feeding station offers lots of cover for birds as well as easy viewing. The protective screen keeps cats from taking birds. *Kevin Karlson.*

in comfort and with minimal risk. A feeder sitting in the middle of a yard, open to the elements and far from protective vegetation, isn't going to be as attractive to birds as a feeder properly placed close to some kind of cover.

Ideally, a feeder should stand on the lee side of something that blocks the wind — a tree, a bush, a hedge, an overgrown garden, an outbuilding, a fence, or your home. It should be close enough to vegetation so that birds can bolt for cover if a hawk is approaching, but not so close that squirrels can use limbs as a launch point to gain access to your feeders or cats can stalk close enough to ambush a bird.

Ten feet from the nearest branch crosses the launch threshold for most squirrels; four and a half feet above the ground is above the leap-limit of the average tabby. Thirty to forty feet from cover seems to make some bird species hesitant. If existing cover is at a premium, plan for the future and put in some sheltering plants. In the meantime, you can build one or more **brush piles** from fallen branches, corn stalks, even a discarded Christmas tree — anything that will offer birds a place to hide when a hawk is closing in or to sit while waiting for their turn at the feeder.

A brush pile sitting in the middle of a back yard isn't exactly in the style of *Home & Garden* magazine, but your birds will overlook that, and you'll probably find (maybe to your chagrin) that the brush pile will be the most bird-active place in your yard.

 ## Glass and Tragedy

Sheet glass is very arguably the most underappreciated lethal threat to birds, and to some species far more than others. Birds act as if they do not see it, and most often the consequences of flying into it are instantaneous death or debilitating injury. My investigations have found that lethal collisions take place wherever birds and glass coexist, and the victims of sheet glass have been recorded the world over at windows of all sizes in residential homes as well as at single- or multistory buildings with entire walls of glass.

There is more than one type of bird-glass collision. One is rarely, if ever, harmful, whereas the other is fatal in one out of every two strikes. Harmless strikes occur when back-yard birds, such as the American Robin and Northern Cardinal, repeatedly bang into and flutter against windows in the spring and summer. This activity is often of concern to homeowners — and, for some, no small annoyance — but except for an occasional bloodied face, the birds seem only to exhaust themselves for a few weeks during the breeding season. This type of strike is the result of male birds defending their territory against their reflected image. By contrast, birds that strike glass as if they are unaware of its presence are so totally deceived and vulnerable that the strike kills them. These birds are attempting either to reach habitat visible on the other side of the clear panes or to reach the perfect illusions of habitat and sky reflected from the glass surface. Glass is an indiscriminate killer, taking the fit as well as the unfit of a species population.

For over twenty-five years I have been studying the glass hazard by conducting extensive observations and experiments at collision sites, both at homes and at various other building types. To put the magnitude of this problem in perspective, assume that one to ten birds are killed at one building over a one-year period. Between 100 million and 1 billion birds are therefore killed each year striking sheet glass in the United States alone. Some of the most informed scientists consider even the upper limit of this range to be excessively conservative, given the amount of sheet glass in almost every human structure, and some office buildings are known to kill hundreds of birds even in a single day. The death toll worldwide is certainly in the billions.

I am frequently asked: If birds are killed at windows to such an extent, why don't we find them heaped in front of the offending panes? Mounds of bird carcasses never appear because strike victims are part of, and disappear with, the 10 billion individuals estimated to die from one year to the next in the overall bird population of North America. The billions that perish by any number of means are simply carried off and eaten by predators and scavengers, or they lie hidden, decaying.

Approximately 25 percent of the birds in the United States and Canada, or 225 species, have been documented striking windows. The species not recorded as **window-kills** are those that rarely occur near human dwellings. The sex, age, or resident status of a bird in any locality has little influence on its vulnerability to windows. There is no season or time of day, and almost no weather conditions, during which birds elude glass. Transparent or reflective windows of various colors are equally lethal to birds. Strikes occur at windows of various sizes, heights, and orientations in urban, suburban, and rural environments, but birds are more vulnerable to large (greater than two-square-meter) panes near ground level and at heights above three meters in suburban and rural areas. Continuous monitoring at single-family homes reveals that bird strikes are more frequent during the winter than at any other time of the year, including the temperate spring and fall migratory periods, when this type of mortality typically attracts the most human attention because victims are often more visible on the sidewalks or around the workplace. Winter strikes are more numerous because more birds are attracted to the vicinity of glass by bird feeders placed near windows.

There are many solutions that effectively reduce or eliminate bird strikes, but none is universally applicable or readily acceptable for all human structures. Protective measures range from physical barriers that keep birds from striking the unyielding surface to detractants that protect birds by transforming the area occupied by glass into uninviting space or a recognizable obstacle to be avoided. Fortunately, an offending window in a home is easily rendered safe for birds when the outside of it is covered with netting (or screen). Detractants include awnings, beads, bamboo, or fabric strips hung on the outside and in front of windows, or stickers, such as silhouettes, of any shape, size, or color placed on the out-

Window strikes kill between one hundred million and one *billion* birds every year. Statistically, the Blue Jay that struck this window (and whose outline is etched in dust) had a 50-50 chance of survival. *Noble Proctor.*

side of the window. These contrast with the glass and, if uniformly separated by two to four inches over the entire surface, will eliminate strikes completely. (My experiments reveal that a single silhouette — a falcon or other shape — will not significantly deter strikes any more than a window without a silhouette.) As long as more than one outside window covering is used, the strike rate will be reduced. If more window coverings are used, strike prevention will be even greater.

We need to take strike prevention measures in remodeled or new buildings if we are to make them safe for birds. Nonreflective glass that gives an opaque appearance is available, but I am told that architects rarely recommend it because it is inefficient in conserving energy. I have proposed the manufacture of a new product, a sheet glass that externally shows creative patterns separated by the requisite distance of two to four inches; from inside the building the glass would provide the same view as contemporary panes. A glass of this type would be especially functional for sunroom additions to homes; my studies indicate that these see-through extensions are deathtraps for resident as well as migratory birds.

Long ago I noted that birds attracted to feeders are much better protected when the feeder is moved *closer* to a window. My students and I were able to quantify this protection by conducting experiments that revealed that feeders placed within a meter or less of a window eliminated all harmful strikes at that window. Alternatively, a feeder placed thirteen feet away from a window resulted in significantly more strike deaths than one closer or farther from the offending window. The closer the feeder is to a window, the safer it is for visiting birds because they focus on landing on the feeder. If they do strike glass when leaving the feeder, they do not build up enough speed to kill or injure themselves.

Whatever means are used to reduce these unintended deaths will be appreciated by those of us concerned about the health of bird populations and biodiversity in general. Most solutions will require humans to tolerate some aesthetic changes to their dwellings, or more bird species will have to tolerate continued losses.

— **Dr. Daniel Klem Jr.**
Daniel Klem, professor of biology at Muhlenberg College in Muhlenberg, Pennsylvania, has studied and written about the subject of glass and bird strikes for more than twenty-five years.

Landscaping for Birds

Artificial feeding stations encourage birds to frequent your yard and direct them to places where they are easily viewed. But if you really want to make your yard attractive to a greater number and variety of birds, particularly during the warmer months, you'll have to landscape for them. This can be done with either a great deal of effort or through benign neglect.

Many trees, plants, shrubs, and grasses are attractive to birds — they provide food, shelter, protection, and nest sites. Most favored are food-bearing plants that offer birds seed, berries, and fruit, such as mountain ash, juniper, sumac, black cherry, American holly, mulberry, little bluestem, desert olive, and wax myrtle. Not only are these plants sought out by birds coming to your feeder, but many are also attractive to reluctant feeder species, like waxwings and thrushes. Some plants that are attractive to birds are not direct sources of food. In April and May, flowering oaks support a host of nectar feeding insects. These in turn draw hordes of migrating (and highly insectivorous) warblers — a seasonal bonus for any back yard.

Flowers, of course, are a food source for hummingbirds. When

Birds can be attracted naturally to your yard with the right plants and the right landscaping. Here, naturalist Pat Sutton and her dog Cody enjoy blooms, birds, and butterflies in her backyard habitat. *Clay Sutton.*

favorites like cardinal flower, penstemon, trumpet vine, and spotted touch-me-not are in bloom, hummingbirds may ignore sugar-water entirely.

Finding some of these plant species may be challenging, although more and more garden centers and bird watching specialty stores are becoming attuned to the importance and attractiveness of **natural plantings.** But nature is perfectly capable of decorating her house if left to do so. One of the easiest things homeowners can do to make their yards attractive to birds is, literally, nothing.

Planting to Attract Back-yard Birds — The Experts' Choices

The best way to attract back-yard birds through landscaping is to choose a diverse mix of trees, shrubs, and flowers. Select plants for their flowers and fruits, but also consider them for their potential as nest sites and protective cover as well. Experts from around the country have provided these lists of their favorite plants to help you get started in selecting plants tailored to your region. When in doubt, "go native." Native plants are well adapted to your soil and climate and well suited to meet the needs of native birds.

BIRD-ATTRACTING NORTH AMERICAN PLANTS BY REGION

NORTHEAST (selections by Wayne Petersen, Massachusetts Audubon Society, Lincoln, Massachusetts)

Birch (*Betula*)
American mountain ash (*Sorbus americana*)
Eastern red cedar (*Juniperus virginiana*)
Cherry (*Prunus*)
Dogwood (*Cornus*)
Virburnum (*Viburnum*)
Hawthorn (*Crataegus*)
Crabapple (*Malus*)
Bittersweet (*Celastrus*)

MIDATLANTIC *(selections by Karen Williams, proprietor of Flora for Fauna, Woodbine, New Jersey)*

American holly (*Ilex opaca*)

Eastern red cedar (*Juniperus virginiana*)

Oak (*Quercus*)

Eastern dogwood (*Cornus florida*)

Hackberry (*Celtis*)

Arrowwood viburnum (*Viburnum dentatum*)

Coral honeysuckle (*Lonicera sempervirens*)

Black cherry (*Prunus serotina*)

Elderberry (*Sambucus*)

Bayberry (*Myrica pennsylvanica*)

SOUTH *(selections by Reese Partridge and Tom Barnes)*

Pine (*Pinus*)

Oak (*Quercus*)

Holly (*Ilex*)

Hackberry (*Celtis*)

Rough-leaf dogwood (*Cornus drummondii*)

Hawthorn (*Crataegus*)

Honeysuckle (*Lonicera*)

Grape (*Vitis*)

Trumpet vine (*Campsis*)

Beardtongue (*Penstemon*)

EAST-CENTRAL/MIDWEST *(selections by Alicia Craig-Lich and Greg Oskay)*

Oak (*Quercus*)

Holly (*Ilex*)

Pine (*Pinus*)

Hickory (*Carya*)

Black cherry (*Prunus serotina*)

Elderberry (*Sambucus*)

Serviceberry (*Amelanchier*)

Viburnum (*Viburnum*)

Coral bells (*Heuchera*)
Purple coneflower (*Echinacea*)

GREAT PLAINS/PRAIRIES (selections by Chuck Otte)

Eastern red cedar (*Juniperus virginiana*)
Crabapple (*Malus*)
Hawthorn (*Crataegus*)
Rough-leaf dogwood (*Cornus drummondii*)
Sumac (*Rhus*)
Elderberry (*Sambucus*)
Wild plum (*Prunus americana*)
Trumpet vine (*Campsis*)
Virginia creeper (*Parthenocissus quinquefolia*)
Sunflower (*Helianthus*)

NORTHERN BORDER STATES/CANADA (selections by Bucky Dennerlein, Minnesota Department of Natural Resources)

Spruce (*Picea*)
Hackberry (*Celtis*)
Oak (*Quercus*)
Cherry (*Prunus*)
Hazelnut (*Corylus*)
Snowberry, coralberry (*Symphoricarpos*)
Sumac (*Rhus*)
Virginia creeper (*Parthenocissus quinquefolia*)
Trumpet creeper (*Campsis radicans*)
Purple coneflower (*Echinacea*)

ROCKY MOUNTAINS (selections by Pat Hayward and Susan Lenard)

Colorado spruce (*Picea pungens*)
Rocky Mountain juniper (*Juniperus scopulorum*)
Cottonwood (*Populus*)
Hawthorn (*Crataegus*)
Chokecherry (*Prunus virginiana*)
Serviceberry (*Amelanchier*)

Currant (*Ribes*)
Trumpet vine (*Campsis*)
Columbine (*Aquilegia*)
Beardtongue (*Penstemon*)

NORTHWEST *(selections by Patty Van Vlack and Carol Pollard)*

Douglas fir (*Pseudotsuga menziesii*)
Pacific dogwood (*Cornus nuttalli*)
Birch (*Betula*)
Elderberry (*Sambucus*)
Red currant (*Ribes sanguineum*)
Raspberry, blackberry (*Rubus*)
Virginia creeper (*Parthenocissus quinquefolia*)
Aster (*Aster*)
Columbine (*Aquilegia*)

SOUTHWEST *(selections by Lynn Kaufman, Tucson Botanical Gardens, Tucson, Arizona)*

Desert marigold (*Baileya multiradiata*)
Baja fairy duster (*Calliandra californica*)
Saguaro (*Carnegiea gigantea*)
Desert hackberry (*Celtis pallida*)
New Mexico thistle (*Cirsium neomexicanum*)
Brittle bush (*Encelia farinosa*)
Chuparosa (*Justicia*)
Wolfberry (*Lycium*)
Penstemon (*Penstemon*)
Red sage (*Salvia greggii*)

SOUTH-CENTRAL CALIFORNIA *(selections from* New Western Sunset Garden Book, *National Audubon Society)*

California bayberry (*Myrica californica*)
Coffeeberry (*Rhamnus californica*)
Strawberry tree (*Arbutus unedo*)
California holly (*Heteromeles arbutifolia*)
Cestrum (*Cestrum*)

Currant (*Ribes*)

Chuparosa (*Justicia*)

Honeysuckle (*Lonicera*)

Salvia (*Salvia*)

California fuchsia (*Zauschneria californica*)
This list was orchestrated by the garden writer and horticultural editor Pat Hayward, who lives in Loveland, Colorado.

BENIGN NEGLECT

Our species likes to impose its peculiar sense of neatness and order upon the world — smooth, grassy plains (called lawns) that are to species diversity what white bread is to nutrition, woodland stripped down to sterile, park-like proportions. Nature is different. Nature *likes* diversity, and she likes clutter too. So do most bird species.

If you have a woodlot on your property, or a wooded edge, *resist the temptation to clear out the* **understory**. A denuded landscape is a bird-free landscape. Many understory trees, shrubs, and plants (like dogwood, holly, wintergreen, even poison ivy) produce fruit that birds eat, and the branches in this strata of the forest are prime nesting places for birds.

If you have a fence, don't trim grass to the edge. Let it grow up as a buffer and a food source for birds. If you have a flower garden, don't cut back the dead plants in the winter. Let them tangle and blow down into natural, sheltering pockets. You'll have more birds if you do.

If you build a few strategic brush piles, you'll soon find a wealth of seed-bearing plants sprouting up through the latticework of branches — the product of seeds that have passed through the digestive system of host bird species and found fertile footing in your yard. This is one way nature spreads her wealth and says thanks for your benign neglect.

Bird-feeding Problems

Engaging the natural world courts risk and challenge. Here are some common problems that back-yard birders face and some methods to redress them.

HAWKS

Feeding stations cause concentrations of birds, and that in turn attracts bird-eating hawks — most commonly **accipiters** like the robin-sized Sharp-shinned Hawk or the crow-sized Cooper's Hawk, but also, in open country, **falcons** like the American Kestrel, Merlin, Peregrine Falcon, and western Prairie Falcon, as well as **harriers** like the Northern Harrier. In some parts of the country some **buteo hawks** are bird-hunting specialists too. Cover is a bird's best defense, but it is a two-edged sword. The same vegetative cover to which birds flee for shelter may also cloak a hawk's approach.

All hawks are justly protected by law, so killing hawks is not an option. Nor should it be.

The solution to the problem of hawks picking birds off your feeder is simple. Stop thinking of it as a problem. Start thinking of the hawk as just another bird coming to the feeder — one that doesn't eat seed. Predators killing prey is one of the natural world's fundamental interactions. While we may not like it, we lack the wisdom or standing to judge or interfere. And for whatever consolation it is worth, when you attract birds to your yard, you are not causing them to be killed. You are only causing them to be killed where you will see them.

HOUSE CATS

House cats are different. Hawks and birds have a natural relationship. House cats and birds have no natural links. Small, bird-catching, feline predators are native only to the American Southwest. Over most of North America, birds are not well attuned to the threat of cats, with the result that in the United States alone an estimated three-quarters of a *billion* birds per year are killed by domestic cats that are allowed to roam free. Feeders should be placed so that cats cannot approach or hide undetected. They should be elevated at least four and a half feet — the limit of a cat's leap.

However, the most effective way of keeping house cats from killing birds is to *keep cats in the house.* Don't let them roam during daylight hours with a yard filled with birds. Don't even think for a moment that your gentle, well-fed, bell-collar-wearing tabby isn't capable of killing birds. It is. It will. If you choose to feed birds and let your cat roam, you have elected to slaughter birds needlessly.

DISEASE

In any population of birds (and other living things), a small percentage carry **diseases** that can be transmitted to other birds. Sometimes disease organisms are transmitted by direct physical contact, and sometimes through fecal matter deposited in and around feeding stations. Rarely do diseases common to birds pose a health threat to humans (unless, of course, you are eating out of the feeder too), but wherever many birds are concentrated (as at bird-feeding stations), bird-to-bird infection is facilitated. The solution is just that — periodic cleaning with a solution of white wine vinegar and hot water, particularly in warm weather. A thorough vinegar-and-water cleaning is warranted every three months or so, but even a periodic rinse with a garden hose will help to keep feeders disease-free.

SQUIRRELS

The squirrel is the animal that back-yard bird watchers love to hate. Squirrels monopolize feeders. They hog the seed. They chew up expensive feeders. They can, through pure esophageal zeal, bankrupt a modest seed budget. To thwart squirrels, position feeders away from overhangs or launch points. Poles that support feeders can be fitted with squirrel guards of PVC pipe or galvanized steel. Some "squirrel-proof" exclusionary feeders are effective (to a point) at excluding squirrels. Once squirrel security measures are in place, you can try baiting the squirrels away from feeders by making offerings of whole, unshelled corncobs. The squirrels will often accept the tribute and go off to enjoy the corn in some private corner.

Squirrel deterrents that may be mixed with the seed, like cayenne pepper additives, sometimes discourage squirrels, but concerns have been raised as to the effect that these irritants have on the digestive tracts and eyes of birds. They may also pose a health risk to pets and children. *Do not use them.* Perhaps the best solution is, simply, acceptance. Squirrels might not be birds, but they are no less envoys of na-

Water is just as important and just as attractive to birds as food. Want birds? Just add water. *Kevin Karlson.*

Attracting Birds with Water

Some bird species get all the water they need from the food they eat. Virtually all back-yard birds, however, need to drink water to remain healthy. Moreover, hardly a bird exists that does not like to bathe now and then. What this means to back-yard bird watchers is that *water is a powerful attractant to birds* — whether it is standing, moving, misting, or dripping. In fact, in desert areas, and during summer heat, water is more attractive to birds than any amount of seed.

Commercial **bird baths** — most typically a basin mounted on a pedestal — are readily available. Placed in a sheltered, shady place, they attract birds that drink from their rim or step in to take a cooling, cleansing dip. Hanging bird baths lose their contents to wind and accelerate evaporation. Birds don't accept them as readily as baths that offer a stable platform.

The American Robin is a compulsive bather, but even for birds as large as a robin, *one to one and a half inches of water is all they want or need.* Keep your bath filled to this level. Put more water than this in your bird bath and you defeat your purpose. Also be sure to change the water frequently.

Even better than a basin on a pedestal is a bird bath placed directly on the ground, where birds are used to finding water. Also available are **drippers** and **misters**. If water attracts birds, moving water is like a siren's call — in fact, just the sound of water running or dripping is an attractant.

A dripper is any hanging vessel that lets water droplets fall at a regulated rate. Birds are drawn to the falling droplets and enjoy standing beneath the drops. Bird photographers have understood the magnetic properties of **drips** for years. Many of the most exquisite photographs gracing natural history magazines owe their existence to a cheap plastic bottle with a pin-prick-sized hole poked in the bottom, left to dangle over a shallow tray in some vegetated place.

Commercial misters are devices that send a fine spray of water into the air. They are especially effective in vegetated areas where water can collect on leaves. Birds drawn to the spray will **leaf-bathe** — the avian equivalent of sponge-bathing among humans.

Chiricahua Mountains Morning

I recall an early July morning spent at Rustler Park — a forest island in Arizona's Chiricahua Mountains. The 9,000-foot elevation offers Canadian zone habitat and a generous mix of Rocky Mountain and Southwestern bird species — at least it did until midmorning, when a hot, dry summer sun brought bird activity to a standstill.

Sitting by a shady stream, more interested in resting than birding, I was delighted when a Hermit Thrush came out of the shadows and proceeded to bathe. It was joined by a House Wren (of the southwestern brown-throated form), a Yellow-eyed Junco (a regional specialty), and a Black-headed Grosbeak. Then a Western Tanager dropped out of the canopy, followed by a Hepatic Tanager. They were joined by a family group of Mexican Chickadees, a Plumbeous Vireo, a Grace's Warbler, an Olive Warbler, several Painted Redstarts, and even the Red-faced Warbler that had eluded me all morning. For over an hour I had many of these forest and treetop species at my feet in full view. It was a picture-perfect example of how magnetic water is to birds.

— **P.D.**

If you are lucky enough to have a stream or natural spring on your property, you can easily dam a section to create a small pool. Fit it out with rocks for perches and a shallows for bathing, and nature could hardly do better herself. (*Caution:* In some places, in these litigation-prone times, an area that holds water in an unfenced or otherwise accessible yard could be construed to be what prosecuting attorneys call "an attractive nuisance." When establishing a bird bathing area, do not make it so attractive — or so deep — that it might constitute a hazard to children or pets.)

If you do not have a natural water source, you can buy a commercial basin, complete with a recirculating pump, or you can construct a pool using a plastic liner and utilizing rainwater directed from a drain spout as a water source. The same rules governing shallow depth and ample perching places apply. Naturally growing vegetation will disguise the artificial nature of the place and in time make it even more attractive to birds (and other living things).

Birds need water in winter as well as summer, but winter poses problems in places where daytime temperatures remain below freezing. Electric water heaters are available to keep bird baths and pools ice-free. In more temperate areas, ice that forms at night can be replaced with water during the day.

Do not under any circumstances put antifreeze in your bird bath water. The mixture is toxic, and the results will be tragic.

Nest Boxes

Many species of birds are **cavity nesters** — they use the defensive confines of tree cavities to protect themselves and their young. Among them are several species of waterfowl, hawks, and owls, as well as woodpeckers, chickadees, titmice, nuthatches, some flycatchers, Tree Swallows, and, of course, Purple Martins and bluebirds.

At some point in the overlapping lives of humans and birds it was discovered that cavity-nesting birds quickly adopt artificial cavities, or **nest boxes.** Note the use of the term "nest *box*," not "*house.*"

Nest boxes (don't call them houses!) are man-made natural cavities. These three, crafted by Coveside Conservation Products of Maine, are all specked for bluebirds. *Coveside.*

Living in houses is something birds do not do. Cavity-nesting birds use boxes to rear young; some will roost in them at night. But they don't live in them the way people live in houses.

Semantics aside, properly sized and properly placed nest boxes will attract cavity-nesting species as readily as any other hole surrounded by wood.

PROPERLY SIZED

Cavity-nesting birds come in all sizes, from House Wrens to Spotted Owls, and each has certain nesting requirements with respect to elevation, cavity depth and size, hole size, and habitat.

Having the right-sized opening will help exclude species you don't want using your box. Having the right dimensions will ensure that young have enough room to grow and will be able to reach the opening when it's time to fledge.

TABLE 1.2: Nest-Box Requirements for Selected Species

SPECIES	INTERIOR SIZE	DISTANCE BETWEEN HOLE AND FLOOR	HOLE DIAMETER	MOUNTING HEIGHT
Eastern Bluebird	4×4×10"	6"	1$\frac{1}{2}$"	4–10'
Western/Mountain Bluebird	5×5×11"	6"	1$\frac{9}{16}$"	4–10'
Chickadee	4×4×10"	6"	1$\frac{1}{8}$"	5–15'
Titmouse	4×4×10"	6"	1$\frac{1}{4}$"	5–15'
Nuthatch	4×4×10"	6"	1$\frac{1}{4}$"	5–15'

SPECIES	INTERIOR SIZE	DISTANCE BETWEEN HOLE AND FLOOR	HOLE DIAMETER	MOUNTING HEIGHT
Finch	4×4×9"	5"	1³/₈"	4–10'
House Wren	4×4×9"	6"	1"	4–10'
Bewicks Wren	4×4×9"	6"	1"	4–10'
Carolina Wren	4×4×10"	6"	1¹/₂"	4–10'
Prothonotary Warbler	4×4×10"	6"	1¹/₂"	4–6' 2' (water)
Purple Martin	6×6×6"	1"	2¹/₂"	8–10'
Barn Swallow	4×4"		shelf	4–15'
Tree/Violet-Green Swallow	5×5×10"	6"	1¹/₂"	4–15'
American Robin	6×6"		shelf	6–15'
Phoebes	6×6"		shelf	6–15'
Downy Woodpecker	4×4×12"	6"	1¹/₄"	6–20'
Hairy Woodpecker	5×5×13"	9"	1¹/₂"	6–20'
Flicker	6×6×16"	14"	2"	6–20'
Other woodpecker species	5×5×14"	9"	2"	6–20'
Ash-throated Flycatcher	5×5×9"	9"	1¹/₂"	8–20'
Great-crested Flycatcher	6×6×10"	7"	1³/₄"	8–20'
Wood Duck	10×10×22"	17"	3"×4" (oblong)	4' (water) 12' (land)
Screech/Saw-whet Owl	6×6×15"	9"	3"	8–30'
Boreal Owl	8×8×16"	10"	4"	8–30'
American Kestrel	7×7×16"	11"	3"	15–30'
Barn Owl	18×20×16"	4"	8"	10–20'
Barred Owl	14×14×26"	16"	8"	20–30'

Most measurements provided by Robin E. Clark, owner of Robin's Wood Ltd., specializing in nest boxes and feeders.

Things to Look for in a Commercial Nest Box

Nest boxes should be constructed of wood. The arguments against using other substances such as plastic or aluminum — nestlings can overheat or be injured by the unnaturally slippery surfaces — are contestable, but one thing seems clear. Birds have been nesting successfully in cavities made out of wood for a long time. You can't go wrong with wood — plain, unpainted, unstained, untreated wood. Pine and cedar are durable and widely available. Exterior plywood is durable but not as easy to work with.

The wood should be about an inch thick (translation at the lumberyard: three-quarter-inch planks). Thicker wood insulates better, keeping interiors cooler in the summer and warmer in the winter for birds (like bluebirds) that use boxes as winter roosts.

Exteriors should be unpainted since paint can be toxic, and interiors should be left rough and unfinished to offer nestlings traction.

Boxes should have slanted tops to shed rain, ventilation slots near the top, and drainage ports at the bottom to vent any water that does enter the box.

Nest boxes should *never* have a perch. It is an open invitation to predators — akin to leaving the key in the front door of your house. In nature, cavity-nesting species do without perches. They are at best superfluous, and at worst life-threatening to brooding adults and young.

As an added defense against the hole-widening incisors of squirrels and the chiseling bills of nest-box usurpers like starlings, nest-box openings may be surrounded with a predator-proof plate of slate, metal, or a double-thick layer of wood.

All nest boxes should have a hinged or removable top or side so that old nest material can be removed at the end of a nesting cycle. Some species (like woodpeckers) that do not line natural cavities with grass or twigs like to have a thin (half-inch) layer of wood shavings cushioning the bottom of the box. Don't let your tidy inclinations overstep their natural proclivities.

Properly Timed

Winter (January and February) is the best time to place nest boxes. Many species start prospecting for good sites weeks before they actually occupy them. Tree Swallows and Purple Martins are very early migrants, establishing themselves in March over much of North America.

Some species (like bluebirds and wrens) **double-** or even **triple-clutch** (raise two or three broods) during the breeding season. Nest boxes put up late, in May or June, may catch these species the second time around.

Properly Placed

Different species prefer boxes in different types of places. What attracts one discourages another. Ideally, boxes should be placed so that they receive some shade during midday heat—as a nest cavity in a live tree trunk would.

Boxes attached directly to the trunks of trees come closest to replicating nature. Fence posts make suitable substitutes for some species, most notably bluebirds. With human-tolerant species like wrens and House Finches, boxes may be affixed to homes or outbuildings.

Many species, including some open-country birds, like a tree or perching surface within ten or twenty feet of the front of the box. (A notable exception is the Purple Martin, which likes unencumbered airspace.) Adults use this as a launch site to gain access; it also gives fledgling birds a safe place to head for when they are learning to fly.

One thing that does not seem to matter a great deal is which direction the opening faces. You can point the box whichever way gives you the better view.

Properly Elevated

Most species are fairly tolerant about the height of a nest site. Boxes placed an easy-to-reach (by us) four to six feet from the ground are acceptable to most species, including bluebirds, chickadees, titmice, nuthatches, Tree Swallows, House Finches, and wrens. Woodpeckers, Purple Martins, and *Myiarchus* flycatchers like their cavities at stepladder height — eight to ten feet. Cavity-nesting ducks, owls, and American Kestrels fall in the extension-ladder range — fifteen to thirty feet (See table 1.2).

Properly Protected

Nesting in a cavity offers a good defense against many forms of predation, but rat snakes, bull snakes, and pine snakes are very adept at finding and entering cavities, where they consume eggs and young. Raccoons and house cats are deft enough to reach into boxes and remove nests and young. Most terrestrial-based predators can be discouraged by three and a half feet of seamless metal flashing or PVC pipe around and above the base of the pole or by a three-foot-wide metal "skirt" placed several feet above the ground.

Cavity-nesting birds, like all birds, face many other threats besides predators: competitive species like House Sparrows; infestations of ants, wasps, or parasites; hypothermia; and starvation. Back-yard birders can mitigate these problems, but there is nothing that can be done to eliminate them.

Everyone engaging their lives with the lives of birds should understand that 90 percent of the birds born in any given year fail to see the next. Nest failure is the first major cut on the way to maintaining the population at a healthy level that does not outstrip resources.

This mortality rate may not seem right or fair. But it is *natural.*

The Other Side of the Fence

No matter how many feeders you place, no matter how many bird boxes you erect, no matter how bird-friendly you make your yard, you will be able to attract only a fraction of the species that occur in North America.

No loon has ever come to a feeder. No Black-crowned Night Heron or Golden Eagle or Yellow Warbler has ever been coaxed into a bird box. To see these species, you usually have to look beyond your own yard. To get the kind of close-up look provided by a bird feeder, you need **binoculars** to see the birds. To identify them, you need a **field guide.** These are the basic tools of birding beyond the back yard. How to choose and use them is the subject of the next chapter.

Summary Birding is immensely popular, enjoyed by 70 million people in the United States alone. Most bird watchers are most interested in the birds they find and attract to their homes. Birds are drawn to food, water, shelter, and suitable nesting sites. The primary tool of back-yard birding is the bird feeder. Black-oil sunflower seed is attractive to the most species of birds, but other seeds, like striped sunflower, peanuts, and white proso millet, are also highly esteemed by birds. Using a combination of basic seed-dispensing feeders and specialty feeders appeals to a greater diversity of birds. Birds can be safely attracted all year by targeting food offerings. While the job of a bird feeder is to get birds close, landscaping for birds — using the plants they need for food and cover — greatly increases numbers and diversity.

Water is a powerful attractant to birds — in some places and at some times it is better than seed. Nest boxes are also attractive to a number of cavity-nesting species. But the overwhelming majority of bird species cannot be found in a typical yard. To engage most of the birds found in North America, you will have to go where they are.

2
The Tools of the Trade — Binoculars and a Field Guide

Of Chimney Swifts and Larceny

The phone was ringing as I reached the door to New Jersey Audubon's Cape May Bird Observatory. It persisted as I switched on the lights, crossed the room, threw my jacket over a chair, and stood, hand poised over the receiver, considering.

It was, after all, only seven-thirty on a Saturday morning, my first day back as director after a six-year hiatus. I'd come in early to gain time to collect my thoughts before opening the door to visiting birders at nine — and I really wanted that time.

I picked up the phone anyway.

"Cape May Bird Observatory," I said.

"Oh!" a voice intoned. A voice that rose and fell like the song of a

Warbling Vireo but in timbre and pitch was as musical as an oriole. "So early — I thought I would get a machine."

"No," I replied, "just a person this mor —"

"Good. I saw a program on the television about Cape May and that it was a good place to see birds, especially hawks, and is it true? because if it is then I want to come, and can you send me information and tell me when is the best time to be there?" She said this in one breath.

Before I could reply, the effervescent caller tossed me one more question.

"And do you know about Chimney Swifts?"

"A . . . little," I stammered. I'm not an ornithologist, one who studies birds as a scientific pursuit. I'm a birder, one whose interest in birds is steeped in fun, challenge, discovery, and adventure. But having birded forty-two of my fifty years, and having seen over twenty species of swifts on five continents (including the Chimney Swift of eastern North America), I figured I could claim to be swift-conversant.

"Well, do you know that Chimney Swifts live in the Bronx? And that they fly to South America in the winter? And they come *back* again?"

I did know this. Chimney Swifts are insect-eating birds, one of four swift species that nest in North America and, as insect-eating birds, vacate the Northern Hemisphere in winter. What interested me more than Chimney Swift distribution was the circumstance that had brought a sixty-year-old Latina grandmother living in the Bronx (as she had described herself to me by then) to become fascinated with swifts in the first place.

"I saw them in a big cloud that disappeared into a chimney outside my window," she explained. "So I went to the bird people at the Bronx Zoo, who told me that they were Chimney Swifts and that they were migrating and that if I went to Central Park I would see other birds, so I did and met a lady with binoculars who told me that if I waited by this pond a Black Night Heron [*sic*] would come and . . . and . . . *it did!*"

"The lady let me see it through binoculars," she added. "It was beautiful."

I didn't respond at first. I was too captivated by her story and found it wonderfully affirming that even in a place as environmentally estranged as the Bronx, birds have the power to touch human lives.

"Do you have binoculars of your own?" I asked.

"No, but my grandchildren are saving to buy me some," she said proudly.

"Do you have a field guide?"

"What is that?" she wanted to know.

"A book with pictures that helps you to identify the birds you see."

There was silence for a time — silence that was the echo of suspended breath. Then a voice approaching that information the way shy desert birds approach water asked, "There *are* such things?"

"Yes," I said, glancing at the scores of guides sitting on the shelves of CMBO's bookstore. "Can I have your name and address?"

After concluding our conversation, I put a standard visitor information packet in a padded envelope and addressed it to her. Before sealing it, I crossed the room, lifted a *Peterson Field Guide to Eastern Birds* off the rack, and slipped it into the envelope.

They'll never miss it on inventory, I explained to my conscience.

So I'm pleased to say that my first act upon returning to my job directing the Cape May Bird Observatory was ushering a new birder into a world of discovery. I'm embarrassed to say it was also larceny.

The Keys to the Kingdom

Binoculars and a field guide are the most important tools of birding. One confers supernatural intimacy. The other is a blueprint to discovery. Together they buy a person passage on a lifelong treasure hunt.

There are hundreds of binoculars on the market. Most are unsuitable for birding. There are more than a dozen popular general

Binoculars and a field guide — that's all you need to be a bird watcher, and you cannot be a bird watcher without them. *Kevin Karlson.*

field guides to birds — all with strengths and weaknesses that add or detract from their usefulness. The balance of this chapter will explain what you should look for in birding binoculars and in a basic field guide to the birds. Make the right choices, and a world of discovery and wonder awaits. Arm yourself with ill-suited optics or a poorly organized field guide, and frustration will be your companion — until you fix the problem or give up birding.

Binoculars — The Defining Tool of Birding

Before optics became refined and widely available, the study of birds was almost exclusively a scientific pursuit called **ornithology.** The primary tool of early ornithology was the shotgun — a tool that, like the binocular, vaulted distance, permitting close study of birds. Ornithologists like Alexander Wilson ("the Father of Ornithology") and John James Audubon (America's pioneering bird painter) "collected" specimens, identified them, and in the case of species new to science, described them.

Shotgun ornithology had several major advantages — close scrutiny, unlimited opportunity for study, and positive proof of the identification of a species. But it had obvious disadvantages too. Shortly after the American Civil War, the quality of optical instruments began to improve, and it finally reached a point where birds could be accurately distinguished in the field without the need to collect them. By the early twentieth century, **field-glass ornithology** was augmenting shotgun ornithology, making it possible for scientists to broaden their studies in the field. Improved optics also opened the door to bird study to broader segments of the population — to people whose interest in birds was aesthetic and conservation-oriented. These were "nature lovers."

Today birders, whose interest in birds is both intellectual and aesthetic, are hybrids of the ornithologist and the nature lover. Their primary tool remains the binocular.

BINOCULAR BASICS

A binocular is a hand-held, twin-barreled telescope. Each barrel contains glass **elements** called **lenses** and **prisms.** These catch, magnify, and direct down the length of the barrels an image that falls as shafts of light upon the user's eyes.

Binoculars are more useful than **telescopes** for birders. They are lighter, more portable, more versatile, and designed to be used with both eyes opened, making them generally easier to use. Telescopes, more commonly referred to as **spotting scopes,** offer higher **magnification** than binoculars and are useful for more specialized forms of birding. (Spotting scopes are discussed in chapter 5.)

Binoculars are hand-held, twin-barreled telescopes. Each barrel houses lenses and prisms that magnify and direct an image to the user's eye. Shown is a cutaway of the very fine Swarovski EL roof prism binocular. *Swarovski Optik.*

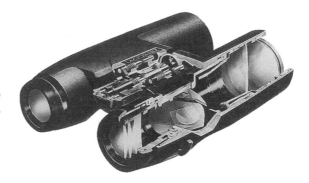

Binoculars are designed with specific uses in mind. Hunters demand rugged binoculars. Yachtsmen want waterproof ones. Backpackers need light and portable instruments

Birders demand all these qualities *and more.* The birding binocular should be light, rugged, portable, and weather-resistant if not waterproof. It should offer a wide **field of view** (to facilitate getting on subjects quickly), exceptional **depth of field** (to aid in finding birds in a maze of branches), **close focus** (so that birds can be viewed in tight, woodland confines), **fast focus,** good balance. . . .

In other words, birding binoculars must meet more stringent requirements than those of any other user group.

Attributes of the Birding Binocular

The most important consideration when choosing binoculars is fit: Does the instrument fit your eyes, your face, your hands, your frame? There is no one-size-fits-all binocular, however much you are willing to spend. Many people have spent $1,000 or more for a binocular only to find that it doesn't work for them.

Doesn't the Quality of the Glass Matter?

Of course it matters. But optical quality, measured in terms of an instrument's ability to resolve detail, pretty much stops being a concern at the $200 to $300 price level — which is (with few exceptions) the least you should expect to pay for a decent, durable, birder-worthy binocular. Low-end (under $100) binoculars commonly use low-quality **BK-7 boro-silicate glass,** or even plastic lenses. Binoculars that begin to approach the optical standards demanded by birders use higher-density, **BAK-4 barium crown glass** or better. Since manufacturers of low-end instruments don't necessarily advertise the glass they use, buyers must often make this determination obliquely — by looking at the sticker price.

The emergence of China as a center for optics production has brought down the cost of midpriced binoculars. There are now binoculars featuring BAK-4 glass that can be had for as little as $100. But setting a low price point often leads to compromises in quality, durability, and performance.

Once you start paying $200 and up for a simple, gimmick-free binocular, you can pretty much stop worrying about acceptable optical quality and concentrate on other performance factors. The performance difference between a $200 binocular and a $500 binocular may be considerable, but it often has little to do with the quality of the glass.

Wide-bodied versus Sleek: Porro Prism and Roof Prism

Binoculars come in two basic designs: **porro prism** and **roof prism.** Each has advantages and disadvantages.

Porro Prism

Porro prism binoculars are wide-bodied with the classic binocular shape. The big lenses in the front, the **objective lenses,** and the smaller lenses that fit over your eyes, the **ocular lens,** are offset, not lined up along a linear axis.

Advantages: Porro prism binoculars are generally less expensive than roof prisms, both to purchase and to repair, and so are very popular among beginning birders. They are also modestly optically superior to "roofs" in design — not necessarily in glass quality — insofar as they incorporate fewer reflecting surfaces, thus reducing light loss and image distortion.

Disadvantages: Porro prism binoculars are generally more difficult to hold steady than a roof prism, and often less rugged.

Roof Prism

The sleeker and generally more favored design among skilled birders is roof prism.

Advantages: The sleeker design fits most people's hands and frames better, making them easier to hold steady. A stable platform al-

Binoculars come in two basics models—the porro prism (or classic) design like these Swarovski 7×42s at left, and the sleeker roof prism design, as profiled by this Swarovski 7×42SLC at right. *Swarovski Optik.*

lows better overall **image quality,** particularly from higher (10×) magnifications. The roof prism system is better anchored to take rough handling.

DISADVANTAGES: The roof prism is optically inferior to the porro prism of comparable quality because of increased light loss and a design-induced light-wave shift that reduces image contrast. (This problem is corrected in more expensive roof prism binoculars by the application of a **phase coating.**) Roof prisms are also generally more expensive than porro prism instruments.

WHICH PRISM SYSTEM IS BETTER?

Until you start spending *lots* of money, neither system is superior if you use image quality (what you see) as the reference standard. Porro prisms offer superior optical performance for the same glass quality; roof prisms offer greater stability. Image quality is the sum of both.

More fundamental than design is:

HOW DOES THE INSTRUMENT FIT YOU?

If your index finger does not fall quickly and easily upon the **focus wheel** when you grasp a binocular, or if you find that you must raise

The Myth of Tens

In 1975 I was a beginning hawk watcher. One piece of wisdom I got from the senior veterans was that nobody could hold 10× (ten-power) binoculars steady. So when I went out to purchase my first premium binoculars, one of the sleek new roof prisms that had just hit the market, I bought a Leitz 8×40; I never considered buying a 10×. Not long after, I chanced to use a friend's 10× Zeiss, another roof, and was astonished at how much better it was for studying distant birds of prey.

I certainly had no trouble holding a 10× binocular steady. I assumed (as all members of the younger generation do) that it was a matter of age. I was young. The old-timers were, of course, old. I could hold a 10× binocular steady. They could not.

But what accounted for the performance advantages of the glass had little to do with youth. It was a matter of technology and design. The older birders had grown up using porro prisms, many of them large and unwieldy instruments that forced users to bring their elbows up and out, exacerbating hand shake, distorting images, and *making lower magnifications more practical.* The new roof prism instruments were much easier for birders of any age to hold steady. In the 1980s, the 10× roof prism binoculars became the glass of choice among a whole new generation of hotshot young birders.

This didn't mean that a 7× roof prism binocular couldn't offer superior image quality. It does, and in the 1990s many 10× binocular users retired their "tens" to reap the inherent advantages offered by lower magnification — such as a wider field of view and superior depth of field. But the introduction of roof prisms meant that 10× optics could be used effectively in the birding arena — so long as they were housed in the ergonomic roof prism design.

It wasn't that the elders were wrong, but that they and their optics had dominated another age.

— **P.D.**

Binoculars are not one-size-fits-all. They must fit your hands. They must fit your face. If your index finger does not fall precisely and easily upon the focus wheel, the glass is not designed for you. Get rid of it. *Pete Dunne.*

an elbow or shift your grip to reach the focus wheel, put it down. The instrument is too large for your hands or is poorly designed. When you raise your elbows up and away from your body, you exacerbate hand shake and reduce image quality.

If you bring the binocular up to your eyes and find that you cannot adjust the ocular lenses close enough or wide enough to let you see a single image, or the image is **vignetting** (i.e., you are constantly plagued with **black flashes**), put it down. The **interpupillary distance** is too wide or too narrow for your eyes (or you haven't adjusted the binocular eyecups properly).

Size and shape directly affect how easily and steadily a binocular may be held. The light, pocket-sized **mini-binoculars** favored by backpackers offer little to grasp, and so hand shake is exacerbated. For this reason, and because mini-binoculars trade off optical performance for size, birders should avoid them. **Marine binoculars** are bulky (forcing users to hold their elbows spread) and heavy (causing muscle fatigue) — conditions that increase hand shake and reduce image quality. Birders should avoid these too.

Binocular Weight
Particularly for people who have neck or back problems, weight can be a determining consideration when choosing binoculars. The most popular birding binoculars range from eighteen to over fifty

ounces — a very wide range. Binocular manufacturers are very conscious of weight and have begun using polycarbon bodies and lightweight metal alloys to shave ounces, but the fact remains that most of the weight in quality binoculars is in the glass. The denser the glass is, the better it is and the more it weighs. Thus, the best-performing birding binoculars are on the heavy side — between twenty-six and thirty-six ounces.

If binocular weight is a problem, you can distribute the weight with a wide, spongy neoprene strap, or you can lengthen the strap and wear the binocular bandolier fashion (over the shoulder, across the chest, binocular resting under one arm). There are also harness systems available that distribute the weight over the shoulder and off the neck entirely. Some are cumbersome, but they work.

FOCUSING

Birding requires constant focusing, from birds close at hand to those fast disappearing over the horizon. All birding binoculars must have a **focus system** that allows you to focus quickly, easily, and responsively with a **center-focus** *wheel* (not lever) that falls where your index finger can easily find it. By moving this wheel, you can focus both barrels of your binoculars simultaneously. Center-focus binoculars incorporate an **individual eyepiece adjustment** ring on one of the oculars, or sometimes an adjustment knob fitted to the binocular bridge. This adjustment control compensates for the small differences between your two eyes. You set it once, then never again (unless, of course, your eyesight changes).

Some military or marine binoculars have individual eyepiece focus systems — focusing rings on each ocular that must be focused separately. This cumbersome system has no place in birding.

Instead of wheels, some instruments feature focus levers or bars, which are touted for their ability to "fast-focus" or "instant-focus." The reality is quite different. Lever-focus systems are undermined by a **range of focus** that is too terse. The instrument's capacity to resolve detail from near focus to infinity is controlled by what amounts to an abbreviated wheel — a wheel with only a 90-degree arc (or looked at another way, a wheel that is 270 degrees short of being a wheel). The levers require a two-handed grip and a great deal of back-and-forth adjustment to get a sharp image. It is easy to get *almost* focused — but time-consuming to get the image sharp (if it is possible at all).

Optimally, focus wheels should cover the range of focus with no less than one and no more than two turns of the wheel. This translates to two to four quick draws of the finger across the wheel to go from close focus to infinity.

"Permanent-focus" or "no-focus" binoculars are prefocused on a set average distance. The user's eye, not the binocular, does the focusing when the object isn't where the average says it should be. As a result, the eyes tire quickly, and the ability to resolve detail at close quarters (like less than seventy feet!) is lost. Instruments like these are fine for sporting events but nearly worthless for birding.

All birding binoculars should be able to focus clearly to *at least* fifteen feet. Some superior instruments allow birders to focus down to ten feet . . . even six feet. These are particularly useful for birding in woodlands and rain forests, where the birds may be very close or the birder's situation precludes moving.

MAGNIFICATION

Binoculars come in different **powers,** designated by the first number of the binomial formula etched on every glass. For example: **6**×30, **7**×42, **8.5**×44, **10**×50. The second number expresses the width of the objective lens in millimeters.

Simply put, a 6× binocular (six-power) makes a distant object appear six times closer than it actually is (or, if you prefer, only one-sixth as far away). A 10× binocular makes objects appear ten times closer.

Buyers often mistakenly assume that higher power (10×, 12×, or . . . [shudder] . . . 15×) is better. This is not so.

Although higher powers magnify the size of distant objects, they magnify the image-compromising effects of hand shake and heartbeat too. The image is larger, but the image quality, in terms of the details that can be seen, remains essentially the same.

Increased magnification also contributes to a reduced field of

Less Power, More Performance

In 1987, five years after I'd switched from 8× binoculars to 10×, I was given oblique insight into the functional limits of higher magnification. Carl Zeiss Optics was introducing a new Zeiss 20×60 binocular that featured an internal stabilizing mechanism and a $4,750 price tag. The engineers set up an eye chart across a parking lot, distributed production model Zeiss 7×, 8×, 10×, and 15× instruments, and instructed us to study the chart and try to read the smallest line of type, line 10.

I could not — 7×, 8×, 10×, 15× . . . it made no difference. My ability to read the print stopped at line 6 or 7.

Then the Zeiss engineers gave us the 20×60 and directed us to try it again. If anything, the results were worse. Twenty-power was too hard to hold steady. The letters danced. Then we were instructed to push the button that kicked the internal stabilizer on line. The result was magic. The dancing letters froze. Line 10 was perfectly readable.

But as impressive as the new product was, what impressed me more was the performance parity evidenced by the other instruments. As noted, *no matter what the power, my ability to resolve detail stopped at the same lines.* In terms of seeing details, the 15× held no advantage over the 10×, or the 10× over the 8×, or the 8× over the 7×. At higher magnification, the letters were bigger but, because of increased image distortion caused by hand shake, no easier to read. No matter what the power, image quality remained fundamentally unchanged.

At that time I was using a 10×40 as my primary glass, and the test begged the question: Why was I using a binocular that offered a much smaller field of view than the 7×, a much shallower depth of field, a very critical (that is, unforgiving and precise) focus, a darker image, and a marginally acceptable close focus of sixteen feet (as compared to the 7×'s eleven feet) if I was not getting any appreciable advantage in return?

There was no reason that I could see. Shortly thereafter I retired my 10×40s, bought a 7×42, and was a much happier birder.

— **P.D.**

view, more light loss and a darker image, a shallower depth of field, and a more critical focus, with the result that *higher-power binoculars are more difficult to use than lower-power instruments.*

Most experienced birders choose binoculars between 7× and 10× — with 7× and 8× binoculars being most favored, particularly among birders who spend a great deal of time in woodlands or rain forests or who want a versatile instrument. Ten-power instruments are preferred by birders who habitually bird in open habitat or who specialize in the study of very distant birds in flight (for example, hawk watchers).

If you cannot decide between a 7× and a 10×, consider a compromise — an 8× or 8.5× — but *never buy a **zoom binocular!*** They are a gimmick. Even at the lowest power setting, zoom binoculars offer a narrow field of view, making it difficult to find birds. As power is increased, image quality deteriorates so dramatically on most models that users find that they rarely exceed the lowest power setting anyway. Virtually all zoom binoculars are heavier than fixed-power instruments of comparable quality; their optical quality is poor; they are mechanically inferior; and they are usually priced higher.

If you look at the optics lines offered by the three companies that specialize in superior-quality, high-performance binoculars — Carl Zeiss Optics, Leica, and Swarovski Optik — you will not see a zoom binocular. This should send a clear message to the discerning consumer.

Stabilized binoculars, instruments with internal mechanisms that reduce vibration and the image-distorting effect of hand shake, are a compelling idea whose field-worthiness remains some years away. Most stabilized instruments available today are cumbersome and offer optical performance that is inferior to that of comparably priced nonstabilized instruments. A stable image of poor quality holds no advantage.

LIGHT AND BRIGHTNESS

A bright image is important to birding since it enables the eye to better discern color and details. Binocular brightness is the product of several things, including the size of the objective lens, the power of the

A lot of birding is done in low-light conditions. A 7× or 8× binocular with at least a 30-millimeter objective lens that features *fully multi-coated lenses* will serve in most birding situations. *Pete Dunne.*

instrument, and the number of glass surfaces that the shaft of light must pass through or reflect off before it reaches your eye. In an optics store, and in an instrument's accompanying literature, brightness is often rated by formulas that measure **twilight factor, relative brightness,** and **relative light efficiency.**

If this sounds confusing, it can be made to sound even more confusing in a store. All you need to know about binocular brightness is how the size of the **exit pupil** and the antireflective **lens coatings** affects light passing through a binocular.

Exit Pupil — The End of the Straw

Here's the problem. Every time light strikes a glass surface (like an untreated binocular lens), approximately 5 percent is lost — either reflected away or absorbed by the glass. Since the average binocular has fourteen to sixteen glass elements, approximately half of the light entering the instrument will be lost before reaching the human eye. The result: a dark image.

In partial compensation, the size of the objective lens can be increased. This size, measured in millimeters, is displayed on binoculars as the second number in the numeric formula: 6×**30,** 7×**42,** 10×**50.** A larger objective lens allows more light to enter the instrument, increasing the diameter of the shaft of light that travels through the glass and falls upon the eye.

If you hold the binoculars away from your face and look at the ocular lens, you can see this shaft of light. It appears as a silver bubble that floats in the center of the lens. Called the exit pupil, its diameter can be calculated by dividing the size of the objective lens by the power of the binocular. For example, for a 7×42 binocular, 42 millimeters (the size of the objective lens) divided by 7 (power) equals a 6-millimeter exit pupil.

The size of the exit pupil is important because the human eye has a pupil too — one that adjusts to changing light conditions. In bright light the human pupil contracts to about two millimeters, and any binocular exit pupil larger than two millimeters will provide enough light. Almost any binocular, even mini-binoculars, can do this. In poor light the human pupil expands to about seven millimeters — setting the functional maximum of a binocular exit pupil. Any shaft of light greater than seven millimeters falls outside the capacity of the human eye to accept it. In addition to providing sufficient light in low-light conditions, a large exit pupil also makes it easier for eyes to get aligned quickly and easily. Looking through binoculars is like looking through a pair of straws. The smaller the exit pupils, or the narrower the straws, the more precise the alignment between your eyes and the shaft of light must be.

Lens Coatings — Bending the Rules of Light Gathering

At the onset of World War II, German scientists discovered that a coating of reflection-reducing material applied to the surface of glass reduces the light loss caused by reflection from 5 percent to almost 1 percent. These coatings, most often magnesium fluoride, appear as a blue, purple, or green glaze on the objective and ocular lenses. Later it was discovered that the application of several thinner layers would reduce light loss even more. Some **multilayer coatings** can cut light loss to less than half of 1 percent per reflecting surface, with the result that light transmission through high-quality, **fully multicoated** binoculars can be close to 95 percent!

As mentioned earlier, roof prism binoculars have an inherent shortfall — the diminished contrast caused by a modest light-wave shift as light is bounced between prisms. The application of a phase coating corrects this problem. Phase-coated or phase-corrected roof prisms offer the same sharp image contrasts as porro prism binoculars.

Seeing the Light

The take-home is this: if you want the binoculars you buy to be adequately bright, be certain that they have an exit pupil of 3.75 millimeters in diameter or more and that *all* glass elements (not just the outside ones you can see) are *fully multicoated.* Not just coated, not just multicoated, but *fully* multicoated. Without this qualifying modifier, there is no guarantee that a less exacting coating process was not used for some (if not most or all) elements.

A larger exit pupil (like the 6-millimeter exit pupil offered by a 7×42 binocular) offers a brighter image in low-light conditions. But under most conditions, and for most people, a fully multicoated 7×30 binocular (4.29-millimeter exit pupil) or even a quality 8×30 (3.75-millimeter exit pupil) will serve.

Field of View and Depth of Field

Looking through binoculars magnifies the size of objects, but it diminishes field of view — that wedge of the world seen through stationary binoculars measured from one edge of the field to the oppos-

Birding binoculars demand a *wide* field of view (to help find things), as well as a generous depth of field, because birds live in a three-dimensional world and make no effort to accommodate people who cannot see them for the blurry maze of branches. Lower magnification (7× or 8×) offers superior depth of field and excels in woodland situations. *Pete Dunne.*

ing edge. Field of view may be described in terms of **degrees of arc** (for example, 6.6 or 5.7) or feet at 1,000 yards (or meters at 1,000 meters).

However it is measured, a wide field of view — one that offers a minimum of 330 feet at 1,000 yards, 120 meters at 1,000 meters, or 6.3 degrees of arc — is essential. A field of view of 400 feet is exceptional; 450 feet or more is prized.

A wide field of view makes it easier to find birds quickly and easily. It makes it easier to get onto fast-flying birds. It makes it easier to scan a wide area.

A wide field is particularly helpful to inexperienced birders, whose greatest challenge lies in *finding* birds through unfamiliar instruments.

Birding binoculars should also offer a generous depth of field — the ability of a binocular to resolve detail, near to far, without the need to adjust the focus. A good depth of field makes it easier to find birds in situations such as woodlands, where the desired point of focus would otherwise be lost in a blurry maze of branches. It also eliminates the need to make constant focusing adjustments every time a bird moves a little closer or farther away.

Both field of view and depth of field are closely related to magnification. In general, the higher the magnification, the smaller the field of view, the shallower the depth of field, and the less user-friendly the instrument.

EYE RELIEF

Eye relief is the measure of distance between the ocular lens and the point beyond the ocular lens where the image is in sharp focus. The actual point of focus is called the **eye point.** Measured in millimeters, this point is also the distance from the lens at which an observer's eye will appreciate the widest possible field of view.

Eye relief differs from instrument to instrument, and it is not necessarily an important concern for non-eyeglass-wearers. When extended, the length of a binocular's **eyecups** automatically directs the user's eyes to the proper eye point for that instrument, *providing that the eyecups sit properly over the eyes.*

Eye relief is a critical concern for eyeglass-wearers (and may be a concern for others too). Eyecups rolled down, Debbie Shearwater of Shearwater Journeys enjoys nearly the same wide field of view that non-eyeglass-wearers get from these venerably old Zeiss 10×40s. *Linda Dunne.*

Eye relief is a critical concern for eyeglass-wearers, whose eyes are already set back twelve to twenty millimeters behind a glass plate. Unless the binocular offers a high eye point (a distance that approximates the gap between the eyeglass lens and the eye), eyeglass-wearers have a field of view that is considerably reduced — the functional equivalent of trying to look through a keyhole with your eye drawn back from the door. The keyhole equals the eye point. With your eye up against the keyhole, you can see a wide portion of the world beyond. Pull your eye away, and the view becomes smaller and smaller.

With binoculars that offer good eye relief or a high eye point, *and with eyecups retracted or rolled down,* eyeglass-wearers should enjoy the same wide field that non-eyeglass-wearers get.

Note: Just because a binocular features adjustable eyecups does not mean that it provides sufficient eye relief. The proof is in the length of the cups. Unless it is at least fifteen millimeters, most eyeglass-wearers will be short-changed.

Not always, however. It is possible to have *too much* eye relief. If your eyes are set fifteen millimeters behind your eyeglass lenses and a binocular offers twenty millimeters of eye relief, the point of focus is beyond your eye! When this happens, users often see "black flashes" — or no image at all! If the eye relief cannot be adjusted (that is, it's a one-size-fits-all roll-down eyecup), try another binocular better suited for your eye relief needs.

WATER AND GRAVITY

By far the biggest threats to the integrity of binoculars are water and gravity. Combating these two enemies of optical performance accounts for much of the production cost that distinguishes $1,000 binoculars from $300 instruments.

Binoculars need not be immersed in water to be rendered dysfunctional in the field. An act as innocuous as taking a poorly sealed binocular out of an air-conditioned car into a steamy Florida afternoon can cause moisture, sucked in by working the focus mechanism, to condense on internal elements — fogging them.

Even binoculars that are well cared for are not immune to accidents. One fall from the kitchen table to the linoleum floor is enough to put the average binocular out of **alignment** — that is, the twin barrels no longer focus on the same point. Even binoculars that are moderately out of alignment will tire eyes and make birding burdensome. Binoculars that are severely out of alignment make you nauseous.

The best birding binoculars are waterproof — meaning immersible — and shock-resistant. Many instruments are armored with a hard rubber or polyurethane outer shell.

THE SUM OF ITS PARTS

Engineering binoculars is an exercise in compromise. Higher magnification reduces field of view. **Resolution** can be absolutely sharp at the center of the field and distorted at the edge, or averaged out across the field, compromising resolution at the center. Binoculars can be made waterproof — but for a higher price.

Different people emphasize different attributes, but here are my basic requirements for a birding binocular:

SIZE— Large enough to be grasped firmly; small enough for your index finger to find the focus wheel quickly and easily.

WEIGHT — No more than you care to bear. Most people are comfortable carrying up to thirty-two ounces (two pounds).

SHAPE — Any size or design that allows a firm, strain-free, shift-free grasp.

INTERPUPILLARY DISTANCE — To fit your eyes.

DESIGN — Porro prisms are optically superior until you start spending $400 and up for phase-corrected instruments.

FOCUS SYSTEM — A center-focus system with a wheel that covers the full range of focus in one to two revolutions.

MAGNIFICATION — A 7× or 8× is best for beginners, all-around birding, and woodland birding. A 10× performs well (but is not necessarily any great advantage) in open country and for hawk watching and sea-bird watching (from land). *Never buy a zoom. Never buy a binocular that features a permanent or fixed focus.*

EXIT PUPIL SIZE — No less than 3.75 millimeters; five to six millimeters is preferable.

OPTICS — BAK-4 glass or even denser; **HD (high-density) glass.**

COATINGS — *Fully* multicoated optics only. Color bias minimal. Roof prism binoculars should have phase-corrected coatings.

CLOSE FOCUS — Down to *at least* fifteen feet, preferably less than ten.

FIELD OF VIEW — No less than 330 feet at 1,000 yards (for conversion purposes, 1 degree of arc equals 52.5 feet at 1,000 yards; 1 meter equals 3.28 feet or 1.09 yards).

EYE RELIEF — For eyeglass-wearers, no less than fifteen millimeters; for many, eighteen millimeters is preferable.

WATER RESISTANCE AND DURABILITY — Waterproof and rugged binoculars are desirable — but expensive. If you bird in the tropics or offshore **(pelagic birding)**, waterproof instruments are essential.

THE BOTTOM LINE: PERFORMANCE

There is, after all is said and done, only one test of a binocular. When you bring it to your eyes, you find what you want to see, quickly and easily.

If you go into a store and find that you are having difficulty with the instrument you are testing, put it down. Reach for another model. There are a number of quality instruments that meet birding specs. One is almost certain to fit you.

Good Glass and the Quality Gradient

"Let me check these out for you, sir," I said, addressing the imminent owner of a pair of Zeiss 7×42 binoculars.

Bringing the binoculars up to my eyes, I trained them on the eyechart across the wall. Line 10, at the bottom of the chart, was set in teeny-weeny six-point type. Nevertheless, I expected to read it with ease. I was wrong. The letters were blurred beyond recognition.

An hour earlier I'd sold a pair of binoculars that retailed for $700 *less* than the Zeiss — and had been able to read the bottom line with ease!

Reaching into the display case, I extracted the display model 7×42 and trained it on the eyechart. Line 10 was perfectly readable. I tried the suspect pair again and got the same blurred results.

Really curious now (and having just received a shipment of instruments), I brought out seven different 7×42s and tested them all. The results were illuminating.

One instrument offered resolution that was clearly superior to all the others. Another was obviously brighter than the rest. Three were functionally fine. One was slightly, but noticeably, darker than the pack, and one, the instrument that had initiated the test, was — generously speaking — not in the same performance class.

So the point is that Zeiss's quality control is poor? No. Zeiss's quality control is good, as most owners of the 7×42s can attest. The point is that there is a range of quality and performance inherent in all mass-produced products, *including optics.*

Since this eye-opening experience, I have discovered many examples of the variation between individual optical instruments — even noticeable and disconcerting differences between the images offered by the different barrels of the *same* instrument.

To repeat: test the instrument *before* you buy it — and you might want to test several.

— **P.D.**

How to Buy Binoculars

FOREWARNED IS FOREARMED

When you go shopping for birding binoculars, there are several things you should know. First, as a birder, you represent the largest consumer bloc in the binocular industry. Over 30 percent of all binoculars are purchased for birding.

Second, binocular manufacturers understand your needs as a birder. The average salesperson may not. *Don't let them confuse you.*

Third, the only way to be certain that the binoculars you purchase truly work for you is to test a number of different makes and models first. Most stores don't offer a good selection. They may carry an assortment of instruments, but many are designed to appeal to other user groups.

If there is a store in your area that is geared toward birders and offers a wide selection, go there. Play with the whole array. If a store is not convenient to you, go to a popular birding spot in your area. Find out what instruments the experienced birders are using. Ask to try them (most birders will be only too pleased to help), and ask them where they made their purchase.

Fourth, not only are there differences between makes and models, there are differences *between individual instruments of the same make and model.* Be certain you examine the instrument you buy and ask the salesperson to check it too — for proper alignment, for optical performance, for any dust or debris in the barrels, for any mechanical problem. If you are very particular and the store has the inventory, ask to test two or three instruments of the same model and select the one that outperforms the others.

TESTING INSTRUMENTS

Testing the performance of a binocular in the store takes about three minutes. Here's what to check for: optical performance (resolution/field), brightness, color bias, close focus, dust, and alignment.

Resolution

Resolution comes into play when you try to read an eye chart or a printed page that offers type of various sizes (such as a newspaper):

the instrument that lets you read the smallest print offers the best resolution.

Check both barrels *individually* and use the same eye. Remember, no two human eyes are identical either.

Field Quality

Instruments often show considerable distortion across the visual field. To test for distortion, focus the instrument on an open newspaper set approximately forty feet away. The print should appear uniformly sharp. Most instruments blur at the extreme edges. Those that show random, patchy distortion or are sharp only at the center of the field are not acceptable.

Field of View

Find a target that offers a number of reference points — for example, a multivolume bookrack, a row of photos on a wall, a bulletin board plastered with notices. Train the left edge of the field onto a fixed reference point. Note where the right edge falls. What you are looking for is the instrument that reaches the farthest to the right — the one that has the largest field of view. There is variation between instruments here too.

Color Bias

Few binoculars offer a totally unbiased image. The coatings used by different companies accentuate different colors, and while some biases are subtle, others are not. For example, amber- or ruby-coated instruments, which are touted as offering better contrast, turn the world a ghastly green. The best way to test the color bias is to train binoculars on a white background. A subtle shift to red, yellow, or brown is acceptable, but not to a degree that affects your perception of natural colors. Bird study, after all, is very much a matter of seeing colors.

Close Focus

Simply a matter of seeing how close an object can be brought into focus.

Dust in the Barrel
Turn the binocular upside down. Look through the objective lens on the ceiling, the palm of your hand — or optimally, a blue sky. Internal dust or debris (and fingerprints and oil) on a lens or prism will be seen as a gray or black speck. *Note:* make certain the dust is not simply on the outside of the instrument.

Alignment
Method 1: To test vertical alignment, stand directly in front of your target and focus the binoculars on a horizontal line — a window sill, for instance, or the top of a wall. Draw the binoculars away from your eyes until the single image splits in two, leaving the left eye to look through the left barrel, and the right eye through the right. If the line is broken in the center but remains horizontal, no problem. If one line is higher or lower than the other, then the binoculars are *out of alignment:* the barrels are not focused on the same point.
Method 2: To test both vertical and horizontal alignment, train the binoculars on some distant object, such as a house. Keeping both eyes open, cover one objective with a piece of paper. Hold and focus the instrument on the target with the free hand. Wait ten seconds. Remove the paper. If the target shifts or jumps, it means your eyes are working to bring the images together. The instrument is out of alignment.

A disturbing number of less expensive binoculars are out of alignment out of the box (sometimes quality instruments too). Buyer beware.

SHOULD I BUY A HIGH-PERFORMANCE INSTRUMENT?
If money is no object, absolutely. Beginning birders even more than experts need good equipment. But for most of us, money is a consideration. Still, don't expect to pay less than $200 for an instrument that is durable and works well in the birding arena.

The rule of thumb: *buy the best binocular you can buy, and buy it as soon as you can afford it.* If you cannot afford the one you want, buy the best you can afford now; then save for the one you want.

In my years of birding I have encountered many birders who

looked forward to upgrading their present instruments. I have never met the owner of a superior instrument who regretted the purchase.

Binocular Use and Care

Binoculars come (or should come) with an adjustable neck strap. Most people adjust the strap so that the binocular rides on the chest or just below the ribs. Some people (like those with neck problems) prefer to lengthen the strap so that it stretches bandolier fashion across the chest, with the binoculars riding at the side. It's your choice.

Adjust the interpupillary distance to fit the distance between your eyes by bringing the binocular up to your eyes and adjusting the barrels until you see a single image. Customize the instrument for your eyes by looking at a distant object, closing your right eye, and turning the center-focus wheel until the image is sharp. Don't labor this adjustment. Once the image looks sharp, it is sharp. Then close your left eye, open the right, and move the individual eyepiece adjustment ring (usually located on the right ocular) or a separate adjustment knob until the image in the right eye is sharp. Now look down and see where the adjustment is set. Remember this setting (in case the adjustment knob shifts). If the setting slips frequently, you can affix a strip of black electrical tape over the adjustment ring to prevent it from moving.

From here on in, all focusing will be done with the center-focus wheel. There should be no reason to change the individual eyepiece adjustment unless your vision changes.

The key to using a binocular is practice. The best way to practice is to go outside and find birds. It's no more complicated than that.

MAKE CAUTION A MINDSET

Binoculars are tubes filled with glass, and glass is not the most durable stuff on the planet. High-quality binoculars require less care than less expensive ones because they are generally more rugged, better sealed, and designed with long years of service in mind. No matter how rugged the design, binoculars should not be dropped or banged about. Mistreat them and you will soon find out how good the manufacturer's warranty really is.

Caution: binocular straps wear and fray, and connection points break. Check your strap periodically and replace it at the first sign of wear.

When not being used for long periods, binoculars should be kept in a case — to prevent dust or corrosives from collecting on the lenses.

Cleaning Lenses

Unless they malfunction, the only maintenance that binoculars require is a periodic cleaning of the ocular and objective lenses. Improper cleaning, however, can do more harm than good.

Coatings can be scratched, abraded, and sometimes even polished off. In an ideal world, the way to clean binoculars is:

- ❧ Use canned air, purchased from a camera store, to blow the lens surfaces clean.
- ❧ Work lens surfaces lightly with a camel-hair brush to remove macro-gritties.
- ❧ Breathe onto the glass to "fog the lenses," then dry them with a clean chamois cloth or soft optical cleaning cloth, using a circular motion and without bearing down.

Warning: never use lens tissue treated with silicone. It breaks down some coatings. If lenses are severely fouled, try applying a small amount of distilled water to a cloth and wiping the lens surface after brushing. Commercial lens cleaners should be used only as a last resort.

But in the real world, you will find that lenses are most often in need of cleaning while you are in the field. What you do is:

- ❧ Blow on the lens.
- ❧ Breathe on the lens.
- ❧ Reach for a soft cotton handkerchief and wipe the lens clean.

No handkerchief? Try the corner of a 100 percent cotton T-shirt. An alternative method, developed by pelagic birders whose lenses were constantly being fouled by salt spray, works well on land too. Just lick the lens and wipe. It's not hygienic. It might not be good for some lens coatings. But it works.

Field Guides — The Rosetta Stone to Birds

Field guides are just that — books that are compact and portable enough to be carried into the *field* and whose descriptive content *guides* users toward a proper identification. How well a field guide works can mean the difference between a challenging encounter with a bird and a frustrating one.

Dozens of field guides are available. Some are very simplistic, containing only the more common birds and catering to casual and back-yard birders. Others are more specialized and detailed, focusing upon specific groups of birds, particularly those that show an array of plumages (like gulls) or are difficult to differentiate (like sandpipers). These specialty guides are discussed in chapter 5.

This section deals with general field guides that cover all the regularly occurring North American birds that you can aspire to find.

The Naming and Ordering of Birds
SYSTEMA NATURAE

Every field guide strives to impose a logical order upon the natural world to make it easier for our species to understand it. The foundation upon which all field guides rest incorporates two articles of faith: that at some biological level, all living things relate only to one of their own kind or **species;** and that each species has traits that both distinguish it from and link it to similar species.

The scientific system of naming and ordering birds and other living things, called **taxonomy,** can be traced to the work of the Swedish botanist Carolus Linnaeus. In 1758 Linnaeus devised a system that assigns two Latin-based names to each distinct species. The first name, called the **genus,** groups organisms with very similar traits. The second denotes the species. Together they confer a unique identity — a sort of scientific last name/first name.

Take, for example, the species *Chaetura pelagica*, the **scientific name** for the bird that captivated the caller from the Bronx and whose **common name** is Chimney Swift. The scientific name is descriptive (as scientific names tend to be) and unique to this species. *Chaetura* comes from two Greek words, *chaite*, a "bristle," and *oura*, a "tail" — an obvious reference to the short, stiff tail that helps swifts anchor themselves to cliff faces and brick walls. *Pelagica* derives from the Greek *pelagos*, meaning "marine" — a reference not to any presumed association with oceans but perhaps to the wayfaring habits of this long-distance migrant. In Linnaeus's time, all great travelers were sailors.

Other species of swifts in North America include the western Vaux's Swift, *Chaetura vauxi* (named in honor of the ornithologist Richard Vaux) and the White-throated Swift, *Aeronautes saxatalis* (*Aeronautes* from the Greek words *aer*, "air," and *nautes*, a "sailor"; *saxitalis*, the Latin word for "rock dweller" — an apt name for this cliff-dwelling western speedster).

Chimney Swift and Vaux's Swift are so similar that they share the same genus. Because White-throated Swift, on the other hand, has traits that are not shared by the other two, it is placed in a different genus.

All three swifts share the same scientific **family,** Apodidae and the same **order,** Apodiformes — a grouping that includes swifts and hummingbirds (Trochilidae).

All birds, of course, share a common **class:** Aves — the scientific grouping that distinguishes birds from other living things.

In a schematic diagram, the breakdown looks like this:

TABLE 2.1: The Taxonomic Order of Birds: Swifts

	CHIMNEY SWIFT	VAUX'S SWIFT	WHITE-THROATED SWIFT
CLASS	Aves	Aves	Aves
ORDER	Apodiformes	Apodiformes	Apodiformes
FAMILY	Apodidae	Apodidae	Apodidae
GENUS	*Chaetura*	*Chaetura*	*Aeronautes*
SPECIES	*pelagica*	*vauxi*	*saxatalis*

There is a level of differentiation below the species level called, appropriately, **subspecies**. These regional forms are sometimes different enough to be distinguished in the field but are not (at least not *now*) thought to be genetically dissimilar enough to be regarded as different species.

Here's the Take-home

Avian systematics is fundamentally simple. Birds that have traits in common are lumped together. The more birds have in common, the more closely allied they are in the taxonomic ordering of birds. The more dissimilar they are, the more space and other species lie between them.

While birders most often refer to birds by their common name instead of their scientific name, birders have generally accepted both the species differentiations established by ornithologists and the taxonomic ordering of species as presented in the **American Ornithologists' Union Check-list of North American Birds**. This document, published by the AOU, is updated periodically.

The problem is — and has long been — that what makes sense in the hand and in the lab does not always make sense in the field.

The Evolution of Field Guides

So What Does Taxonomy
Have to Do with Field Guides?

Back when Linnaeus began grouping and ordering the natural world, the traits he used to relate, distinguish, and order species were anatomical. Some of these traits were easy to see — like the xygodactyl feet of woodpeckers. (Most birds have three toes in front, one in back; woodpeckers have two toes in front, two in back.) Some traits are not readily apparent, like the fused vertebrae that help distinguish falcons from other birds of prey. Today scientists are looking even closer in their efforts to distinguish species, comparing the very genetic makeup of birds.

Field guides order and group birds too. As in ornithological tradition, field guides arrange species on the basis of shared traits, frequently the same anatomical traits used by scientists. But the tradition of ornithological taxonomy hinges upon traits that can be distinguished *in the hand or in the lab*. The objective of field guides is to establish relationships between species that help distinguish them *in the field*.

A Brief History of Field Guides

Books about North America's birds have a long tradition. Notables include works by the English naturalist-painter Mark Catesby, who explored the American Southeast in the first half of the 1700s; by Alexander Wilson, author of *American Ornithology* and "the Father of American Ornithology"; and by John James Audubon, whose *Birds of America* is a visual masterpiece.

But these were ornithological and artistic treatments. None of these works even pretended to be a field guide. The very nature of bird study at the time, conducted over the barrels of fowling pieces, precluded the notion of carrying reference books into the field, much less the need to do so.

In 1895 Frank M. Chapman, curator of the New York Museum of Natural History, published *Birds of Eastern North America*, a compact accounting that he called a "handbook." It was written (as the 1926 third edition states) to meet the needs of the "bird student" who primarily demanded information concerning the bird in nature. Unfortunately, Chapman's use of a dichotomous key to distinguish species, backed up by painfully detailed descriptions, probably broke more hearts among aspiring "bird students" than it did new ground. Take, for example, this species description from Chapman's third edition:

> Top and sides of head black, a white spot above and below the eye; rest of upperparts grayish slate color; margins of wings slightly lighter; tail blackish, the outer feathers with white spots at their tips; throat white, streaked with black; rest of the underparts rufous (tipped with white in the fall), becoming white on the middle of the lower belly; bill yellow, brownish in fall.

Few, in their first reading, would recognize this as the common American Robin.

The first true field guide was the famous *Chester Reed Guide to the Land Birds East of the Rockies*, published in 1906. A western version was published in 1913. It was pocket-sized (3½-by-5½-inch) and featured thumb-sized portrayals and a descriptive text.

The painted illustrations were good, portraying birds as they might appear at a distance, with details muted. The text fell short of today's field guide standards but was a revolutionary leap ahead of the pedantic descriptions of Chapman.

Millions of copies of Chester Reed's guides were purchased, one by a thirteen-year-old "bird student" living in Jamestown, New York, who carried it into the field along with a 4× Le Maire opera glass. His name was Roger Tory Peterson. Twelve years later, in 1934, he would publish *A Field Guide to the Birds*. The first two thousand copies sold out within three weeks. Now in its fifth edition, the Peterson field guide and its western companion volume have sold over ten million copies.

New Guide for a New Age

Roger Tory Peterson (1908–96), the once and forever "grand master" of North American birding, never claimed proprietary rights to the breakthrough that made his *Field Guide to the Birds* so useful. In his first edition, Peterson acknowledges the catalytic influence of Ernest Thompson Seton's *Two Little Savages* and the "pattern charts" drawn by Seton (attributed to one of the book's characters) that depict ducks seen from a distance. The illustrations show the bold plumage patterns that distinguish them — what Seton called "uniforms" and birders today call **field marks.**

The few illustrations found in Chapman were too detailed — they showed the marks that might be seen on hand-held birds. Chester Reed depicted distant birds but failed to appreciate how distance affects plumage. Details disappear, but contrasts sharpen; patterns not evident in close quarters emerge. These patterns are the "trade marks of nature" that are the cornerstone of Peterson's identification system.

What Roger Peterson did was to take the field mark approach pi-

Roger Tory Peterson, author, illustrator, teacher, and naturalist, ushered in a new age of bird study with the publication of his first field guide in 1934; the fifth edition was published in 2001. He is pictured here with a young Osprey near Old Lyme, Connecticut, in 1961. *Alfred Eisenstaedt, courtesy of Virginia M. Peterson.*

oneered by Seton and apply it to all eastern birds, codifying in his depictions and in the text the marks that distinguish one species from another.

Peterson did not discover all the field marks described in his book. There were a number of other eager minds trying to solve the riddle of bird identification during the first decades of the twentieth century — among them Peterson's fellow members of the Bronx Bird Club. What Peterson brought to the table was a winning blend of artistic talent, communication skill, a cutting-edge understanding of his subject, and a utilitarian vision of purpose that to this day others have merely refined (and in some cases obscured).

Systema Naturae Revisited

Most field guides to North American birds nominally follow the **taxonomic order** established by the AOU but diverge from it when the primary focus of a field guide — differentiation between similar or confusing species — dictates a more pragmatic order.

For example, in the fourth edition of the Peterson guide, the Alcidae, or alcids — penguin-like birds most often seen along rocky coasts in winter — follow the grebes, a family of lobe-toed diving birds. The species are visually similar enough that they might be confused, although by taxonomic standards alcids are only distantly related to grebes. In the AOU's taxonomic order, many bird species (including ducks, hawks, grouse, shorebirds, and gulls) lie between alcids and grebes.

Kenn Kaufman's *Focus Guide to Birds of North America* tempers the taxonomic order by incorporating an element of probability. Birds that are common and widely distributed (and more likely to be encountered) are depicted first. Similar species less likely to be encountered follow.

Several field guides have departed radically from the AOU taxonomic order (and from the other guides too). Two use a habitat approach — grouping and comparing species that share a common habitat. Another divides birds into groups distinguished by behavior and shape and then further subdivides them by color.

CHARACTERISTICS OF A GOOD FIELD GUIDE

With so many from which to choose, what should you look for in a field guide?

- ✺ SIZE: A field guide should be small enough to be carried easily in the field.
- ✺ SCOPE: A good field guide contains all the birds you are likely to encounter where you are birding.
- ✺ FOCUS: A good field guide has one aim — to impart key information relating to the identification of birds.
- ✺ TIMELINESS AND ACCURACY: Staying up-to-date is a challenge for even the best field guides.
- ✺ ORGANIZATION: An intelligent organization and presentation of material accommodates the needs of birders who are being challenged in the field.
- ✺ DESIGN: A field guide cannot impart information effectively without a utilitarian design.
- ✺ ILLUSTRATIONS: Illustrations that present birds as they appear in the field.
- ✺ PROCESS: A field guide should convey to readers the process of identifying birds as well as provide a means to identification.

Size

It has been many years since anyone has been able to squeeze all that is useful to know about bird identification into the format of a Chester Reed field guide. But among the most popular guides, most will fit (snugly) into a hip pocket. For those that do not, a jacket or a vest with big pockets or a belt pouch designed to hold a large guide will serve. Barring this, slipping the book between your belt and the small of your back is a time-honored technique.

Scope

Field guides should be all-inclusive: all the species that regularly occur within the geographic scope of the book should be depicted. Guides that try to second-guess nature by excluding less common species in the name of simplification are a formula for frustration.

A more workable approach to simplification involves the grouping of birds into eastern and western volumes. Birds that are unlikely to occur in one part of the country or the other are eliminated, thus reducing variables. Some guides, however, house all North American species in a single volume.

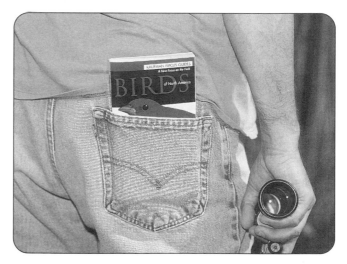

Field guides are just that—books small and portable enough to accompany birders in the field. *Linda Dunne.*

First Guide Frustration

My first field guide was a hip-pocket-sized paperback with robins on the cover and 112 species depicted within. Another 148 were mentioned in the text but not illustrated.

I loved this little book, but several things frustrated me. First, there were birds in it that I knew I'd never see — western birds like the Black-billed Magpie and Brown Towhee (now split into two species: California Towhee and Canyon Towhee). Second, there were birds like the Red-headed Woodpecker and Bobolink that were supposed to be found where I lived but that I could never find. The **range maps** had been drawn according to distribution, not habitat — a fine point of distinction I didn't appreciate.

But what *really* frustrated me were the birds I saw that weren't in the pages of the book — and there were lots of them, especially in spring. Lots of brightly colored ones that moved like quicksilver. It occurred to me that some of these birds were the ones whose names were mentioned but not illustrated. But I couldn't be sure. If a bird was common enough to be seen, it should have been in the book.

What I never appreciated was that the book had been highly simplified to make it easier to use and more appealing to a general audience. The birds shown were those that nested widely across North America and occurred in a variety of habitats — not just the woodlands behind my parents' home. Migrants, which could be very common in those woodlands at times of migration, were omitted.

So, even though the book was simple, it didn't save me from frustration, and it held back my development as a birder. Somebody with an eye toward simplification or market appeal had tried to determine what birds I was most likely to see.

And they had guessed wrong.

— **P.D.**

Focus

The species accounts within a field guide should have one aim: to impart key information relating to the identification of birds. The elements of identification include: an accurate depiction, a concise description summarizing the distinguishing field marks, information relating to a species range, **seasonal occurrence, relative abundance,** and additional distinguishing information relating to habits, habitat, behavior, and **vocalizations.**

Accuracy and Timeliness

No field guide is flawless, but errors horrible enough to prevent a correct identification are few. More troublesome is the battle that all guides have with time and change. Books in print are static. Science is not. Species are constantly being reevaluated, reclassified, and renamed.

Sometimes two species are determined to be genetically similar and **lumped** into a single species. For example, the Baltimore Oriole and Bullock's Oriole were lumped in 1973 to become the Northern Oriole. Sometimes a species is **split** — that is, it is recognized, after study and debate (or in the case of the orioles, more study and debate), to represent two or more distinct species. In 1995, for example, the Northern Oriole was "split" back into Baltimore Oriole and Bullock's Oriole.

Since the first Peterson field guide was published in 1934, there have been scores of name changes. The only sure way to remain current on names and species classifications is to own a recently published or updated field guide. Changes, as they occur, can be noted in the margins.

Organization

This is where the guides begin to differ markedly and fundamentally. Most use a modified AOU checklist approach — that is, going from water birds to passerines, from primitive species to those more evolutionarily advanced. Some books take a different approach, however: they use some standard other than anatomical traits to group birds in an effort to make it easier for beginning birders to match a bird in the field with its likeness in the book. These might be called "process approach" field guides.

While process-oriented field guides have good points, they generally fail in their goal — simplifying bird identification. A process that combines and compares birds on the basis of habitat or behaviors or colors is still a system that must be learned to be effective.

Guides that follow the standard taxonomic order of birds established by the AOU have several advantages over process-oriented guides. First, this order is widely accepted. Once you familiarize yourself with the standard order of families and species, you can pick up any other guide (or checklist) that uses it and find a bird quickly and easily. Second, the anatomical characteristics used to group birds — like bill shape and wing shape — are easily seen in the field. Third, easily confused species with similar physical characteristics — like the webbed feet on loons and the lobed feet on the similar grebes — are often found in comparative proximity in the field as well as in the standard guide.

When beginning birders say that they cannot use the traditional field guides, what they are really saying is that they haven't troubled to familiarize themselves with it. The remedy is simple. Take the time to make yourself familiar with the birds and with your field guide.

Design
The design of field guides makes them more or less utilitarian. Guides that include all the information needed to identify a species on one page — illustration, text, and range map — or on a two-page spread are easier to use than guides that separate text from illustrations or text from maps. Guides whose layout provides direct comparisons between a number of similar species facilitate identifications and learning.

Illustrations
The most important consideration in choosing a field guide is the depiction. A bird must be illustrated *as you see it in the field* to be identified accurately.

Some field guides use painted illustrations. Some use photographs. Some use both. For many reasons, illustrations generally work better than photos.

- Illustrations are idealized depictions that show a bird and its field marks to best effect. A photo shows only a representative member of a species and its field marks to best effect. Thus, a photo shows only what an individual bird looked like at one moment in time, under a certain lighting condition, in a certain plumage, at a certain angle, using a particular film.

- The quality of photos used in field guides differs markedly — from excellent to poor. The quality of painted illustrations also varies — between artists (in guides using multiple artists) and between print runs, but not so markedly as in photo guides.

- An illustrator can easily portray and arrange birds to show relative sizes between species. Photo guides cannot accomplish this easily or well, and most fail utterly in this regard.

- The background that best illustrates a subject for the purpose of identification is no background at all. Unmanipulated photos complicate identification by presenting birds against a virtual kaleidoscope of backgrounds.

- Those who illustrate birds almost always know their birds well. Not everyone who photographs birds or who edits and selects photos for field guides is necessarily as knowledgeable.

- Photographers strive to take supernatural images — pictures that show extreme detail and colors that pop under perfect lighting. Illustrators depict birds the way they are seen in the field — at a distance, through binoculars.

This is not to say that photographic guides are not without merit, that the information they contain is not good, or that photos (when correctly identified) inaccurately depict. But among the field guides available today (and with the exception of *Birds of North America* by Kenn Kaufman, which circumvents many of the shortcomings of photo-driven guides by using digitally manipulated photos and a very thoughtful arrangement of subjects), painted illustrations work better for identification and learning the discipline of identification.

The Take-home of Learning to See Critically

For some queer reason, I didn't discover field guides until I was in my teens. What filled this niche, from the age of eleven to eighteen, was a two-volume set published by the National Geographic Society entitled *Song and Garden Birds of North America* and *Water, Prey, and Game Birds of North America,* both edited by Alexander Wetmore. The books had an informative (but not very identification-oriented) text and a mix of photos and illustrations that were sometimes (and sometimes not) useful for identification purposes. The books had one other serious shortfall: they were too big and too expensive to take into the field. Instead of looking at a bird and then leafing through the pages of a guide, I developed the technique of looking critically at each new bird, memorizing the details (color, shape, size; wing bars, tail spots, eye-line), and then running home (literally running) with the image fresh in my mind.

Sometimes I'd discover that there were two (or more) species with the features I'd remembered and that the way to tell them apart was to look at the feet or the quality of the eye ring or something else I hadn't noticed. So I'd run back and try to locate the bird again.

Not having a real field guide may have prevented me from identifying some of the birds I saw. But it also forced me to see critically and memorize details. In the process I learned the best lesson any guide could hope to impart, one I have used all my life.

— **P.D.**

Process

This is a subjective consideration. It has little to do with the identification of a single unknown bird. It has everything to do with how a birder learns the mechanics of bird identification — the process of seeing and assimilating detail that is the foundation of making an identification.

In part, process is linked to how the author of a field guide imparts information — the order of significance he assigns to key information — abundance, range, habitat, most prominent feature, and supportive field marks. In part, process is projected by the illustrations — how the birds are grouped. Do they facilitate comparison? What possibilities do they suggest?

But the essence of process is not comparison. It is critical thinking. All field guides, to a greater or lesser extent, can be used to help identify a puzzling bird. This is a static approach to bird identification. But bird identification itself is a process. The guides that work best are those whose format is not so much anchored in a process as an embodiment of it.

Choosing and Using a Field Guide

There is no single guide that does everything best. They vary in complexity, regional bias, and usefulness. There is also no reason to own just one field guide. They are inexpensive and a treasure trove of valuable information.

In all likelihood, however, one field guide out of the many is destined to become *your* primary guide — the one that fits your approach to birding and will become as familiar to your hands as your binoculars are.

Many guides come in a hardcover or softcover edition. Softcover guides, wrapped in weather-resistant material, are more kick-around tough than hardbound guides and can bend to fit more easily in a pocket.

Using Your Field Guide
Don't let the name fool you. Field guides are not just to be used in the field. In fact, in some places (most notably the United Kingdom) the use of guides in the field is discouraged. Birders coming upon an unfamiliar bird are encouraged to sketch the bird from life, to use field time to study the bird, and to make a description of all pertinent details — more or less what I did before I got my first true field guide.

Here in North America field guides are widely used in the field.

The first step in using a field guide is becoming familiar with it *before* taking it into the field. *Kevin Karlson.*

You can cut crucial seconds, even minutes, off the identification, however, by becoming familiar with your guide before you go birding.

READ THE INTRODUCTORY MATERIAL: Learn how to quickly find and interpret what you need in the text and illustrations.

LEARN THE ORDER IN WHICH GROUPS OF BIRDS OCCUR and where species fall on the page.

LEARN BIRD TOPOGRAPHY, the names that distinguish the parts of a bird.

READ THE SPECIES DESCRIPTIONS: You don't need to memorize them, but try to learn the key field marks of key birds so that you know what to look for when a glimpse is all you get.

CUSTOMIZING YOUR GUIDE

Whatever guide you choose, you can customize it to make it more useful. Quick key indexes can be glued inside the covers of books to help locate target species, and index tabs can be affixed to pages to make it easier to find particular bird groups. You can buy these indexes ready-made, make your own, or devise your own system using color bars running along the pages of the book.

If your guide is more far-ranging than you are, you can underline or highlight birds that are likely to occur in your area or use masking tape to cover those that aren't. As your skills grow or your search for birds expands, the tape can be peeled away.

Of course, the best way to customize your guide is to mark each species you find with a check mark, followed by the date and the place — the particulars of your first encounter with the species — an encounter known among birders everywhere as a **life bird.**

In Praise of Peterson

You might bet that any text on birding published by Houghton Mifflin would tout the merits of the Peterson field guide — the flagship of its field guide series and the guide that ushered in the age of birding. I won't disappoint you. In point of fact, I heartily recommend both the Peterson eastern and western bird guides, but for reasons that have nothing to do with the colophon this book shares with them.

When experienced birders recommend a field guide, they most often recommend the one they themselves started with — because that is the one with which they are most familiar, and the one whose process they have wittingly or unwittingly made their own. I did not start with Peterson's, but I wish I had. Through my experience with beginning birders, and through my efforts to increase my own identification skills, I have come to appreciate the utilitarian ease of a Peterson field guide.

There are several reasons why this guide serves beginning birders well. First, the text is simple and friendly, written with the beginning birder in mind. Second, the illustrations are very thoughtfully laid out to make comparisons with similar species easy. Third, the text and the illustrations were crafted by a single hand and a single mind, so there is perfect accord between what the author wanted to say and what the illustrator wanted to depict. Most of the popular guides are committee efforts.

I have other favorite field guides that I am pleased to recommend when their advantages seem tailored to someone's need. For beginning birders who travel widely but whose birding is conducted primarily in the East, *Birds of North America* (the "Golden Guide" written by Chandler Robbins and his colleagues) is a wonderful choice.

For birders who are already grounded in the basic birds and are searching for uncommon and elusive species all across North America, the National Geographic Society's *Field Guide to the Birds of North America* is a favorite. Owing to its focus on western subspecies, beginning birders who live anywhere from the Rocky Mountains west (particularly Alaska, which hosts many vagrant birds from Asia) might want to consider this their primary guide.

A guide that incorporates intelligent design, the sum of current knowledge concerning bird identification, and superb illustration skills is *The Sibley Guide to Birds*. The *Kaufman Focus Guide to Birds of North America* is a scion of Peterson, combining utilitarian ease with digitally altered photos — a technique that vastly improves the usefulness of photos.

The Sibley guide will most appeal to accomplished birders. The Kaufman guide offers easy footing for back-yard birders who want to make the avocational leap to field birding.

The needs of the birding community, like its skill levels, are vast. No guide can hope to do it all or satisfy everyone. But for most people, for my money, the guides that serve the beginning birder (even the intermediate birder) best are the eastern and western Peterson field guides.

Roger Peterson grew up and learned his skills in the formative years of birding. His skills advanced as birding advanced, but his grounding is very much in the age when seeing a bird *close* and *well* and identifying that bird was the challenge. It's the very same challenge that beginning birders face today.

The books, like the man who crafted them, are mated to that fundamental challenge in simple, sympathetic accord. Users don't have to understand why these guides work so well, but like the millions of users before them, they cannot help but appreciate them.

THE BOTTOM LINE
One thing every new birder should know is that no matter how good your field guide is, there will be times when you find a bird that doesn't look like any of those in the book.

In every species, individuals vary in size, shape, and particularly plumage. Occasionally, too, birds of two different species mate and produce hybrid young with characteristics of both parents. Or birds become stained — by tar, paint, and even the dyes applied by ornithologists to study bird movement.

And of course, a guide is limited to a defined range. Birds sometimes wander far outside their normal range.

A field guide is just that — a guide. It is not the final word.

BIRDING CD-ROMS — NOT YET BEYOND FIELD GUIDES
Software is available for bird identification and for listing birds (discussed in chapter 3). Some programs are technological offshoots of printed field guides. (The best current example of this type is Houghton Mifflin's *North American Birds* with Roger Tory Peterson.) Others are rooted in the electronic information culture.

All birding CD-ROMs combine informative text with illustrations (often multiple illustrations) and have the advantage of recorded vocalizations (not just the descriptions of bird sounds found in printed guides). CD-ROM technology also provides for attractive asides (like bird quizzes).

Identification software can be a useful learning tool, but CD-ROMs continue to have one fundamental shortfall: they cannot realistically be taken into or used effectively in the field. However, with the advent of hand-held computers, we may soon have portable electronic field guides.

Clothing
QUIET, CRYPTIC, AND COMFORTABLE
Birding doesn't have a dress code. The standard garb is shorts or slacks, T-shirt, polo shirt, or flannel shirt, and sneakers or walking shoes, but almost any casual outdoor wear will serve. You will enjoy birding more and see more birds if you wear clothing that is quiet, cryptic, and comfortable.

"Quiet" means rustle- and crackle-free so that you can hear birds while walking with your arms swinging at your sides — and so birds and other wildlife won't hear you and beat a premature retreat.

"Cryptic" means not garishly bright or colorful. Clothing doesn't have to be camouflaged — although the camouflaged patterns popular among hunters are becoming more popular among birders. But clothing should be a cool, neutral, or natural color — like tan, brown, green, or smoky gray — that makes a figure blend into a landscape, not stand out.

Birds see colors, and bright colors advertise your presence and may even startle birds. Imagine, for a moment, being a ground-foraging, shadow-loving Hermit Thrush and having a hooded figure in a full-length yellow rain suit suddenly swing into view.

One color you should absolutely avoid is *white*. Across much of the animal kingdom the color white is visual Esperanto for "Hey, lookee here! Danger! Take cover!" This message is flashed from a deer's raised tail, or from the underparts of schooling bait fish turning to avoid a predator's rush. Since your objective is to get close to birds, it's not a message you want to send.

Casual clothing for casual birding on the island of Attu. *Linda Dunne.*

Good Birders Don't Wear White

On October 14, 1991, I spent several hours crouched by a trail in Ramsey Canyon monitoring a nest. Most birds in southeastern Arizona had fledged their young months earlier, but these were no ordinary birds. These were Eared Quetzals — handsome, rare cousins to the Elegant Trogon — and this was the first nest ever recorded in the United States.

These Eared Quetzals had arrived in the Huachuca Mountains in early August, among several that crossed the Mexican border that summer. News of this sighting worked its way through the birding grapevine, and soon birders were flooding into Ramsey Canyon in hopes of spotting this treasure from the Sierra Madre. But the birds were extremely wary, disappearing into the dense forest at the first sign of human intrusion.

On October 10, a group of visitors videotaped the female trogon entering a cavity in a dead maple easily visible from the trail. A member of the same group returned on October 12 and watched as the male carried a caterpillar into the hole, confirming the presence of nestlings.

The nest was a two-mile hike from where I lived and worked at Ramsey Canyon Preserve, so on October 14 I took a day off to watch the nest and record every detail of this historic event. At 12:44, an hour since the previous feeding, the male signaled his return to the nest with several *squeal-chuck* calls, silencing the six birders patiently awaiting his return. After two breathless minutes, the male landed at the nest entrance with a caterpillar in his bill, then immediately flew to a nearby tree. There he sat squeal-chucking in alarm, each call accompanied by a flash of his white outer tail feathers.

On previous feeding visits, the arriving parent had entered the nest almost immediately despite the presence of several observers, so what caused this delay? Over the next eight minutes the male flew back and forth across the clearing, calling constantly, before landing once again at the nest entrance. Through the spotting scope I saw his head turn briefly toward the trail before he flew off again, still squealing in alarm. I followed the direction of the quetzal's gaze to a recently arrived birder sitting apart from the rest but in plain view of the nest. The man's white long-sleeved shirt and cap glared against the dark forest background. The problem suddenly became clear.

Though movement might have disturbed the bird even more, I quickly sidled over to the birder in white and asked him to remove his shirt and cap. Taken aback at first, he quickly complied when I explained the reason for this odd request. I crept back to my spotting scope, and after six tense minutes the male quetzal finally entered the cavity. After less than a minute inside, he left again, returning to the tree a few minutes later with another insect; this time there was little hesitation as he slipped inside the nest to feed his young.

That evening a colleague and I cut a few yards of camouflage cloth into simple ponchos for loan to inappropriately dressed trogon seekers, allowing dozens of people to observe the nest with minimal disturbance to the parent birds. The nestlings died in an early storm just two weeks later, but what we learned in that short time has made many birders aware of how something as seemingly innocent as a white shirt can affect the birds we watch.

Though Eared Quetzals are unusually sensitive, they are not unique. Most birds are highly visual creatures, and color plays a significant role in their lives and behavior. Elegant Trogons also flash their white tail feathers to signal alarm. A Northern Cardinal's parental instinct is triggered by the gaping orange mouths of its young. Male Red-winged Blackbirds keep the peace in winter by concealing their provocative red epaulets. Blue-crowned Motmots instinctively recoil from the red-black and yellow-ringed pattern of coral snakes. As sensitive as birds are to such visual cues, is it logical to expect them to ignore white shirts, red hats, and fluorescent yellow day packs? Yet unlike hunters and wildlife photographers, the average birder still doesn't give much thought to field wear. Trading in that white birding festival T-shirt for a camo jumpsuit and face paint is a little extreme, but selecting neutral colors that blend with the environment can reduce the impact of birding on birds and other wildlife and improve birding success for all.

— **Sheri Williamson**

Sheri Williamson, a consummate naturalist, is codirector of the Southeast Arizona Bird Observatory in Bisbee, Arizona. Before that, she and her husband, Tom Wood, were stewards of the Nature Conservancy's Mile-Hi/Ramsey Canyon Preserves.

Other Things You'll Need

Unlike backpacking and photography, birding doesn't require much equipment. Over time I've pared what I carry down to a minimum.

A cotton handkerchief for cleaning optics (particularly when it's raining)
Lip balm and sunscreen
Insect repellent (when necessary)
Sunglasses (particularly for hawk watching or sea-bird watching)
Pocket notepad and pencil
For longer jaunts, a small daypack, a water bottle, a field guide, and extra clothing (depending upon conditions and need)

A jacket featuring several large pockets or a lightweight vest designed to carry equipment can often eliminate the need for a daypack. Some jackets and vests are especially designed for birding.

Other apparel that birders would do well to add to their kit includes knee-length boots (Wellies), a brimmed hat, and light and high-quality rain gear.

Summary Binoculars are the essential tool of birding, but few makes and models meet its demands, which include sharp, bright optics, a wide field of view, an adequate depth of field, close focus below fifteen feet, a responsive focus mechanism, and an **ergonomic design.** Lower magnification — 7× (seven-power) or 8× — is more user-friendly than higher magnification.

The best place to buy binoculars is a store specializing in meeting the needs of birders. Test a variety of makes and models, and give the instrument you buy a particularly good workout. The rule of thumb is: buy the best binocular you can afford, and buy it as soon as you are able. Expect to pay no less than $100 for an adequate birding binocular; $200 to $300 for a decent entry-level pair; and $600 to $1,400 for a top-performing instrument.

Field guides are key to bird identification. The guides that follow the standard taxonomic order, based on the shape and anatomical traits of birds, and use illustrations rather than photos work best. Field guides should be studied at home as well as taken into the field. All guides have useful information, but for sheer utilitarian ease the Peterson eastern and western guides seem to work best for most beginning and intermediate birders.

Field clothes are casual, loose-fitting, and comfortable. Fabrics should be quiet so that birds can be heard. Colors should be cryptic so that birds will not be startled.

3

The Fundamentals of Birding

Like Grosbeaks for Purple Finch

It was sunny but cold. Buds, not leaves, were in season. I was birding the Great Swamp National Wildlife Refuge — a federally designated wilderness area smack in the middle of suburban North Jersey. Ahead of me was a birding couple. Their binoculars were new, their field guide too, their clothes casual but coordinated. By all the signs, beginning birders.

They were feverishly scanning the branches above them — branches animated by a flock of Purple Finch, mostly females and immatures. Boldly patterned, charcoal brown on white, they filled the air with their single, sharp call notes, broadcasting their identity to anyone with experienced ears.

"Seen anything 'good?'" I asked — a near-universal greeting among birders.

"Yes," the gentleman said, smiling widely. "A whole flock of Rose-breasted Grosbeaks. All females. We're trying to find a male."

"Huh," I said, trying to decide whether to correct an obvious but understandable misidentification. Female Purple Finch and female Rose-breasted Grosbeak are similar — at least, similar in plumage.

And plumage is the characteristic that beginning birders usually focus upon — because this is the trait that most field guides emphasize and because, as distinguishing characteristics go, it usually works.

Not this time. By relying solely upon plumage, the couple had overlooked several other salient clues. For instance, they'd failed to note that the birds they were looking at were finch-sized — a distinction that would have eliminated Rose-breasted Grosbeak from any list of possible candidates. Rose-breasted Grosbeaks are twice the size of Purple Finches.

The couple had also failed to note the less than "gross"-sized beak on the birds. Grosbeaks aren't called "gross beaks" for nothing, and while the conical bills of Purple Finch do recall a grosbeak's bill in shape, they fall short in both size and relative proportions.

Even more significant was the date. Purple Finch are winter residents over most of New Jersey. Rose-breasted Grosbeaks, on the other hand, are summer breeders and rarely found in the state before May 1. A whole flock in late March — indeed, the very fact that the birds

A birding couple test-drives binoculars and their field guide in the shorebird-rich environs of the "old" South Cape May Meadows. *Pete Dunne.*

were flocking at all — should have planted seeds of doubt. While Purple Finch commonly gather in large, tight flocks, Rose-breasted Grosbeaks are almost never found in tight flocks — even during migration.

That the birding couple was troubled by the absence of the rhubarb-bibbed male grosbeak was encouraging. I figured that this concern would eventually lead them to discard their initial identification and get onto the right track. No reason to preempt the educational process with a heavy-handed correction.

But since the couple was leaning in the right direction, I figured it wouldn't intrude too much to give them a nudge.

"Nice male Purple Finch up there," I remarked, directing them to the wine-stained bird perched in a nearby tree. I knew they'd be able to work things out from there.

Where, When, and How to Go Birding

You have binoculars. You have a field guide. You have a free morning, and all your socially suppressed hunter-gatherer instincts are tugging at the leash. Now what?

That's easy. Just go birding. It's not a first date. It's not the oral defense of your thesis. It's an act as simple and engaging as a walk along woodland paths or viewing paintings in a gallery. *Except,* unlike paintings, birds have free will. They choose to be in certain places, at certain times. Go there and your birding will be more productive.

ALMOST ANY OLD NATURAL PLACE WILL DO

You don't have to travel to the Amazon Basin just to see birds. You don't even have to go to a national park or a migratory bird refuge. (But if there is one nearby, by all means take advantage of it.) As mentioned in chapter 1, birds are everywhere — even in habitats drastically modified to meet the needs of our own species. There are birds to be found even in cities.

But while some species of birds have acclimated themselves to

Birds and trees go together. This trio of birders is heading down the mangrove-lined Snake Bight Trail in Everglades National Park. You can almost hear the Mangrove Cuckoos calling. *Linda Dunne.*

urban habitats, most birds are more at home in natural surroundings. Different species are specialized for and apportion themselves in different habitat types. The habitat where you go birding largely determines what sorts of birds you will find and what sort of identification challenges you will face.

NOT ALL HABITATS ARE EQUAL IN THE EYES OF BIRDS

Here's a basic hint: birds like trees. Not all birds, and not all trees, but the largest and most abundant scientific order of birds in North America is the order Passeriformes, "the perching birds." Sometimes they perch on wires. Sometimes on weeds. Sometimes they "perch" on the ground. But overwhelmingly, **passerines** choose to perch upon trees.

So, if you are a birder looking for birds, even (and maybe especially) in places where trees are few and far between, you can hardly go wrong heading for a tree-rich landscape. In urban or suburban areas, this can be a riverside park, an environmental center's grounds, even a cemetery. In more rural areas, choices are broader (but not necessarily better).

In a large park or natural area dominated by mature trees, you are likely to find such representative woodland birds as woodpeckers, nuthatches, jays, and chickadees. These are permanent residents, and they can be found here anytime.

No Trees? Be at Ease

Birds have diversified and become specialized to occupy almost every conceivable habitat type. Some species are most at home in grasslands; a morning afield in one of the prairie states might turn up such grassland and open-country specialists as meadowlarks, Horned Lark, or one of several grassland sparrow species. Rivers, lakes, and coasts offer different possibilities — among them loons, grebes, waterfowl, and gulls.

Freshwater marshes, which are sort of a habitat cross between a meadow and a lake, are home to rails, bitterns, herons, and egrets; and tidal wetlands, which expose their muddy or sandy bottom at low tide, attract a host of sandpipers and other shorebirds.

Desert, tundra, chaparral, sagebrush plains, spruce bogs, open seas, mangrove swamps — each habitat has its own peculiar flavor and its own special species. So no matter where you are, there is a nearby habitat that hosts a variety of birds.

The Subject Is Sewage Ponds

Sooner or later (but sooner is better), you will learn that some of the best birding anywhere, at almost any time, is upwind of the local sewage treatment plant or collection site.

These epicenters of effluvium are attractive to birds of many persuasions and divergent feeding habits. Species may vary geographically or seasonally, but there is hardly ever an ornithological void near such a site.

Bird diversity is often indicative of the level of present-day technology in the management of organic waste. For instance, where the cleanup proceeds from pond to pond, eventually to be deposited in adjacent fields via spray heads, and with the natural addition of man-made fresh marsh or even emergent vegetation, you might find an astounding variety of birds, with one or more species representing virtually all the expected families: grebes, cormorants, herons, ducks, terns, gulls, rails, shorebirds, birds of prey, flycatchers, swallows, wrens, warblers, sparrows, and black-birds.

Sewage plants and ponds can be located by calling your county or local pollution control commission or wastewater management district, or by asking other birders. You may have to request permission to bird the area. (Some have relatively open access; others have locked gates and sign-in sheets.)

By virtue of one or more astounding birds, some sewage lagoons are justifiably famous. The humble pond at Starkville, Mississippi, was the site of the first and only record of a Citrine Wagtail in the Western Hemisphere; the operation in Baltimore, Maryland, made the newspapers when a Ross's Gull visited for a few days. Some treatment plants, like that in Jackson County, Mississippi, keep a guest book and are as accommodating to birders as any official wildlife refuge.

In addition to sewage lagoons, there are other habitats favored by birders that others might give a very wide berth: cemeteries, industrial parks, landfills, and impoundments — anywhere a few good birds may be found even on a bad day.

— **Judith Toups**

Judith Toups is a writer, field trip leader, and birding instructor who birds mostly where she lives, in Gulfport, Mississippi.

When to Go

How about now? There is never a time when birds are not around. Over most of North America the calendar determines what species you will encounter, not whether birds are present at all. There is a seasonality to bird distribution. In summer the ranks of permanent residents are augmented by summer residents. These are species that migrate to warmer areas in the fall, returning to their breeding grounds in the spring to establish **territories,** find a mate, nest, rear their young, and then retreat again before winter closes over the land.

The retreat is not necessarily far. Some birds go from higher elevations to lower ones. Some go from inland lakes to ice-free coasts. Some retreat a few hundred or a few thousand miles but remain in North America. Depending upon where you live, the diversity of species in winter may equal or even surpass that of the summer.

The best time to see the greatest diversity of birds is during **migration.** While migration is a very protracted phenomenon, the peak migratory periods over much of North America range from March to June and from August through November.

Not all species migrate at the same time. In spring, in some places, waterfowl and birds of prey are migrating north in late January and February; the last straggling **shorebirds** and songbirds may not reach their northern nesting territories until June.

The first southbound shorebirds begin their "fall migration" during the third week in June. Assorted **raptors,** sea birds, and hardy winter finches anchor the autumn retreat, reaching their winter ranges in January.

Bird populations are dynamic, and the seasons determine the mix. Because there is almost never a time when bird populations are not shifting, every day afield offers birders the possibility of something new.

How Early Is Now?

Active birds are easier to find than quiescent birds. Different species have different activity patterns. But for most species, early morning and late afternoon are the times when they are most active. Everything you might have heard and dreaded about the early bird catching the worm is true. But look on the bright side. One of birding's unspoken benefits is the number of extraordinary sunrises you are destined to see.

How to Find Birds

First, give yourself every advantage. Pick a birding location that offers good light, a little room to maneuver, and vantage points that allow you to see birds from far enough away that they don't retreat.

Stay out of the deep woods: shadows mask color, and even birds standing still disappear in a blurry maze of branches. Search along woodland edges, in mixed field and patchy woodlands, or on paths or roadways that offer lots of room on both sides and an avenue of sky above.

You don't have to stalk. Just walk quietly and naturally, keeping your eyes alert for motion and your ears attuned to **call notes** and **song.** Even if you don't know bird vocalizations well enough to identify birds, vocalizations can still alert you to their presence.

You don't have to keep your hands on your binoculars at all times. When you see a bird, stop. Reach for your binoculars with both hands and raise them to your eyes. If you are approaching a place where you suspect or know there are birds to be found, you can shave seconds off your reaction time by keeping one or both hands on the binocular.

If you flush a bird, freeze. It may fly a short distance and perch to get a look at the intruder, or if it disappears, it is very likely to reappear. The bird has wings, but you have the strategic advantage: you are standing where that bird wanted to be. Be still. Be patient. You may get the look you want.

Caution: if the bird is behaving in a very agitated manner — calling, moving branch to branch, doing everything it can to draw attention to itself — back off! The bird is telling you that you are too close to its nest or its young. The ethical practice in birding is to respect the bird's territory and retreat to a comfortable distance. The bird, by its actions, will tell you when you've gone far enough.

If you spot a bird that is too far away to see field marks, walk up on it slowly, stopping every few steps to take another look. The essence of birding is getting close enough to identify a bird without getting so close that the bird flushes.

Different birds have different **flush points.** Some, like hummingbirds, will let observers get amazingly close — sometimes closer than binoculars can focus. Some, like many birds of prey, will not let you approach closer than one time zone. This gray area, between close enough and too close, is where the whole game of birding is played out.

Getting Between the Lines

Whether a bird flushes is a matter not only of distance but of how birds are approached. Knowing how *not* to push a bird's panic button will let you get closer.

RULE 1: Choose a birding area where birds are used to people (for example, a park where people exercise, or a beach where people stroll). Birds become habituated to a normal human traffic pattern, and as long as you don't break the pattern (like leaving a trail to approach them), they will usually be tolerant.

RULE 2: Don't rush. Take it easy. Let the birds get used to you. If they seem agitated and about to flush, wait. Give them time to relax.

RULE 3: Don't walk directly toward a bird but approach obliquely, making it obvious that, on your present course, you are not going to crowd or intercept it.

RULE 4: Don't get between birds and their escape route. Do not, for example, approach birds resting on a beach from the water's edge. Many of the species that frequent beaches seek safety by flying over open water. If you seem intent on cutting off their escape route, they will flush sooner. Similarly, don't approach a flock of ducks or gulls from the upwind side. Birds like to take off into the wind, and if you approach from upwind so that they have to cut across your path or fly *toward* you to get airborne, they will flush sooner.

— **P.D.**

NOW YOU UNDERSTAND WHY YOU BOUGHT BIRDER-WORTHY BINOCULARS

Okay. You've found a bird with your naked eyes. Keep your eye on the bird. Now bring the binoculars up so that they fall in line between your eyes and the target.

Don't be surprised if your aim is off — particularly if the bird is very close. Bringing binoculars up to your eyes and having them point where you want takes practice.

Don't swing your binoculars wildly around trying to find the bird. You are probably closer to being on target than you think, and a lot of wild gyrating isn't going to instill confidence in a bird whose suspicions are already aroused.

Move the focus wheel until the bush — or limbs or wires or whatever the bird is sitting in or near — is clear; then move your binoculars slowly left and right and up and down. If you don't find the bird after a short search (three to five seconds), lower your binoculars slightly and peer over the top. Confirm that the bird is still there. Fix your gaze on the bird. Try again.

Look for an obvious reference you can use to locate the bird — an oddly forked branch, for instance, or a discolored leaf. If the bird is near a tree trunk or on a branch, you can move your binoculars along the length of the trunk or branch until you reach the bird.

Basic Bird Identification

I See It!

Congratulations. Now comes the hard part.

Ten Steps Away from an Identification

Much of the fun and challenge of birding is bound up in identifying birds. For a birder to master the challenge of identification, he or she must do some sleuthing. Birders approach this challenge in much the same way that Socrates sought the essence of truth — by asking a series of questions. Each answer parries away possibilities and builds a case until all the questions are answered and all the answers point to one bird's name. The questions are:

1. How large is the bird?
2. What is the shape of the bird?
3. What are the bird's field marks?
4. What are the bird's mannerisms?
5. How does the bird fly?
6. How does the bird sound?
7. What kind of habitat does the bird prefer?

8. Where in North America was the bird seen?
9. When was the bird seen?
10. What is the bird's relative abundance?

The first seven questions are real-time queries: they must be asked in the field while studying the bird. The last three are reflective qualifiers that serve to eliminate possibilities from consideration and guide an observer to a probable identification.

HOW LARGE IS THE BIRD?

Birds vary greatly in size, but size is often difficult to determine. Distance can make birds the size of eagles look tiny; close proximity makes smaller birds seem unnaturally large. Misjudge the distance and you misjudge the size.

A good trick when trying to estimate the size of an unfamiliar bird is to compare it to a bird you are familiar with. Is it as big as a sparrow? Robin? Crow?

Many birds are gregarious and gather in **mixed flocks** that allow direct comparisons. If the bird is alone, or the flock is uniform in its species composition, try comparing the birds to some other reference of known size. For example, if the bird is perched on a fence post, is it as long as the diameter of the post? If it is perched next to the insulator on a utility line, is it larger or smaller?

A backlit falcon, perched on the crossbar of a telephone pole, might be an American Kestrel, a Merlin, a Peregrine Falcon, or, in the

Size constitutes the first cut in the identification process. After ascertaining that a bird, like the Great Blue Heron shown here, is very large (standing about four feet tall), you have already eliminated all but a few of North America's 900 or so bird species from consideration. *Linda Dunne.*

The Fundamentals of Birding **101**

West, a Prairie Falcon. If the bird is more than twice the length of the average insulator, however, be assured that it isn't the diminutive American Kestrel.

Determining the size of birds in flight can be a real challenge, but even here comparisons are possible. Soaring birds in particular often join other species in turning circles in the sky. Solo birds are more difficult, but the way they fly can sometimes offer an oblique reference to size. Large birds turn in wider circles than smaller ones. Their flight is more deliberate and less acrobatic, and their wing beats are slower.

Bryan and the Red-faced Feeder Bird

Bryan Bland, a birder in Cley, England, received a call from a local resident who was perplexed about a bird at her feeder. Its most distinctive characteristic was a "red face."

"You have a goldfinch, Madam," Bryan told her. Goldfinch, *Carduelis carduelis,* is a common English resident, similar in many respects to North American goldfinches but distinguished from them (and all other birds commonly found in England) by a bright red face.

"No," the woman said, "I don't think it is a goldfinch."

"There aren't many other options here," Bryan explained, asking her to describe the bird again.

The woman obliged, saying nothing inconsistent with the identification of goldfinch, which Bryan offered again as the most likely possibility.

"No," the woman asserted, "I'm quite certain it isn't a goldfinch."

Perplexed, Bryan offered to stop by the woman's house on his way home — which he did. There, standing next to the woman's feeder, was a four-foot Sarus Crane, a bird whose normal range doesn't come much closer to England than India but that does indeed have a bright red head.

"She neglected to mention the bird's size," said Bryan.

— **P.D.,** *for* **Bryan Bland**

Shape is another key piece in the identification puzzle because shape, the sum of a bird's physical characteristics, is the quality that most closely links a bird to others in the same biological grouping. Placing a bird in the correct grouping greatly simplifies the identification process.

For instance, is the bird lanky like a crane or stocky like an owl? Are the legs long like a wading shorebird's or short like a duck's?

Is the tail long like a Mourning Dove's or short like a meadowlark's? Blunt-tipped like a gull's or forked like a tern's? If so, how forked? Deeply forked like the tail of Forster's Tern, modestly forked like a Royal Tern's, or hardly forked at all like a Black Tern's?

Are the wings long, tapered, and pointed like a kestrel's or short and blunt like a Sharp-shinned Hawk's? Is the bill thin and pointed like a warbler's, thick and down-hooked like a vireo's, or short and conical like a sparrow's?

Shape is the most important and most determining element in the identification process. Sometimes shape alone can identify a bird. More often it helps the observer place the bird among a defined group of birds. Long and snaky? How about a cormorant or Anhinga (like this female Anhinga). *Linda Dunne.* Big and blocky? Could be an owl (like this Great Gray Owl). *Ted Swem.*

Remember, birds are grouped largely on the basis of structural similarity. Knowing those traits — like the thin bills of warblers or the conical bills of sparrows — will help you quickly place the bird you are studying into its proper family.

What Are the Bird's Field Marks?

Most birds have conspicuous plumage patterns that are visible at a distance. These plumage field marks include: eye rings, eye-lines (or lines above the eye), stripes on the crown, bars or patches on the wings, spots on the tail, and spots, stripes, or bibs on the chest, to name a few basic ones.

Some field marks are most visible, or only visible, when a bird is in flight. For example, the red **epaulets** of an adult male Red-winged Blackbird may be partially or totally hidden beneath covering feathers until the bird goes aloft. A juvenile Black-bellied Plover can be confused with a juvenile American Golden-Plover until the bird flies — exposing a white rump and black patches on the wing pits, which golden plovers lack.

Some plumage characteristics are not useful field marks. The orange crown on the Orange-crowned Warbler is very indistinct, difficult to see even with the bird in the hand, and not something to be looked for in the field. It's better to use the bird's faint breast streaks and to distinguish it from the similar, cleaner-breasted, immature Tennessee Warbler.

Size helps you get to the church. Shape gets you to the right pew. Plumage helps you find the right seat—or in birding terms, make the identification. If all field marks were as obvious as the red epaulets on a displaying adult Red-winged Blackbird, birding would be all too easy. *Kevin Karlson.*

We recognize friends from a distance by the way they walk or sit or stand, and birds can be distinguished this way too — by their movements and by the way they feed or run.

Sandpipers, for example, feed on the run; plovers walk, stop, pick ... walk, stop, pick (as robins do). Flycatchers dart from a perch, snapping insects from the air, and return to a perch; swallows and swifts sweep insects out of the air and keep going.

Woodpeckers hitch themselves *up* the trunks of trees; nuthatches clamber up, down, and sideways. Terns dive into the water headfirst or swoop low, snatching prey from the water; gulls plop to the surface.

Orange-crowned Warblers are hyperactive acrobats, darting quickly from branch to branch, stre-e-e-etching to reach some insect just out of reach, fluttering their wings to vault those last few centimeters. Kinglets are hyperactive too, **wing flicking** nervously.

Vireos are slower, more methodical, dropping branch to branch like a leaf on a windless day, pausing to search the foliage around them; they reach up and deftly remove caterpillars trying to pass themselves off as part of a leaf — and failing.

A bird's mannerisms can identify it at distances from which other field marks are not visible. The Eastern Phoebe, a flycatcher that frequents woodland edges, and the Eastern Wood Pewee, a forest species, are very similar; they are distinguished most readily by their wing bars. Pewees have them and phoebes do not — except in the fall,

Sometimes the way birds move, feed, or behave leads directly to an identification. Several groups of birds cling to the trunks of trees. While all can hitch themselves up the trunk, only the nuthatches (like this White-breasted Nuthatch) can descend head down. *Frank Schleicher.*

when young birds, called **birds of the year,** sport pale, buffy wing bars.

But if the bird is pumping its tail up and down, the wing bars become superfluous. Phoebes engage in **tail-wagging;** pewees do not. With the flick of a tail, phoebes sign their name.

How Does the Bird Fly?

Knowing how a bird flies permits identification at distances from which color, field marks, even shape, are not discernible.

Soaring birds, like gulls, pelicans, and birds of prey, seem to turn lazy circles in the sky without moving a wing. Other birds, like ducks and shorebirds, are more energetic in their flight, moving quickly and directly with wings constantly moving. Still others, like the rails (a family of marsh birds), fly like the Wright brothers — their feeble efforts are ground-hugging, labored, and end with a controlled crash. Crows fly in the proverbial straight line. The flight of the Pileated Woodpecker, a crow-sized bird, is like an undulating roller coaster.

Nighthawks are stiff-winged, erratic, bat-like in flight. The wing beat of a loon is loose and elastic, its flight purposeful and direct.

Great Blue Herons glide and fly with their wings cupped down. Bald Eagles soar on flat wings. Golden Eagles hold their wings slightly raised in a **dihedral** or V. Turkey Vultures hold their wings in a dihedral too, but they rock in flight — like a tightrope walker of the sky. Golden Eagles don't rock.

Some birds, like hummingbirds and most birds of prey, fly solo. Others, like swallows, fly in loose-knit flocks. Still others fly in large

Flight helps not only to define birds, but to identify them. Some birds move their wings steadily. Some flap and glide. Many species, including adult Thayer's Gulls, soar. *Linda Dunne.*

numbers and large, tightly packed groups (like starlings and grackles) or well-ordered chevrons (like waterfowl and many shorebird species).

How Does the Bird Sound?

Bird sounds are a form of communication for them, and an audio fingerprint for us. Even nonbirders recognize the *caw-caw-caw* call of the American Crow or the resonant two-note honk of the Canada Goose. The song or call of a species can identify it as accurately as any visual field mark — sometimes even more accurately.

For instance, American Crow and Fish Crow are very similar in size and shape. Even expert birders, with ample time for study, find the species difficult to tell apart visually. But if the bird's call is nasal, two-noted, and has the quality of a denial (*Uh-uh),* the bird is telling you it isn't American Crow.

Some birds, like the *Bob-white* quail, the Black-capped *Chick-a-dee,* the Eastern *Pe-wee,* and the Long-billed *Curlew,* say their names — or at least a phonetic approximation.

Some bird songs can be phonetically rendered in a way that helps us remember them — for example, the song of Common Yellowthroat is *witchity-witchity-witchity.* Even if you don't recognize the song or call or fail to recall all its elements, just noting the dominant qualities — whether it was a note-blurring trill, a distinct series of chip notes, a single phrase repeated over and over, an ensemble of notes and phrases — can help you to distinguish similar species.

Birds distinguish themselves by their vocalizations, and a knowledge of bird songs and calls is often the best means of locating and identifying birds in the field. Challenging as this is, it is almost certain that you already include several bird vocalizations in your repertoire, including the sound of this bird. *Kevin Karlson.*

For example, the two dowitcher species, Long-billed and Short-billed, can be a difficult identification challenge, particularly when the birds are in **basic** (nonbreeding) **plumage.** Their calls are very different, however, and of course they don't shed them with the season. Long-billed Dowitchers most often utter a sharp, single-note *keek;* Short-billed Dowitchers have a more mellow-toned, three-note stutter, *Tu-tu-tu.* One note versus three notes — you need not have perfect pitch or the audio recall of an Igor Stravinsky to recognize the difference.

WHAT KIND OF HABITAT DOES THE BIRD PREFER?

Birds are not just creatures of habit, they are creatures of habitat. They fit, hand in glove, the habitats for which they are specialized and even in migration will seek out habitat that most closely approximates these.

The widespread Marsh Wren, as the name implies, seeks out open, wet, well-vegetated places. The western Rock Wren prefers rocky slopes and canyons. Although both are wrens, where their ranges overlap neither is likely to occur in the habitat of the other.

Some species are very adaptable — able to acclimate themselves to a variety of different habitats. A stellar example is the Red-tailed Hawk. A common raptor with a wide range of prey, this species is at home in marshes, prairies, farmland, deserts, open woodlands, roadside suburbia, even city parks.

Birds are creatures of habitat. Water birds are usually found near water. Grassland birds are keyed to open, grassy areas. And while many sandpipers are attracted to mud flats, the aptly named Sanderling is a true lover of sandy beaches. *Pete Dunne.*

Some species are very discriminating: they are found only in habitats that offer specific plants or food items. A prime example is the Kirtland's Warbler, a bird specialized to nest in young jack pine thickets whose nesting range, accordingly, is largely limited to several counties in north-central Michigan.

The habitat preferences of birds can be an aid to identification. Take again the example of the Long-billed and Short-billed Dowitchers. Short-billed Dowitchers readily forage in saltwater; Long-billed Dowitchers have a preference for fresh.

A momentary glimpse of a hawk preying on songbirds at your feeder may not be enough to determine whether it is a falcon (like a Merlin) or an accipiter (like a Sharp-shinned Hawk). Falcons are birds of open areas; accipiters are woodland specialists. If the hawk beats a retreat into the woods instead of heading for the open, it isn't a falcon.

WHERE IN NORTH AMERICA WAS THE BIRD SEEN?

If you look at the range maps in your field guide, you will discover quickly that very few bird species occur all over North America. Most are confined to specific regions and only occasionally encountered outside the boundaries of their normal range. Distribution is one of the easiest ways of narrowing down identification.

For example, there are four species of yellow-cheeked warblers in North America: Townsend's, Hermit, Golden-cheeked, and Black-

There are four species of yellow-cheeked warblers in North America. Only one is commonly found in the East—this one, Black-throated Green Warbler. *Kevin Karlson.*

throated Green. All have similar traits and might easily be confused one with another. But Townsend's and Hermit are western species that are rarely seen east of the Rockies. Golden-cheeked is even more restricted in its range, breeding only on the Edwards Plateau of central Texas.

Only one of these yellow-cheeked warblers commonly occurs in the eastern half of the continent — the Black-throated Green. So if you are birding in Minnesota and you encounter a yellow-cheeked warbler, you would want to check the field marks of the Black-throated Green Warbler first.

While some birds do wander outside their normal range — particularly when migrating, and especially in the fall when young, inexperienced birds are migrating for the first time — birds can usually be depended upon to be where they are supposed to be, when they are supposed to be there.

When Was the Bird Seen?

Field guide range maps are multicolored to show where birds are at different seasons. As already discussed, most species redistribute their entire populations over the course of the year, moving from their summer range to their winter range along established migratory

Separating the spot-breasted thrushes is challenging. But in North America, in winter, the season simplifies the identification process by eliminating variables. Only the Hermit Thrush winters where snow regularly falls. All similar-appearing thrushes winter south of the U.S. border. *Frank Schleicher.*

pathways. Seasonal distribution, marking a temporal line that falls between probable and improbable, can be a useful clue to the bird's identity.

For example, in North America there are six spot-breasted thrushes: Wood, Hermit, Swainson's, Gray-cheeked, Bicknell's, and Veery. All but Gray-cheeked nest in New York State, and all may be found there during migration. But in December any spot-breasted thrush encountered in New York (or anywhere in North America for that matter) is almost certain to be Hermit Thrush because the other five species migrate to the tropics in the fall. Only the Hermit Thrush winters so far north.

Knowing the migratory period and seasonal distribution of a species is not just a clue to support an identification, it is a scheduled appointment. By knowing *when* and where to search for *which* species, birders can plot a strategy to intercept them.

What Is the Bird's Relative Abundance?

Some species are more common than others, and many that are uncommon look much like their more common kin. Probability is a very salient clue to a bird's identity, and while uncommon species (like rare coins) are avidly sought, the more likely possibilities should

Sure, you'd love to turn this bird into an Ivory-billed Woodpecker. But the odds greatly favor Pileated Woodpecker, and the head pattern and absence of white in the wing confirm it. *Frank Schleicher.*

be considered and eliminated before less likely possibilities are examined.

A large, red-crested woodpecker showing white flashes in the wings as it disappears in the forest might be an Ivory-billed Woodpecker or it might be a Pileated. Insofar as Pileated is common and widespread and Ivory-billed is believed to be extinct, the odds overwhelmingly favor Pileated.

The probability of encountering a species is not wholly determined by its numbers. There are other contingencies, such as weather, climate, distribution, time of year, as well as the propensity for a species to wander. Some birds travel great distances, some do not. Great travelers are more likely to turn up in unlikely places.

But the rule of thumb is simple: if it looks like the more common of several possibilities, then it probably is. Or as one birding tour leader of my acquaintance puts it: "If you are in North America and you hear hoofbeats, think horses, not zebras."

Learning to See Critically

In principle, there is nothing fundamentally difficult about bird identification. You see a bird. You note its distinguishing features. You look for its likeness in the field guide.

But in practice, learning how to see birds critically, to note key field marks under less than ideal circumstances, and to find the right match amid pages of bird pictures that may differ only by degrees and shades, is no easy task.

It takes discipline. It takes practice. And it takes preparation.

FIVE THINGS TO BEAR IN MIND
1. Don't go into the field with an open mind.
Go into the field already armed with an arsenal of information you can bring to bear quickly — such as the knowledge that bill shape is used to distinguish the species of loons, that bill color is key to separating the several species of medium-sized terns, and that identifying

sparrows depends upon noting first whether the bird does or does not have a streaked breast.

When a glance is all you get, knowing where to direct that glance can make the difference between an identification and a missed opportunity.

2. Learn to look broadly before you look critically.

The identification process begins *before* binoculars are brought to bear. Size can be measured best with the unaided eye. Family is something that can often be established at a glance — ducks look like ducks; ducks that dive beneath the surface define themselves as one of the diving ducks, telling you it isn't necessary to consider any of the nondiving puddle ducks when making your identification.

Bird identification is a process of elimination. It starts not by noting small details but by putting each bird in a probable group — a broad-brush approach that paints birds into a corner with similar species where they can be easily compared.

3. But learn to look critically, too.

Look for obvious traits first — anatomical peculiarities, color, and any obvious field marks. Many birds project very obvious characteristics that give you shortcuts to an identification.

If obvious traits are lacking, examine the bird systematically, starting at the bill, working back along its length, then returning to the bill. Study the underparts, beak to tail, finishing with the **soft parts** (legs and feet).

Make this process of study second-nature — something you do every time you see a bird. Drawing the bird in the field is an excellent way to develop this discipline. Not only does a field sketch prompt you to note detail and think critically, it provides evidence for later analysis.

Don't worry if you aren't an artist. The sketch is for reference, not sale.

Paul Lehman (left), Jon Dunn (center), and Wayne Petersen (right) rank among North America's finest field birders. You would have to spend the rest of your life to equal the number of birds that they have misidentified on the way to gaining the skills they are famous for today. *Kevin Karlson.*

4. Use every opportunity for study.

Field guides (as well as CDs and videos) are very useful. But there is no substitute for studying real birds, in real time, in the real world. Whether you can identify a species or not, whether you have seen it a hundred times or more, *use every opportunity to study birds in the field.*

A studied intimacy with common birds allows you to identify them quickly and accurately. It offers a familiar backdrop against which rare or unfamiliar species will stand out.

The planet's most accomplished field birders pay as much attention to the birds they see all the time as the ones they are seeing for the first time. This is how they became accomplished in the first place.

5. Experience has a price; everyone antes up.

Birding should be, above all else, fun. No one should ever go into the field worried about making a mistake or misidentifying a bird. There isn't a birder on the planet who hasn't misidentified a bird. The difference between a beginning birder and an experienced one is that beginning birders have misidentified very few birds. Experienced birders have misidentified *thousands.*

Making mistakes and learning from them is the essence of experience. The obvious question is: "So how do I know when I've made a mistake?" For that insight, you rely on your friends — the subject of the next chapter.

Keeping Records

Keeping records of the birds you see and recording the birds you find will help you learn, provide evidence that can be reviewed later, and help you see patterns of occurrence or activity.

There are three ways to record your encounters in the field: **checklists** or **field cards;** a **life list** (and other composite lists); a **journal.**

CHECKLISTS

The easiest way to keep track of the birds you see is to fill out a checklist every time you go birding. A checklist cites the birds found in a defined area, in standard taxonomic order. They are distributed free at many popular birding locations, or they can be purchased at nature

Record keeping reinforces the learning process and caps each special sighting. Making field sketches allows birders to spend field time in study, committing key field marks to paper instead of memory. It also produces a keepsake that captures the triumph of the moment. This sketch of a Two-barred Greenish Warbler ensures that this British birder will always recall this first record for England. *Pete Dunne.*

centers and birding stores. Checklists differ in length, the birds listed, and the information about each species they try to impart. (Many are information-packed, offering not just a species listing but information about relative abundance and seasonal occurrence as well.)

All checklists have at least two things in common: convenience and editorialized simplicity. All the birds you might expect to see are already written down. All that do not occur have been excluded. All *you* have to do is put a check mark next to the birds you find, although it is useful to note the date, location, weather conditions, and names of any birding companions.

LISTS AND LISTING

Part of birding's appeal is acquisition. Many birders go beyond daily checklists to keep cumulative lists of the birds they see. In fact, the very act of keeping track of birds has a name. It is called **listing**.

Some birders keep a **yard list** — a list limited to the birds seen in (or from) their yard. Some maintain **state lists** or **county lists**. Others keep a **year list** — a list of birds seen during the calendar year — or **month lists** or **trip lists**. Some lists are even more esoteric.

Dear to the hearts of many birders is their life list — the cumulative list of all those species that they have encountered since the day they started birding. Some North American residents put a geographic boundary on their life list — including only those species found in North America (a North American life list). Others maintain a world life list.

There are any number of ways to keep lists — from homemade loose-leaf binders to commercially available checklist journals or diaries, to computer software programs that not only keep track of your sightings but cross-file them any way you like.

Some birders simply note in their field guide where and when they saw each species. Just one word of caution for those who use a field guide as the vehicle for their life list — *Keep your record-bearing book at home or keep updated photocopies of the pages.* Even cherished field guides sometimes get left on lunch counters or automobile rooftops.

Listing Software — An Introduction

Listing programs are "relational" databases that require inputting data (species you identify), which then can be grouped by various criteria to generate lists of species and related information. As such, listing software offers much more than life lists, which simply record the species you identified and when you first encountered each one.

Most good listing programs include all the world's bird species. (Abridged versions covering limited regions are usually offered at slightly reduced prices.) Some offer lists for other creatures, such as butterflies, dragonflies, damselflies, herps (reptiles and amphibians), and mammals. These typically cover limited geographic regions, and many are free Website downloads.

How do you find the best listing software? That depends on what you want to do with your data. If you simply want to know when and where you identified certain species, any decent program will do. If you want to track species seen during various times over multiple years in specific habitats during differing weather conditions and phases of the moon, you will need a more powerful program. Most of us want something in between, and the better programs can do it all.

INSTRUCTIONS

Some programs come with a well-written, illustrated user's guide; some come with animated instructions; and some come with the tool bar "help" option only. (The last may suffice, but the first two are usually more user-friendly.) Most programs also include technical support by phone or online. Some companies charge for tech support, and some do not.

REQUIRED DATA

All listing programs require three types of data for each entry: species, date, and place. Finding a species in the included list may sound easy, but it may be buried amid ten thousand other birds. Species also may be listed taxonomically or alphabetically. Most programs help you find species by reducing the list, for example, limiting it to the birds of your state. Some allow you to find species by typing part of its name or its initials or by "jumping" to its family. The date can usually be typed in or selected from a calendar. Places should be linked ("related") to other places. For example, on September 2, 2001, I saw a Clay-colored Robin at Santa Ana National Wildlife Refuge, Hidalgo County, Lower Rio Grande Valley, Texas, United States, North America. Good programs allow you to enter such a sighting once and have it included in each of these regions. (The ease of establishing such links varies considerably.) Programs with hand-held subroutines allow you to enter data in the field and then transfer them to your main computer.

RANGE DATA

Most programs come with at least some range data (where the species occur), and the better ones provide worldwide range data or allow you to use such data from other companies. Periodic range data updates are offered by various services for minimal fees. With these you can better prepare for trips by generating lists of birds seen and not seen in an area.

UPGRADES, UPDATES, AND EDITS

Most companies offer periodic upgrades, often as free downloads. The better programs also provide downloadable updates (for example, after taxonomic changes have been made) and allow you to make your own edits.

CONVERSIONS

Some programs can convert entries from a competitor's program, but usually very poorly, and much additional editing is often required.

CUSTOMIZING YOUR PROGRAM

Some programs allow you to add notations that can be used to sort data. For example, I can add "/p" to show I photographed an individual, "/f" to denote I saw it at a festival, "/g" while golfing, etc.

SPEED

Anyone who used a computer in the early 1990s knows they were *slow*, especially as newer, bigger programs were added. Today computers tend to be much faster, as are today's listing programs. Thus, speed is not the concern it used to be (unless you have an old computer).

OTHER OPTIONS

Some programs allow access to CD-ROM instructional software, create maps of where your sightings occurred, offer multiple taxonomies and lists of species names used around the world, and allow you to add photos with your entries.

Given these choices, it pays to do your homework. Before you buy, read reviews, talk with other users, and consider what you want from a listing program.

—Michael R. Hannisian

Michael R. Hannisian is associate naturalist at the Cape May Bird Observatory and executive director of the Valley Land Fund.

JOURNALS

Some birders go beyond checklists to keep a journal or diary that offers a detailed account of each day's birding. Weather, habitat conditions, places visited, nests discovered, and the number of individuals seen of each species are often included.

There is no right way and no wrong way to maintain a journal. There is only your way. What is significant to you and appeals to you is all that matters.

Encounters with other birders, descriptions of curious behavior (on the part of birds or birders) or aberrant plumages (again, on the part of birds or birders)—all such impressions provide grist for the mill. Illustrations or thumbnail sketches that highlight key points or simply enliven the pages add to a journal's significance and charm.

Summary Birding can be done anywhere, but some places are more attractive to birds than others, and different species are attracted to different habitats. Bird populations shift seasonally. Regions have winter, summer, and year-round residents as well as migratory birds making a stop on their journey. Bird activity is greatest in the

The Fundamentals of Birding **119**

early morning and late afternoon. Finding birds demands attentiveness to color, motion, and sound; seeing birds requires patience and practice.

Bird identification is a challenge that involves sight, sound, and mind. Identifications are made by building a case for a certain species. Characteristics to consider include size, shape, field marks, behavior, manner of flight, vocalizations, habitat, distribution, time of year, and relative abundance.

All these characteristics should be recorded, on paper, in the field. Record keeping is part of birding. Daily lists, cumulative lists like a birder's life list or year list, and journals are all means to this end.

4
Resources — Dipping into the Pool of Knowledge

The Man of the Mountain

The man with the billowing white beard and flowing mane stood and extended his hand. "Floyd Wolfarth," he said. "Pete Dunne," I replied, taking his hand. I was twenty-four, and Floyd was forty years older. We were standing atop Coon Ridge, a denuded outcropping of New Jersey's Kittatinny Ridge that was a celebrated hawk-watching junction where birders gathered each autumn to witness the river of southbound birds of prey.

I had learned of Coon's existence from a newly printed book about hawk watching. Floyd, I was soon to discover, was virtually synonymous with the place.

Floyd Wolfarth, retired teamster, who used to adjust his pickup and delivery runs so he could spend his lunch hours hawk watching.

Floyd Wolfarth, who had invested "five thousand hours" studying gulls in the Hackensack dumps.

Floyd Wolfarth, who was founder of the Boonton Christmas Bird Count, former region 5 editor of *Records of New Jersey Birds,* and one

Floyd P. Wolfarth, retired teamster, master birder, mentor to this author and a host of other young birders (including photographer Mark Wilson).

of seventeen charter members of the august Urner Ornithological Club.

In short and in sum, I was speaking with one of the pillars of the birding community — someone whose knowledge of birds and birding was part of a parallel universe of information and friends that I hardly knew existed.

I'd grown up in New Jersey, learning the rudiments of birding alone. I had traveled widely in search of birds (most recently to Alaska), studied my field guide, worked out my share of difficult identifications, and considered myself a pretty competent birder. But I'd never considered seeking the guidance of other birders, and I'd never dreamed that birding's true horizon lay beyond my grasp — even my imagination. All that was about to change.

"Got a bird," Wolfarth intoned. "Over 'Stigs.'"

I found the distant speck with effort, because I didn't know the geological lay of the land.

"Accipiter," said Wolfarth after brief study, naming one of the three broad groups of hawks I knew from my book. There were buteos, the large soaring hawks; falcons, the fast, open-country pursuit artists; and accipiters, the short-winged, long-tailed hunters of woodlands.

How can he tell that's an accipiter? I wondered. The bird was just a speck, indistinguishable from all the Broad-winged Hawks I'd been seeing all day.

It was September. Broad-winged Hawks, a forest buteo, were the principal migrants, along with the occasional Sharp-shinned Hawk (an accipiter) and American Kestrel (a small falcon). Broad-wingeds had a wide white band on the tail (at least the adults did) and flew in flocks. Sharp-shinneds were small and had short, round wings; kestrels were small and had long, pointy wings.

Most of my identifications were made at close range — as the birds made their way down the ridge and passed close enough for me to see field marks. This guy had just pinned a name to a bird that seemed beyond the limit of conjecture.

"Watch this bird," Wolfarth commanded. "*This* is going to be something *good.*"

The bird got closer and closer. As distance shortened, I began to see details — large size . . . sort of long, sort of pointed wings . . . mottled brown back . . . lots of streaks on the underparts. To me it looked much like the immature Broad-winged Hawks (the ones without the white band on the tail) that were mixed in with the adults.

The bird drew abreast, then continued down ridge — a large, brown-backed, streak-breasted bird of prey.

"Well," Wolfarth asked, "what did you think?"

"Broad-winged Hawk," I said, falling back on probability.

"Goshawk," said Wolfarth. "Unquestionable," he added. I'd never seen Northern Goshawk before. But with this catalytic identification to guide me, all the things I had seen but not properly noted began to fall into place: the underparts that were much more blotched than streaked, the long, rudder-like tail, the bulky shape that was more accipiter than buteo.

Clearly this guy Wolfarth was an exceptional birder. In time I discovered that he was also an excellent teacher. But on this day, on the spine of the Kittatinny Ridge, I knew only that he knew more about birds than I had ever dreamed of knowing and that I had just flunked my first exam.

As we stood, a migrant flock of chickadees swept by, calling as they went. Among the expected chatter of Black-cappeds I picked out one call that was slurred and slower. Having just spent several weeks in Alaska, it was a call I'd grown familiar with.

"Boreal Chickadee," I announced as the flock moved by.

"What!" said Floyd, spinning around, regarding me with an expression that suggested I'd just confessed to the murder of ex-Teamster boss Jimmy Hoffa.

"Boreal Chickadee," I repeated, suddenly aware that this was New Jersey, not Alaska, and that I'd never seen a Boreal Chickadee in New Jersey — didn't even know if they occurred here.

But Floyd knew and could probably have recited, from memory, the five winters marked by incursions of this northern bird. The winter of 1975–76 was also destined to be noted for its Boreal Chickadee incursion, but nobody knew this yet.

"Wa-ellll," he rumbled. "Boreal Chickadee is a good bird. What made you say Boreal?"

"I heard it," I explained. "I learned the call in Alaska."

"Tough call," he added, to give me some wiggle room in case I wanted to back down. It was clear that Floyd was skeptical. The afternoon wore on. I listened to him talk about birds I'd only dreamed of seeing. The people and places he named were part of a culture I wanted to belong to — now that I knew it existed.

As we were preparing to leave, a wiry figure bounded down the trail. One of Floyd's protégés. He'd been photographing hawks down ridge.

"Had a good bird," he told us. "About two hours ago a Boreal Chickadee went by with a flock of Black-cappeds."

Floyd looked stunned. Then he looked bemused. Then he looked at me. The photographer's credentials were good. Mine had just gotten better.

"That was a good call," he said. The skepticism in his eyes was gone. I found there instead a new respect and something else.

I'd just found my mentor.

Clubs and Chums — The Social Link

You can go birding on your own. In fact, and for reasons that will be explained, you should. But birders can learn a lot by going out with more experienced birders.

Experienced birders can take the guesswork out of identification — by focusing attention quickly on key field marks, affirming correct identifications, and correcting misidentifications before they become entrenched in your mind.

Experienced birders know how, when, and where to find birds and can advise new birders on clothing, optics, publications, and other sources of information.

There are thousands of institutions throughout the world that cater to the social and informational needs of birders. They range from international organizations to local clubs. The best way to meet other birders is through a local club or birding organization. Membership is open to all. Shared interest, not experience or skill, is the coin of the realm.

First Contact

The telephone directory has no listing for "Mentors" or "Bird Clubs." But there are listings for "Bird Feeders and Houses." Under this listing

Birding, like all avocations, has a social network. Bird clubs and organizations help keep birders connected and informed, and most serious birders belong to several. *Linda Dunne.*

you may find a retail store in your area that specializes in meeting the equipment needs of birders.

Some stores are independently owned and operated; others are run by organizations such as Los Angeles Audubon or the Cape May Bird Observatory. There are also franchise stores operating under one of several store chains that cater to birders, including Wild Bird Centers, Wild Bird Marketplace, and Wild Birds Unlimited. All of these stores should be in contact with the local birding network and will be able to put you in touch with it as well.

Another way to make contact with the birding community is through your local newspaper. If it has a column that specializes in birds, nature, or the outdoors, the columnist is almost certainly in contact with the local birding community and may post notices of meetings, trips, courses, and events.

Local park systems, refuge "friends" groups, and outdoor recreation departments often offer bird identification classes, bird walks on-site, or birding field trips off-site. Community colleges and high schools sometimes offer birding or field ornithology courses, and some museums and zoos have such programs too. The people who teach these courses or lead these walks are almost certainly linked to the birding community at large. Through them, so are you.

A Birder's Guide to Field Trip and Bird Tour Survival

Going on a first field trip is a little like attending your first dance. You can either step onto the floor and let someone else lead or you can learn a few dance steps beforehand. Both approaches are fine.

But for those who like the assurance that knowledge brings, here is a list of field trip dos and don'ts I have collected from field trip participants, leaders, and my own experiences in the field.

Take them to heart and on your first field trip you'll spend more time enjoying the birds and less time tripping over your (or a fellow birder's) feet.

Dos

Do ask questions about the trip *before* the trip. Find out what the weather conditions will be like, how much walking is involved, how bad the bugs will be, and whether you should bring your scope. Most organizations will provide you with a list of what to bring and how to prepare for the trip. If they don't, ask.

Do make sure the leader knows before the trip about any special physical needs or limitations you may have. Many times such needs can be accommodated with advance notice.

Do honestly evaluate whether you are physically up to a particular trip or portion of a trip. Don't leave it to the leader to say, "I really don't think you should come on this hike — it's going to be tough." Normal birding is not particularly strenuous, and most trips and tours are suitable for anyone in good general health, but some trips may involve night sessions or arduous hikes.

The bird field trip is a favorite institution among birders. But just like all assemblies united by a common purpose, there are rules and standards that serve to keep a group successful. *Linda Dunne.*

Do be early, or at least on time.

Do make sure you know how to get to the meeting place. Some leaders are ruthless and will leave without you, but most will wait at least a little while, delaying the trip for everyone else.

Do let the leader know whether there is a particular bird you would like to see. If it is a common bird but you would really like a good look at it, say so! Leaders are happiest when they make people on their trips happy. However, *don't* harp on the birds you are missing.

Do feel free to ask questions about a bird — how to identify it, where it lives, what it eats. Field trip leaders love to have people along who are truly interested in birds and who ask questions about them.

If someone calls out a bird and you cannot find it, say so! Leaders and other trip participants will always be glad to help you get on the bird.

Do call out yourself if you see a bird, say a raptor overhead. One of the chief advantages of birding with a group is having multiple sets of eyes all looking at once.

Do learn how to give and receive directions to a bird's locations (see "Directions, Please," page 219).

Do know when to be quiet. Being quiet means more than not talking loudly. It means not moving unnecessarily and moving quietly when you have to move. Watch the leader. If he or she stops suddenly with head cocked, *stop*. Undoubtedly the leader heard a bird — maybe your next life bird.

Do stay with the leader. This is particularly important when the group is intently looking for a particular target bird or when the leader is pishing. **Pishing** brings birds to the pisher, and good leaders generally choose places to pish where birds are easily attracted and easily viewed.

Do wear quiet clothing in quiet colors. It can be hard to get good looks at shy birds, and it becomes doubly hard in a group garbed in neon nylon.

Do be prepared for less than adequate bathroom facilities. There may be long periods between bathrooms (drink less coffee), or the only bathroom may be the great outdoors (know how to handle this). If the absence of a man-made toilet facility is a concern, ask about making "pit stops" before the trip.

Don'ts

Don't be a scope hog. Even if the leader's scope is trained on your dream lifer, step up to the eyepiece, take an identifiable look, and step away to let others have their chance. If you've already seen the bird with binoculars and someone in the group has not seen it at all, let that person have first crack at the scope. If the bird moves, *do* try to follow it with the scope (so that the leader doesn't have to waste time finding the bird again). *Don't* bump the scope when stepping aside for the next person.

Don't be a complainer. If something about the trip is bothering you, carefully evaluate whether the problem is worth mentioning. If it is, speak to the leader in private.

Don't monopolize the leader. Others may want to share the leader's expertise, and the leader can hardly look for birds if he or she is locked in a dialogue.

Don't insist on a particular seat if traveling in a van. Offer to rotate seats with other participants. This is customary procedure on many field trips, especially for window and front seats.

Don't insist on driving alone. If the field trip has space on the van, ride in it. If carpooling is possible, do it. The fewer vehicles involved in a birding trip, the better.

Don't drag significant others along on a birding trip unless they are eager to come and understand what is involved. Make sure they have binoculars. Uninterested people tend to drag the trip down.

— **Don Freiday**
In addition to being director of New Jersey Audubon's Scherman-Hoffman Sanctuary, Don Freiday is a consummate birder, an exceptional naturalist, and a field trip leader whose followers are legion.

Going Direct

There are two national organizations that cater to the information and social needs of birders — the **American Birding Association** and the **National Audubon Society**.

American Birding Association

Founded in 1969, ABA has over twenty thousand members, most of them avid birders. ABA services include excellent birding periodicals, publications, mail-order merchandise, and a membership directory and yellow pages — containing the names and addresses of members by state and zip code as well as listings of clubs, organizations, festivals, stores, and so on. ABA is a storehouse of information about birds and birders across North America. Membership information can be had by writing (Box 6599, Colorado Springs, CO 80934–6599), calling (800-850-BIRD), or visiting the Web site (www.americanbirding.org).

National Audubon Society

Founded in 1905, National Audubon is a national organization whose membership is served by local chapters, nature centers, and (in most states) state offices. Chapters hold regular meetings and organize field trip schedules. Some chapters are more focused on birds than others, but most have at least a bird-watching component. Membership information can be had by writing (700 Broadway, New York, NY 10003), calling (800-274-4201), or visiting the Web site (www.audubon.org).

National Audubon is not to be confused with independent, state Audubon societies.

State Audubon Societies

Several states have their own independent Audubon societies (most founded before 1900). These state societies differ in focus and the intensity of their bird orientation. But birders living in these states would do well to consider them a primary resource and an avenue to the birding community. State offices are listed in appendix 3.

OTHER ORGANIZATIONS

Many other independent clubs and organizations cater to the interests of birders. Some are primarily social, giving birders a forum in which to discuss matters of interest. Examples include the Nuttall

Club of Massachusetts, the Kansas Ornithological Society, and the Delaware Valley Ornithological Club serving birders from Delaware, New Jersey, and Pennsylvania.

Others are more informational or mission-focused, disseminating information to a geographically dispersed membership and engaging in research and education focused upon birds. An example is the Cornell Laboratory of Ornithology, which orchestrates national programs involving back-yard bird feeding (Project Feeder Watch), offers a home-study ornithology course, and publishes a quarterly journal on birds, *Living Bird.*

Some are focused upon specific interests, for example, the Hawk Migration Association of North America and the Purple Martin Conservation Association.

Another kind of independent organization is the bird observatory — a membership-supported institution whose primary focus is research, education, and conservation. These include the Cape May Bird Observatory in New Jersey, the Long Point Bird Observatory in Ontario, and the Point Reyes Bird Observatory in California.

The American Birding Association lists the names and locations of birding clubs and organizations in its membership directory and yellow pages, which are published annually and distributed to members of ABA.

STATE OR PROVINCIAL BIRDING ORGANIZATIONS

Almost every state or province has one or more regional organizations that cater to both the social and information needs of birders. Some meet regularly, some annually or semiannually. Some offer a regular field trip schedule.

Most of these organizations also publish a journal or newsletter with information about bird distribution and occurrence. Their functions often include maintenance of official state bird lists and review of bird sightings through **rare bird committees.**

Another function that these organizations often perform is the upkeep of **bird sighting hotlines.**

Almost every state and province has a bird sighting hotline, and many have multiple hotlines for different regions. Many are supported by statewide organizations. Others are sponsored by clubs, Audubon chapters, and individuals or stores. They provide information about rare bird sightings, seasonal distributions of birds, programs, and bird walks, and they are a link to the local birding community.

Hotline numbers change frequently. An updated summary is periodically published by the American Birding Association, or you can go on-line and call up the listserver that provides information on state and regional lists: http://server1.birdingonthe.net/mailinglists/.

Hooking into the Publication and Communication Network

Numerous publications cater to the interests of birders. Some are the communication link that binds organizations and members. Some are regional, some are national in scope.

BIRDING

Published six times a year and distributed to members of the American Birding Association, *Birding* is aimed at avid birders who want to improve their skills and whose interest in birds is continental in scope. Regular features include a bird species focus ("A Closer Look"), "Building Birding Skills," "Tools of the Trade," "Book and Media Reviews," and the ever-popular bird "Photo Quiz." Write: Membership, PO Box 6599, Colorado Springs, CO 80934.

Members also receive the monthly newsletter *Winging It*, which specializes in more timely information — including upcoming national birding festivals, meetings, and events of interest to birders, and recountings of rare bird sightings.

Bird's-Eye View, ABA's newsletter for its student members, tailors its message for birders ages eight to fifteen. *Field Notes*, published quarterly by ABA, is a continent-wide summary of noteworthy bird concentrations, trends, and occurrences.

BIRD WATCHER'S DIGEST

Published six times a year, this friendly, excellent magazine appeals to birders across the entire range of interest — from casual back-yard bird watching to adventure birding — but its principal focus is on the fun of birding. Feature articles range from the humorous and anecdotal to the informative and species-specific. Regular columns include "Bird Watcher's Question Box," "Far Afield" (travel), "Watching Bird Behavior," and "Quick Takes" (news and issues summary). One of the strengths of this publication is the quality of the writing and the attitude of the publishers. They are birders writing for birders, and it shows. Write: *Bird Watcher's Digest*, PO Box 110, Marietta OH 45750 (800-879-2473).

BIRDER'S WORLD

Published six times a year, *Birder's World* has the diverse focus of *Bird Watcher's Digest* but places less emphasis upon back-yard birding and more upon the nuances of birds, their behavior and biology. Celebrated for its superior bird photography, *Birder's World* is the most visual of the birding magazines. The department editors are excellent. Regular columns include "ID Tips," "Gardening for Birds," "Field Identification," "Book Reviews," and "Those Amazing Birds." Write: *Birder's World*, Kalmbach Publishing Company, PO Box 1612, Wailesja, WI 53187-1612 (800-533-6644).

LIVING BIRD

A quarterly publication distributed to members of the Cornell Laboratory of Ornithology, *Living Bird* is visually arresting and well written. Conservation and bird ecology are common themes, but birding and the needs of birders are perennial topics. Feature articles explore subjects in depth, and columns add a light touch. Like *Birder's World*, quality photography is a hallmark. The Laboratory of Ornithology is anchored in birding and ornithological tradition, and *Living Bird* has long served as a bridge between these parallel disciplines. Write: Cornell Laboratory of Ornithology, 159 Sapsucker Woods Rd., Ithaca, NY 14850 (607-254-BIRD).

A bimonthly publication with the widest readership, *WildBird* is broad-brush in its scope and appeal. New and casual birders find the magazine particularly appealing.

Features often have a travel focus. Departments include "Backyard Birder" and "Birder's I.D." Equipment reviews treat hiking and camping items (attesting to the publication's broad scope). Write: *WildBird* Subscription Department, PO Box 52898, Boulder, CO 80322-2898 (800-365-4421; fax 303-604-7455).

www.birding.fun

While I firmly believe that the best use of the Internet is the dissemination of good (and awful) jokes, it is also a great source of birding information: hotlines, reference material, places to bird, and Web sites where you can virtual-bird anytime, day or night. As a birder, I find these Internet features most valuable: quick access to any state's (or country's) rare bird alert hotline; e-mail to fellow birders, both friends and friends-to-be; selected articles from magazines such as *Bird Watcher's Digest* as well as e-mail-only "newsletters" like the *Beakly News* and the *Dick E. Bird News.*

Large birding Web sites like www.Petersononline.com provide links that can zip you automatically to other birding sites. From this site alone, Internet infinity awaits you.

Two other helpful features of the Internet are "BirdChat" and bird chat rooms. "BirdChat" is a mailing list to which you subscribe. As a subscriber to the Arizona–New Mexico portion of the western "BirdChat," I receive three to fifteen posts (e-mails) each day on sightings and **birding hotspots,** sometimes accompanied by recommendations on food, lodgings, and accommodations, as well as detailed discussions of tricky IDs, **rarities,** and bird behavior.

If you're a beginner birder, a regional "BirdChat" will give you a quick feel for what birds are typical or rare for your area and who the expert birders are. While the more scientific discussions can be daunting, as you become more involved in birding, you'll find them invaluable when you are suddenly confronted with a rarity or a hard-to-identify bird.

New subscribers are not able to post for a couple of weeks, so that they can get the feel of the language and subject matter that is considered appropriate. After this introductory period, you will be e-mailed that you have been given posting privileges. As a subscriber, you will also receive your regional hotline of significant bird sightings and directions to the site.

Bird chat rooms are different from "BirdChat." "BirdChat" is a mailing list that sends e-mails automatically; while prompt, it is not live. Chat rooms are.

A popular one to visit is AOL's Birding Community site (keyword: Birding), which features hosted chat rooms, message boards, chat transcript archives, and more bird-related Web links.

As for actually "birding the net," tune your computer to www.virtualbirder.com/vbirder to go birding at Mount Auburn Cemetery in Cambridge, Massachusetts, during spring migration, or look at waders in southwest Florida, or take a tour of Churchill, Manitoba, where, with luck, you may get that special virtual life bird, the Ross's Gull. As you follow a map showing various paths, different birds appear. You can zoom in for a closer look, even hear some songs. Depending upon the quality of your monitor and the position of the bird, some birds can be surprisingly difficult to identify, making virtual-birding more realistic than you might think. Points are awarded for correct identifications, and you can post your score when you finish. Besides additional tours, the site offers bird photo galleries and bird ID quizzes, including some that test your bird-song skills.

The Web definitely has much to offer to birders of all levels, but remember, sitting in front of a computer screen just can't compare to watching your life Magnificent and Broad-billed Hummingbirds cavorting around a feeder at Santa Rita Lodge, a dance of so many colors that no monitor could possibly capture the moment.

— **Peggy Wang**
Peggy Wang is the owner of Middle Mountain Designs, a graphics company specializing in layout and design. She is also a birder, Web surfer, and resident of Tucson, Arizona.

Birders love to travel in search of birds, and the bird tour industry caters to this interest. This group on a WINGS Tour, led by David Sibley, searches for migrating birds on the grounds of Fort Jefferson on the Dry Tortugas. *Pete Dunne.*

Birding Tours

Before "ecotourism" was a household word, birders had already discovered the excitement of traveling to different areas to see new and exotic birds — and travel companies tailored to meet their interest soon discovered them. Today the three principal birding tour companies catering to North American birders are Field Guides, Victor Emanuel Nature Tours (VENT), and WINGS.

Many birding organizations, like Massachusetts Audubon, have their own travel programs, and there are scores of smaller, more specialized birding tour companies like Alaska Wilderness Birding Adventures (accent on adventure birding) and Shearwater Journeys, specializing in California pelagic birds. Most of these companies advertise in the national birding magazines or have their own Web page. Tour costs range from several hundred dollars for a long weekend excursion to a regional hotspot to over $10,000 for a cruise to Antarctica or a three-week tour of Papua New Guinea.

ADVANTAGES OF BIRDING TOURS

Tours offer two very compelling advantages. They take care of the planning and logistics, allowing you to relax and focus on the birds, and they are (or should be) led by experts — bird tour leaders who have an intimate knowledge of the birds of a particular region and are skilled at responding to the needs of clients, whether helping them locate a bird, describing its distinguishing field marks, or ensuring their safety and comfort.

Finding a good company and a good leader is the responsibility of the client. You can attempt this by trial and error or you can ask other, more seasoned birders for their recommendations.

Choosing a Bird Tour Company

A birding tour can be one of the most productive and delightful ways to enjoy the birds of an area and to learn about them — if you choose the right tour. Here are some of the factors to consider when making your choice.

LEADERSHIP

This is the single most important factor. A quality leader is essential for a successful tour. It is particularly important that the leader have extensive experience in the area and knowledge of its birds and how to find them; be skilled at handling trip logistics and any surprise situations that may arise; and be a good communicator, a skilled teacher, and a "people person" who likes all types of people and genuinely enjoys sharing birding and natural history experiences with them.

COMPANY PHILOSOPHY AND STYLE

It is important to pick a company that has a philosophy and style of birding that most closely matches your own. Important considerations include the pace of the tour and its approach to birds and nature. Some tours are very fast-paced, covering lots of ground in a day and seldom spending more than two or three nights in a location. Other trips have a more relaxed pace, with longer stays at one location and time off in the early afternoon.

The philosophy of a tour attracts certain types of birders. A tour that emphasizes getting the highest species total is attractive to hard-core listers. A tour that emphasizes bird appreciation and study attracts birders who enjoy looking at common, widespread species as well as rare ones and who want to learn more about bird identification and the lives of birds. Some birding tours combine birding with other aspects of natural

Birding workshops are like tours, but with an accent on acquiring skills (as well as acquiring new bird species). This group of young birders is attending Camp Chiricahua—an outdoor workshop organized by Victor Emanuel Nature Tours and, in this case, led by Victor himself (fourth from right). *Pete Dunne.*

history — butterflies, reptiles and amphibians, mammals, and wildflowers. Others focus exclusively on birds.

CREATURE COMFORTS

Birders vary in the level of creature comforts they desire, and you should choose a tour that offers the level you want. Some birding tours stay in the least expensive places and do not include food in the cost of the tour. Other birding tours place an emphasis upon quality accommodations and good food.

REPUTATION

You are more likely to have a good experience if you choose a tour operated by a long-established company with a good reputation. If these companies weren't doing a good job, they probably wouldn't have been in business for so many years. Such companies typically have full-time professional bird tour leaders who are aware that repeat business is essential to their livelihood. They put the interests of clients first.

To find a tour company that meets your interests and needs, check the company's catalogs and Web site and ask other birders. Many birders are well traveled and have enjoyed the services of more than one bird tour company. Ask for their recommendations of companies, tours, and leaders.

— **Victor Emanuel**
Victor Emanuel is director of Victor Emanuel Nature Tours in Austin, Texas, one of the "Big Three" U.S. birding tour companies. Operating since 1976, VENT offers tours all over the planet.

DISADVANTAGES OF BIRDING TOURS

Tours have disadvantages too. The first is cost. In general, an organized tour is going to be more expensive than traveling to a birding destination on your own. But if costs are measured in terms of bird sightings per dollar spent, costs go down — in fact, calculated this way, the cost of a bird tour will probably save you money.

The other disadvantage is personal freedom. Members of a tour necessarily forfeit a measure of self-determination once they become part of a group. Individuals who are very controlling and very particular about how things should (or should not) be done would do well to consider not subjecting themselves (and other tour members) to unnecessary frustration.

Events, Functions, Festivals, and Other Birders

There are now nearly three hundred birding festivals in North America that promote bird-related natural events. Some, like "The Bird Show" in Cape May, New Jersey (October), and "The Hummer/Bird Celebration," Rockport, Texas (September), attract thousands of attendees. Others are smaller.

All offer a blend of field trips, displays, indoor programs, outdoor demonstrations, and celebrity speakers. Most are advertised

Birding festivals are a great way to savor the birding opportunities of an area by taking advantage of the local expertise. Shown are some of the field trip and program leaders who volunteer their expertise to the Bird Show Festival, held every October in Cape May, New Jersey. *Clay and Pat Sutton.*

both locally and in targeted birding publications. Two on-line festival directories are currently available; they are from the ABA and *Bird Watcher's Digest:* www.Americabirding.org/resources/evntfestgen.htm and www.birdwatchersdigest.com/festivals/festivals.html. Many festivals are advertised in the major birding periodicals.

ONE ON ONE

Among all the avenues leading to the birding community, nothing beats teaming up with more experienced birders, one on one. Other birders who can answer the questions that plague you are the ultimate primary resource. Most are very pleased to help less experienced birders.

If you go to any of the prime birding locations mentioned in the next chapter, you are bound to come across other birders who share your interest. You may even find a mentor.

The birding community provides a social and informational network from which beginning birders can draw. Points of access include wild bird retail stores, nature centers, local bird clubs and Audubon societies, some museums and zoos, and community colleges. They sponsor activities such as morning bird walks, birding courses, field trips, regular meetings, and guest speakers. Information about these activities is found through newspaper columns that feature birding and other outdoor activities, birding telephone hotlines, and the Internet.

In addition, national and international organizations cater to birders, and a vast amount of information is lodged in birding magazines and books. A number of birding tour companies, led by experts, specialize in taking customers to domestic and exotic birding hotspots. The Web is a prime link to all of the social and organizational facets of birding, but the next birder you meet may become your primary source of information.

5
Expanding Horizons — Finding and Facing New Challenges

That Story About the Harrier

I was seated atop a very uncomfortable rock — the only kind there is on the North Lookout of world-famous Hawk Mountain, Pennsylvania. Before me was a vista that is emblazoned in the minds of every ardent hawk watcher... and two novice hawk watchers.

They had a single not very useful pair of binoculars to share and an array of basic field guides spread in a semicircle around them, all turned to the pages depicting birds of prey. Every passing Turkey Vulture became an object of scrutiny, the cause of much page flipping, and considerable but understandable frustration.

Hawk watching is challenging. Like all bird identification, it relies upon the use of field marks to distinguish one species from the next. But unlike most birding, identifications in the hawk-watching arena are often made at distances beyond the functional range of traditional field guides and standard field marks such as wing bars and tail spots, eye-lines and leg color.

In hawk watching, identifications are often made on the basis of overall shape (stocky versus lanky), overall color (cold brown versus warm), and the character of a bird's wing beats (quick and snappy or slow and stiff). It's a subtle art and a subjective one too, requiring study and experience to gain a measure of competence.

It also requires more specialized field guides — guides that illustrate and describe birds flying at the limit of conjecture — and superior optics to help vault the distance.

Me? I was pretty inexperienced myself, but better armed and better prepared than my neighbors. For one thing, I'd virtually memorized *Feathers in the Wind,* a book published by Hawk Mountain that focuses specifically upon the identification of hawks in flight. I'd also brought along a spotting scope mounted to a custom-made shoulder stock — a versatile combination that offered high magnification, stability, maneuverability, and portability.

I was also dedicated to the challenge at hand. Hawks had captivated me. During the autumn of 1975 I spent virtually every day hawk watching, which explains why I was seated atop Hawk Mountain under bluebird conditions — conditions that don't produce appreciable flights. **Scanning** ardently, I succeeded in finding a hawk.

W-a-a-a-y out there. A phantom form that drifted in and out of the heat waves and owed at least half of its existence to the very force of my will. After several minutes of study, I convinced myself that what might be a bird was in reality a bird and very probably a hawk. Fixing the position of the bird in my mind, I reached for my spotting scope and managed to find the phantom again in the heat and haze. At that point I concluded, happily, that the bird was eminently raptorial.

"I've got a bird," I shouted to the assembly. "Off the slope of One. Half a [binocular] field up. Way out," I cautioned.

Everyone on the lookout brought optics to bear. Some very experienced folks located the bird. Most could not. The guy in front of me was in the majority. First he looked up . . . then he panned right . . . then left.

He turned around, curious to see whether I was serious about there being a bird out there. Convinced by my look of concentration, he resumed his search. The guy might not have been experienced, and he might have had lousy optics, but he was nevertheless serious about finding this hawk.

Time passed. The bird got closer. I began to see more and more details — suggestions that coalesced into discernible features.

For instance, the set of the wings began to appear less than horizontal; in fact, they angled upward in a V. Only a few species of hawks that frequent Hawk Mountain fly with a pronounced dihedral: Turkey Vultures, Golden Eagles, Red-tailed Hawks, and Northern Harriers — a slim-winged, bantamweight predator of open spaces.

The bird I was looking at was too pale to be a vulture or an eagle, both of which appear almost black at a distance. It also seemed to have more dihedral than a Red-tailed Hawk should — particularly a Red-tailed flying in light-wind conditions. And . . . was it my imagination, or did this bird rock ever so unsteadily in flight?

Given still-wind conditions, only a bird with very light wing loading would be flying so unsteadily — a point that would eliminate the burly, even-keeled Red-tailed Hawk.

It seemed that I'd narrowed the possibilities down to one. So I stuck my neck out.

"It's a Marsh Hawk," I yelled. (We called Northern Harriers Marsh Hawks back then.)

At this disclosure, the gentleman up front spun around and glowered. Turning down ridge once more, he *jammed* the ocular lenses of his binoculars into his eyes, fixing them once again on the horizon.

My suspected harrier kept coming, shedding uncertainty along the way. Wings that seemed to be held in a dihedral became clearly held in a dihedral. A flight that might have been tippy became noticeably tippy. The bird's profile, such as could be seen, seemed gratifyingly long-limbed and slim.

All these traits are harrier traits.

The bird was still too far away, and the angle too acute, to make out the classic white rump patch, the textbook field mark that would have certified the bird as a Northern Harrier. But it wasn't necessary. By projection and deduction, through compounded hints and clues, the bird was as much a harrier at a mile out as it would be if I'd held the bird in my hand. The trick with hawk watching (as with anything else) is knowing the tricks.

Abruptly, the bird left the ridge, angling off over the valley — a classic bluebird day maneuver. A mile off was as close as the bird was going to get. As I watched, studying the bird, trying to learn as much as I could about harrier shape, size, and manner of flight, a vagrant updraft caught the bird, tipping it on its side, exposing bright, white underparts.

Young harriers show cinnamon underparts; adult females are tawny. But . . .

"Adult male!" I sang out. "It's an adult male Marsh Hawk!" Not as commonly seen as immature or female harriers, the bird was then, and remains today, my favorite bird of prey.

At this pronouncement, the gentleman in front of me released his binoculars, lowered his head in his hands, rocked back several times, then, righting himself, leaned toward his wife and whispered:

"I can't believe this son-of-a-bitch behind me. I can't even *find* this bird, and *he* can see its genitals."

The fact is that you can't see the genitals on migrating birds of prey. But if your objective is identification, and if you know the tricks, you don't have to.

Reaching for New Sights and Sounds

Having learned the rudiments of identification and gained a working familiarity with the birds that occur in their regular haunts, most birders want to reach for new birds and challenges that lie beyond their immediate horizons. These challenges could include finding new birds whose identity lies beyond the range of binoculars; tackling new identification challenges, such as bird vocalizations; and expanding horizons in a very literal sense by traveling to new places to see birds. The world is a big and bird-filled place. Discovery, excitement, and challenge lie in every direction. As birders expand their horizons, they discover a need for new tools and equipment — optical, electronic, and informational.

Sight — Spotting Scopes and Tripods

Binoculars may be the primary tool of birding, but they have their limits. Picking up where binoculars fall short is the spotting scope.

SPOTTING SCOPES

A spotting scope permits birders to study details beyond the effective range of binoculars. This single-barreled optical instrument offers a view through one eye. Fitted to a tripod or some other stabilizing platform, it allows the effective use of greater magnification, which enhances the details that can be seen.

Spotting scopes are not as quick, versatile, or portable as binoculars, and they are not a substitute for binoculars. (Birders who have inadequate binoculars and who think that buying a spotting scope

Spotting scopes are less portable and less versatile than binoculars, but invaluable when the challenge involves viewing birds across great distances or seeing very fine detail of birds close at hand. *Linda Dunne.*

Prism spotting scopes (like those pictured in the previous photo) are popular among birders because of their size, portability, ease of use, and rugged nature. Reflecting scopes, like this Questar, are most popular among planet watchers but offer a superlative image of earth-bound objects (for a price). *Clay Sutton.*

will make the difference had better think again.) They are also not useful for some types of birding — for instance, most woodland birding.

They are nevertheless invaluable when birds must be studied at great distances, like distant waterfowl on a lake, or when a tricky identification dictates very detailed scrutiny, as with similar shorebird species.

Spotting scopes are also a portal to gaining supernatural intimacy with birds. Some very fine instruments today offer images of birds at close range that are *even better than can be seen in the hand.*

Mirror Versus Prism Scopes

There are two types of spotting scopes: **reflecting scopes,** or mirror scopes, which use mirrors to capture and direct light, and **refracting scopes,** which use prisms and lenses.

Mirror scopes are generally short and bucket-shaped and commonly have an angled or look-down **eyepiece.** They are lightweight, provide good to excellent resolution even at high magnification, and are exceptionally bright. Unfortunately, they are not rugged, waterproof, or particularly user-friendly — deficits that would render them unpopular among birders even if they did not reverse the image (because they use mirrors) or tend to burn the colors out of subjects (particularly at the center of the field).

Reflecting scopes serve well for observing stars and planets, but only the highest-quality (and -priced) reflecting scopes have ever won a place in the hearts of birders.

Prism scopes are infinitely more popular among birders because of their ruggedness, simplicity, high image quality, and portability. Prism scopes are classically tube-shaped. Many models come with a choice of an angled eyepiece (for restful, long-term viewing) or a straight-through-view eyepiece (which is generally easier to aim).

Prism scopes come in two size classes — those offering a 60-millimeter objective lens and those with a 77- to 82-millimeter objective. The 60- to 65-millimeter scopes are lighter and more compact; those with the larger objective offer marginally superior brightness and image quality — but much also depends upon the quality of the instrument. A superior-quality 60-millimeter spotting scope — one that employs very-high-quality glass — can outperform lesser-quality 80-millimeter scopes.

ED, HD, and APO Lenses — How They Work

Lenses work because light rays bend as they pass through glass (or any other transparent material that is significantly denser than air). Daylight is a mix of many colors, and each color is bent at a slightly different angle when it passes through glass. Each object in the image formed by a simple glass lens is thus surrounded by a rainbow halo (reds, blues, greens, and purples) of unfocused light.

Early on, lens designers discovered that if they made lenses from two pieces of glass (elements) with different densities, they could bring two colors of light, red and yellow, to the same focus. Since red and yellow account for most of the energy in daylight, in most situations you can't detect the blue, green, and purple halos that are left in an image.

Most modern spotting scopes use a two-element, or **achromatic,** objective lens and produce an image that is clean and sharp enough to provide a satisfactory image 95 percent of the time in the field. Still, that unfocused light does bleed over from one object in the image to another, muddying the colors and blurring the edges. In critical situations (such as at great distances, while using the highest powers, or in low light), a standard achromat may show you less than you want to see of the bird.

Using something denser for one of the elements can help to tighten contrast. Modern objectives use **extra-density (ED)** glass, made by adding heavy metals or rare earths to the glass mix. In Europe, ED glass is sometimes called **high-density (HD),** but it is essentially the same. Some spotting scopes use a fluorite element made from a transparent mineral that is also denser than glass.

Scopes with ED (HD) and fluorite objectives eliminate all but a tiny fraction of the unfocused halos in an image. Compared to the image formed by a standard achromatic objective, the ED or fluorite image appears sharper, brighter, snappier, and more intense. You will see the difference most in critical situations, but the extra measure of clarity can add to your enjoyment of birds all day long. I would guess that an ED or fluorite spotting scope shows you all you want to see of the bird 99 percent of the time. You do pay a price, of course. ED and fluorite scopes can cost up to one-third more than standard achromats. (Thirty-three percent more money for a 4 percent gain in performance . . . only you can figure out if that equation is acceptable to you.)

To eliminate the last bit of unfocused light and produce absolutely the purest image, it is generally necessary to add a third element to the objective lens and use a third type of glass. Lenses that bring all the colors of daylight to the same focus are called **apochromatic (APO).** They are featured only in top-end astronomical scopes and a few (two that I know of) of the very finest (and correspondingly expensive) spotting scopes for birders.

— **Steve Ingram**
A resident of Kennebunk, Maine, Steve Ingram is the editor of Better View Desired, *a newsletter whose focus is optics and the optical needs of birders, and is "Tools of the Trade" department editor for* Birding.

Power and Performance
Power and performance are what using a spotting scope is all about. The considerations used to measure binocular performance generally apply to spotting scopes too — brightness, field of view, eye relief, depth of field.

But at the core of the spotting scope is power — the ability to vault distances and magnify distant objects so that details may be seen. Remember, hand shake is no longer a diminishing factor. The scope rests on a tripod, not in your hands. In an ideal, vibration-free world, image quality comes down to a simple matter of magnification and the quality of the glass.

How Much Power?
Spotting scopes offer a range of magnification most often determined by the power of the interchangeable eyepiece you buy and fit to the scope. Popular powers include 15×, 20×, 22×, 25×, 30×, 32×, 40×, and 60×. Not all manufacturers offer all these options for all instruments — and some offer even higher magnifications. In general, anything between 20× and 32× will serve for both easy scanning and con-

Most spotting scopes offer a choice of eyepieces, ranging in power from 20× to 80×. Most experienced birders use 20× or 30× or choose a zoom (15×–45× or 20×–60×) eyepiece. Zoom eyepieces in the high-quality lines of spotting scopes do not suffer the shortfalls associated with zoom binoculars; in fact, some zoom eyepieces offer resolution every bit as good as fixed eyepieces. *Courtesy of Leica.*

centrated study. Wide-angle lenses are superior for scanning. Higher-power lenses (40× and above) enhance detail at the expense of field of view.

There are also zoom spotting scopes. Some scopes have an internal zoom mechanism, and others include a zoom lens among the array of lens options. While internal focusing zooms offer generally inferior optical performance, *some zoom eyepieces on the market offer optical performance that is every bit as good as that offered by their fixed-magnification counterparts.* Unfortunately , the field of view on quality zoom eyepieces is not generous, even at the lowest magnification setting, but their ability to resolve details is often stellar.

For years the standard for spotting scope magnification was 20× — a power that for most makes and models provides a good, sharp, bright image that does not push a scope past its performance limits.

Magnification increases not only image size but optical shortcomings. A spotting scope that offers a nice, bright image at 20× may well produce a dingy image and poor resolution at 40×.

What do I use? Armed with a very high-quality 77-millimeter instrument that can take the challenge of higher magnification at no performance loss, I like a 32× wide-angle eyepiece. To my mind, it offers the best balance of high power (for detailed observation) with a bright image and a wide field of view (for easy pickup and comparative study of birds in flocks).

Other Considerations

Optical performance is the primary but not necessarily the only quality that a field-worthy spotting scope should offer. As with binoculars, other attributes are also important to a scope's usefulness in the field.

DEPTH OF FIELD/CRITICAL FOCUS: As critical a concern in spotting scopes as binoculars, a shallow depth of field will make studying flocks very difficult, even physically exhausting. When you use a scope whose image is blurred everywhere but at the precise point of focus, your eyes try to compensate for the instrument's shortcomings — and quickly tire.

CLOSE FOCUS: Close focus is not as great a concern for scopes as it is for binoculars. Nevertheless there are times when a close-focusing spotting scope can be useful — when studying very subtle distinctions, for instance, like the scapular feather patterns that distinguish Western and Semipalmated Sandpipers, or the tail feather patterns that separate Cassin's and Botteri's Sparrow. However, the greatest advantage of close-focusing instruments is the supernatural intimacy they offer viewers. While all scopes should focus down to at least thirty feet, there are some on the market that focus down to ten feet or less!

So what? Well, imagine a cardinal or a bluebird perched at ten feet and viewed with a 32× eyepiece — the equivalent of viewing a living, breathing creature from a distance of less than four inches. Not only can you see the creature's eye, you can see your reflection in its eye.

FOCUS SYSTEMS: Whether a ring around the barrel or, more commonly, a focus knob, the focus system should move smoothly and responsively. Fast focusing is not the concern with spotting scopes that it is with binoculars since subjects are generally more sedentary.

Caution: Because the focus mechanism of some spotting scopes gets stiff and truculent in cold temperatures, it can be difficult to focus without moving the scope off-target. If the scope you are considering seems hard to focus in the store, it will only be worse when the lubricants gel.

ANGLED EYEPIECE VERSUS STRAIGHT-THROUGH: Whether to choose a scope whose eyepiece is angled or straight-through is a matter of preference, not optical performance. There are advantages to both, and these may determine which style you prefer.

ANGLED EYEPIECE ADVANTAGES
1. It generally provides easier, more restful long-term viewing.
2. The scope is set lower than your raised eyes, allowing you to scan over them (not around them) with binoculars.
3. Two or more individuals of slightly differing heights can better share the instrument with less physical strain, acrimony, or tripod manipulation.

4. Observers can study birds high overhead without having to crouch or buy a super-extending tripod.

ANGLED EYEPIECE DISADVANTAGES

1. It's more difficult to learn to aim and find the bird than with a straight-through eyepiece.
2. The angled eyepiece's greater exposure to rain, mist, or snow can distort the image in inclement weather.
3. It's not serviceable on a shoulder-mount system or easily used on automobile window mounts.
4. It projects the line of sight several inches below eye level. If the bird you want to study is perched beyond some vegetative barrier (such as a hedge or reed bed), the line of sight may not be high enough.

Most American birders prefer the straight-through system, while Europeans favor the angled eyepiece. There is a reason for this. In Europe standard birding practice calls for prolonged study of birds from a hide or long-term scanning (for example, sea-bird watching). In the United States, owing perhaps to more diverse habitat and greater birding possibilities, birders shift position quickly, moving from bird to bird and site to site. The angled system is better suited for long-

Angled eyepiece versus straight-through viewing —there are advantages and disadvantages to both. You choose.
Courtesy of Leica.

term viewing; the straight-through system is faster, particularly for those not skilled at finding birds through a scope.

RUGGEDNESS: Even more than binoculars, scopes must be rugged. Binoculars hit the ground by accident. Spotting scopes go down routinely, the victims of wind gusts, mechanically deficient tripods, or collisions with object-challenged individuals. Scope bodies, particularly scope bodies in the larger classes, 77 millimeter and above, should be housed in metal. Polycarbon bodies are seductively light, but when they fall, a disturbingly high percentage break. Be warned and be mindful of the limitations of a scope's warranty.

How Many $$$?
You can buy a serviceable spotting scope for around $300. You can buy a decent spotting scope for $500 to $600, a good spotting scope for $700 to $800, and a superior spotting scope for $1,000 and up. But no matter how much you spend on the scope, do not skimp on the . . .

TRIPOD
Tripods are the literal foundation of power, the vibration-free platform that makes higher magnification possible. No matter how much over budget you go on your spotting scope purchase, *do not even think about balancing the budget by buying an inexpensive tripod*. You are better off with a $300 spotting scope and a $190 tripod than with a $3,500 spotting scope and a $90 tripod. A light, flimsy tripod is not going to remain stable in even a modest wind, and wind-generated vibration will make a shambles of your image quality.

There are high-quality, high-performance tripods, *made of aluminum*, that can be purchased for under $200. They are fairly heavy (weighing, depending upon models, between five and nine pounds), but they will perform as well as light, strong, graphite tripods costing over three times as much, and their weight is an asset in the wind.

Simplicity is the rule of thumb. Photographers seem to dote on tripods that offer multiple adjustment controls. The ideal spotting scope tripod has just one lever that controls all movement and a head that pans up and down, left and right, smoothly, easily, without disconcerting skips or jumps.

Tripods are the foundation that makes higher magnification work. Whatever you do, *don't buy a cheap, flimsy tripod.* You'll only compromise the usefulness of the scope. *Linda Dunne.*

Legs should sleeve easily and extend so that you do not have to stoop to bring the spotting scope eyepiece to eye level. If you travel frequently, you may want to be certain that the tripod can fit in your travel bag.

There are other very useful mounts for spotting scopes, including window mounts that sleeve over a half-open car window and use the car for stability, and commercial shoulder stocks that optimize portability.

But a good tripod is essential, and very few manufacturers make tripods suitable for birding. Don't expect to go to your average camera store and find a birder-worthy tripod. What you will most likely find is a tripod designed for photography.

Find out what other birders are using. Find out where they bought it. Follow their lead.

Sound — Birding by Ear

Birds are not merely a visual presence but an audible presence as well. They disclose their existence, location, and identities through sounds, many of which are vocalizations that emanate from the bird's **syrinx,** or voice box. They include chips, grunts, wails, warbles, trills . . . and, of

Birding by ear is a two-part challenge. First, you have to hear the bird; then you must link the sound to a species. Cupping hands behind ears will help catch and direct the barely discernable notes of distant birds. *Linda Dunne.*

course, song — one of the natural world's most celebrated offerings.

Bird sounds can also emanate from an alchemy of air and feathers (the **drumming** of grouse and the **winnowing** of snipe) or from percussive manipulation (the drumming of woodpeckers).

Birds make a number of sounds for a variety of reasons. Together, they form an avenue that leads to a greater awareness and understanding of birds. Separated, they are an audio-fingerprint that distinguishes one species from another. Learn which sounds are made by which birds and you'll be able to identify them with your ears as accurately as with your eyes — and in many cases, even more accurately.

Sifting Through Sound

You pull into the parking lot at Warbler Woods and Backseat Sylvia — you know, your birder friend with the perpetual smug look on her face — starts calling out birds: "Black-and-white Warbler, Wood Thrush, Scarlet Tanager, Rose-breasted Grosbeak, Chipping Sparrow . . ." And she hasn't even gotten out of the car!

While Sylvia didn't exactly walk on water, she has performed an apparent miracle: she has identified most of the birds in the area without

Insights

even raising her binoculars. Along the way her flippant audio IDs may just have discouraged every beginning birder within earshot.

To many beginners, Sylvia's auditory talents appear more like a divine gift than an acquired skill. Because most folks come to birding with little or no appreciation for bird song, getting a handle on even the most rudimentary facts of bird vocalization may seem a daunting challenge. And anyway, the name of the game is bird *watching*, isn't it? To be fair, the beginners already have their hands full learning the visual characteristics of birds, and even when the birder becomes dimly aware that bird song may be of some use in birding, he or she usually just lets the bird-song challenge slide. This is a big mistake. Let me tell you why.

Ask almost any experienced or expert birder, and they will tell you that knowing bird song is a critical component of their skill. One survey suggested that between 75 percent and 90 percent of bird identifications are based on bird vocalizations. Think of all the situations in which you are likely to hear a bird before you see it: bitterns in a marsh, sparrows in a hedgerow, warblers in the treetops... The list goes on and on. Also, our ears are turned to 360 degrees — they constantly monitor *all* of our immediate environment while our eyes focus on only a small portion of the area. Once you know most of the common bird songs, your ears will tell you whether there is something different in the area — then you can put your eyes to work to "find" the bird. The sooner you begin learning bird song the more quickly you will develop into a competent birder. So how do you get started?

I suppose most of us, largely for reasons related to maintaining our sanity, pay little or no attention to bird song before we become birders. Apart from the occasional noisy crow or barnyard rooster vocalizations, bird songs are just not a part of our day-to-day reality. It's as though we are born with certain sensory filters and a conscious decision is needed to remove one of those filters. As fledgling birders, however, we are soon made aware that birds are vocal critters. And herein arises the initial problem: a spring morning can deal out a bewildering symphony of bird sounds. Unfortunately for the beginner, the result is not enlightenment but rather sensory overload. Just as you focus on one bird at a time with your binoculars, you need to retrain your hearing to focus on one bird song at a time. So a good way to get started is to learn the vocalizations of one or two of the most common birds in your area and concentrate on their songs. House Finches, Northern Mockingbirds, and American Robins are good candidates.

You also need to develop a system for representing bird song. While the means for representing the visual characteristics of birds — size, color, plumage patterns, and so on — are familiar, methods for representing vocalization require a little practice. Two forms of representation are most helpful: description and phonetic representation.

Let's use the American Robin to illustrate both methods. The American Robin's song can be described as a lilting up-and-down tune. The rhythm is sing songy. Let's add a phonetic representation — *cheerily, cheerup, cheerily.* Try singing (or whistling) the phonetic and give it an up-and-down rhythm. (Don't worry, nobody is listening.) Now you have a good representation of the American Robin's song — one that you can mentally compare to the robin singing in the back yard. Just as you compare a field guide illustration to the bird in the field, you compare the bird song representation to the song you hear. The list of descriptive words you can apply to bird song is limited only by your imagination. Squeaky wheels, flutes, rusty hinges, whistles, Ping-Pong balls dropping on tables — all these are used. In my experience, the more bizarre the description the more likely you are to remember it.

Did you know that Bobolinks sound like R2-D2 (of *Star Wars* fame) with his wires crossed? Also, adding emotional content to your description — for example, the *haunting* song of the Veery — seems to reinforce the description. You will find dozens of descriptive and phonetic representations in field guides and on bird song tapes, but don't be bashful about creating your own. Most bird song learners find that the most helpful representations are the ones they devise themselves.

Keep a notebook of birds you hear and representations of their songs. One other method for representing bird song is to use simplified drawings. Graphical representations might include dotted lines for a trill, wavy lines for an up-and-down rhythm, and upward- and downward-pointed arrows to indicate changes in pitch.

There you have it! A crash course in bird-song learning. A few final tips. Don't try to learn too many songs at once. Start with the common birds first, then relax. This is supposed to be fun. Soon you will be sug-

gesting to Sylvia that she may have missed the Black-throated Green Warbler singing in the background!

— Dick Walton

> Dick Walton is a skilled naturalist and coauthor of the Birding by Ear
> tapes and several natural history videos, including Hawk Watch. Well
> known on the birding (and butterfly) lecture circuit, he lives in Concord,
> Massachusetts.

BUT . . . DO HEARD BIRDS COUNT?

Of course heard birds count, whether you are enhancing your appreciation of a bird or adding it to your life list. You might just as legiti-
mately ask whether a bird that is momentarily seen and identified visually can be counted if you didn't hear it sing or haven't yet seen it in
all its various plumages.

Some species, particularly many nocturnal species, are virtual
disembodied spirits anyway. They are heard, filling the night with a
rich blend of sound, but rarely seen. For years I thrilled to the sound
of Black Rails not far from my home without ever making an effort to
see one. I didn't want to risk disrupting their nesting (or for that matter, the nesting efforts of other salt-marsh birds), and so I was content
merely to listen. A momentary glimpse of a small black bird in a
night-darkened marsh would hardly have mattered.

AWARENESS FIRST

The first step in learning to identify birds by ear is simple awareness.
Whether you are in the field or inside your home with the windows
open, train your ears to be as attentive to sound as your eyes are to
motion. Learn to pick up sounds that are new; condition yourself to
isolate individual songs the way you pick out individual instruments
in a musical ensemble.

You probably know more bird vocalizations than you think —
such as the raucous *caw-caw* call of an American Crow, the resonant
Ah-honk of a Canada Goose, or the seven-note, two-part hoot of a
Great Horned Owl. Perhaps you live in the suburbs and recognize the

You say birding by ear is too difficult for you? If you live in North America and you can't recognize this bird by its call, I agree with you. *Kevin Karlson.*

liquid cascade of notes that is a House Wren's song, or on a farm where meadowlarks sing from fence-post perches.

To build the basic foundation of an audio repertoire, start by listening first to the common everyday birds around you — the ones whose songs and sounds form the audio-fabric of your world. Once you've linked the sounds to the singers — a rising and falling flow of phrases automatically conjures "robin" and a rapid trill means Chipping Sparrow — you can move these back-yard birds to the back burners of your mind and listen for new and unfamiliar sounds.

BUILDING YOUR AUDIO REPERTOIRE

Learning bird sounds is like anything else: the more you know, the easier it gets. The more attuned you become to the nuances of bird sounds, the easier it is to compare an unfamiliar vocalization with a familiar one and to distinguish between them.

With practice you learn to hear critically, distinguishing the elements of a song — volume, pitch, frequency, cadence, phrases — much the same way wine lovers learn to appreciate the subtle qualities of a wine.

Once you know a bird song, you can call it up from memory and use it as a comparative reference to help distinguish and even lock away the elements of a new song. Many species have vocalizations that are similar to those of other species.

Take, for example, Chipping Sparrow, a very common, very widespread bird whose very elemental song is a rapid series of dry chip notes — all on the same pitch, all on the same frequency. There are other birds whose song is a trill, among them Dark-eyed Junco, Orange-crowned Warbler, and Worm-eating Warbler. But the trill of the Dark-eyed Junco is more musical than that of the Chipping Sparrow; that of Orange-crowned Warbler is flatter and lower-pitched at the end; and Worm-eating Warbler's is faster, dryer, sharper, with opening notes that lack volume and closing notes that lose force.

In each case, knowing the song of Chipping Sparrow offers a comparative reference. Knowing that one broad category of bird vocalizations is "trilling" helps give some structure and order to the complex world of sound.

M N E M O N I C S : S O U N D S L I K E . . .

Some people are audio-gifted; they can hear a bird's song once and lock it into memory. Most of us are not so fortunate. We hear a song, strive to memorize it and the name of the singer, and fail to recognize it (and the singer) two minutes later.

"I've got to relearn warbler songs every spring" is a common lament among birders.

Many people find it helpful to remember *mnemonic* phrases that capture the pattern of a bird's song. At its most simple and accurate, the song of Prothonotary Warbler is a loud, ringing *sweet! sweet! sweet! sweet! sweet!*

Hardly more complex and no less phonetically apt is the call of Scarlet Tanager, *chick-burr,* or the song of White-throated Sparrow, *oh, sweet, Canada, Canada, Canada.*

Some mnemonics can be more complex and very creative, including the song of Indigo Bunting — *What-what-where-where-here-here-see it-see it.* And that (perhaps my favorite) of Warbling Vireo, which taunts its caterpillar prey with the boast *If-I-see-it, I-can-seize-it, and-I'll-squeeze-it, till-it-squir-r-r-rts.*

When You Can't Find the Words

Some bird sounds that don't lend themselves to mnemonic phrases may remind you of other familiar things. For example, one of the common vocalizations of the Gray Catbird is a petulant whine that is reminiscent of a cat. The cry of Sandhill Cranes recalls an ungreased hinged opening on a wooden gate. Yellow Rails make a call that recalls two quarters being struck together. The **nocturnal flight call** of Swainson's Thrush might easily be confused with the call of the spring peeper, a small eastern frog.

But while spring peepers, like migrating thrushes, are nocturnal, frogs don't fly. Spring peeper sounds emanating from the heavens over much of North America in May are much more likely to be Swainson's Thrush.

. . . Which Brings up an Interesting Point

Birds vocalize all year — to communicate with other members of a flock, to warn of enemies or intruders, to disclose the location of food. Most birds are most vocal in spring and early summer, when males are establishing and defending territories and advertising for mates with song.

Nesting season can be a very protracted affair in some parts of the continent, and there are some species (like Carolina Wren) that sing all year. But over most of North America, birds are "singing" (not "calling") from March through early July, with April through June the period when many nesting birds are in full chorus.

Off-season, the audio-fingerprints offered by birds might be hardly more than fragments — single-note chips, nasal whines, or the mumbled and barely audible **whisper song,** a shadow rendition of a bird's territorial repertoire. And for inconvenience's sake, remember that it is usually only the male bird that sings. Half of the adult population of most songbird species doesn't advertise its presence or identity itself on the airways in song.

Although birds can be identified by vocalizations other than their songs, the best time to tune your birding ear is spring, when birds are singing. Peak vocalization periods run from dawn until midmorning and again in the evening (although many birds vocalize all day — some even at night). During the height of the breeding season, males are bonded to their territory — backed into a geographic corner. If approached too closely, they won't fly far. For those who, like me, find that repetition is the key to learning, it is helpful to know that male birds sing frequently, often two to three *thousand* times a day.

Once the unidentified singer is located, bring your binoculars to bear. Identify the bird. Then watch and listen, fusing the image of the bird to the elements of the song.

The bond might not hold the first time, or the second, but sooner (if you are audio-gifted) or later (if you are like me), the name and sound will be linked.

No Shortage of Aids

Ornithologists and birders have developed numerous aids to learning bird sounds. Descriptions and mnemonics are helpful, but they are not the audio equivalent of an illustration in a field guide. **Sonograms** — mechanical constructs that use lines on paper to replicate sound visually — are accurate but require study and a working familiarity with bird song to be truly useful.

Sound recordings are by far the most useful aids. An assortment of bird sound recordings, with different focuses, are available on cassette tapes and CDs.

Some recordings, like the ensembles produced by the Peterson Field Guide Series, are offered as an accompaniment to printed field guides. For the most part, the order of bird sounds follows the order in which birds are depicted in the books — a utilitarian marriage that facilitates learning.

Some, like *Sounds of the Warblers of North America,* produced by Donald Borror and William Gunn, have a specialized species focus; others are geographic or site-specific in focus (*Voices of the Peruvian Rain Forest* by Ted Parker; *A Bird Walk at Chan Chich* by John More; Houghton Mifflin's *Backyard Birds*).

More useful to those who are just learning to find their way around the world of bird sound are recordings that group similar-sounding birds together — those that trill, those that buzz, those that use short phrases, those that repeat their notes — so that they can be compared and contrasted. The popular *Birding by Ear* and *More Birding by Ear* recordings produced by Dick Walton and Bob Lawson, and published by Houghton Mifflin, are classics.

Invaluable and brilliant in its scope and execution is *Flight Calls of Migratory Birds.* Produced by William R. Evans and Michael O'Brien, this multimedia CD-ROM contains audio recordings, spectrographic portrayals, and information on migration for 211 species of migratory land birds in eastern North America.

The problem with recordings is that the sounds are disembodied. Without the anchoring reference of the bird making the sound, recordings go in one ear and out the other without finding a home in between. CD-ROMs and videos, which mate the sound to a visual depiction, are superior educational aids.

If you want to hear what species X sounds like, a bird identification CD-ROM allows you to call up an image and description of X and to click on the icon that makes it sing. The image might be poor-quality, and the bird depicted might be a female (not the male), but at least the vocalization is backed up visually.

Videos, while not interactive, have the advantage of being closer to life. Birds move as freely as they do in nature, and the sound that is

You can buy tapes that replicate the call of Green Jay (and most other species), but nothing beats seeing (and hearing) the real bird, in real time. *Linda Dunne.*

heard emanates from the bird being shown. The reference standard among videos is *Watching Warblers,* produced by Michael Male and Judy Fieth. The intimacy is surreal, and the projected situation between the bird captured on video and the viewer is almost as good as being in the field.

HOWEVER, NOTHING — REPEAT *NOTHING* — BEATS THE REAL THING

The array of devices that replicate bird sounds are useful, and they purport to be getting better. There are systems being developed that use bar codes, affixed to field guide illustrations, that key to and play the songs of birds with the wave of a (light) wand — a sort of book-to-CD-ROM conversion kit. It will not be long before birders will be able to record songs in the field whose digitalized translations will call up an identification.

But when it comes to learning to identify birds by their vocalizations, nothing is as effective as listening to real birds, in real time, in real outdoor situations. It is, after all, why you started birding in the first place.

Travel to New Birding Locations

Just as you once left your back yard in search of new birds and new discoveries, most birders are eventually inspired to take their avocation on the road to search for birds whose normal range does not overlap with their own.

More than nine hundred species of birds have occurred in North America north of Mexico. In most states and provinces, less than half this number are accounted for as resident or regular transients. And while birds often turn up hundreds, even thousands, of miles outside their normal range of occurrence, pursuing birds in their native environment is more productive, and arguably more satisfying, than relying upon accident and chance.

Your search for birds can take you *everywhere,* even to the ends of the earth. Linda Dunne trades birding tips with some of the locals on the island of South Georgia. *Bruce Hallet.*

TRAVEL . . . WHERE?

The flippant answer is — almost anywhere. As a general rule, the farther you travel, the more unfamiliar the birds become. But you do not necessarily have to travel across the continent to see new birds. Habitat can be as important as distance where bird distribution is concerned. In some places where **physiographic regions** are found in close proximity, a trip of one hundred miles can dramatically change the birding landscape. For example, the distance between Rocky Mountain National Park and the Pawnee National Grasslands of Colorado is about one hundred miles. But the differences — in the nesting bird life and between western forest species like Hammond's Flycatcher, Western Tanager, and Lincoln's Sparrow and prairie specialties like Mountain Plover, Lark Bunting, and Chestnut-collared Longspur — are dramatic.

While many locations offer exciting birding possibilities, there are birding "hotspots" that offer easy access to large numbers of the endemic and specialty birds of a region. They have the advantage of being well known and well documented and are generally found in proximity to places that meet the needs of travelers.

No two lists of birding hotspots are identical, but every birder would agree that the following locations offer great birding. Some are famous for their endemics, some host large or unusual numbers of wintering species, and some attract vast numbers of migratory birds. Taken in sum, they cover most of the bird species found in North America.

Massachusetts: Newburyport — Parker River National Wildlife Refuge

For winter specialties with an Atlantic Coast flavor. *Some species to see:* Great Cormorant, Common Eider, Barrow's Goldeneye, Harlequin Duck, Purple Sandpiper, Iceland Gull, Glaucous Gull. *Period:* Late November through February. *Contact:* Massachusetts Audubon Society, South Great Rd., Lincoln, MA 01773, 617-259-9500. *Also recommended:* Coastal Maine; New Hampshire; Montauk Point, Long Island. *Reference Guide: A Birder's Guide to Eastern Massachusetts* by Bird Observer (American Birding Association).

Cape May, New Jersey

An autumn migratory concentration point famous for its songbird **fallouts,** hawk migration (average: sixty thousand birds of prey per year), and one-million-bird sea-bird migration. *Period:* August through November. *Contact:* Cape May Bird Observatory, 600 Route 47 North, Cape May Court House, NJ 08210, 609-861-0700. *Also rec-*

Cape May, New Jersey, is best known for its autumn concentrations of birds, but birding is excellent in spring and good in summer and winter. Here, hawk watchers view one (or more) migrating hawks atop the spacious hawk-watch platform at Cape May Point State Park. *Pete Dunne.*

Point Pelee National Park in Ontario is a mecca for spring warbling aspirants in the spring. Trams run birders out to the peninsula's tip. *Linda Dunne.*

ommended: Cape Charles, Virginia; Hawk Mountain Sanctuary, Kempton, Pennsylvania. *Reference Guide: The Birds of Cape May* by David Sibley (Cape May Bird Observatory).

Point Pelee, Ontario

The spring counterpart to Cape May, Point Pelee offers massed concentrations of spring migrants (particularly warblers) in full color and full song. *Period:* Mid-April through May. *Contact:* Point Pelee National Park, RR 1, Leamington, Ontario, N8H 3V4, 519-322-2371. *Also recommended:* Crane Creek State Park, Ohio; Presque Isle State Park, Pennsylvania; Whitefish Point, Michigan.

Everglades, Southern Florida

A winter getaway that offers the opportunity to see many species that rarely occur outside of Florida. *Some species to see:* Snail Kite, Short-tailed Hawk, White-crowned Pigeon, Mangrove Cuckoo, Black-whiskered Vireo. *Period:* December through February. *Contact:* Everglades National Park, Box 279, Homestead, FL 33030, 305-247-6211; also Florida Audubon Society. *Also recommended:* National Audubon's Corkscrew Swamp; Ding Darling National Wildlife Refuge. *Reference guide: A Birder's Guide to Florida* by Bill Pranty (American Birding Association).

The Texas coast offers great birding (except, perhaps, in the heat of summer) but is best known for its spring fall-outs of cross-gulf migrants. This very tired-looking Black-billed Cuckoo just dropped in at Sabine Woods, maintained by the Houston Audubon Society. *Linda Dunne.*

Texas Coast/High Island

A place with great winter diversity and celebrated for its spring songbird fallouts. Birders are courted from High Island (near Port Arthur) to South Padre Island. *Period:* December through March for wintering species; April for migrants. *Contact:* Houston Audubon Society, 440 Wilchester, Houston, TX 77079, 713-932-1639; and Texas Parks and Wildlife Department, 4200 Smith School Rd., Austin, TX 78744-3291, 800-772-1112, www.tpwd.state.tx.us. *Also recommended:* Cameroon Parish, Louisiana; Dauphin Island, Alabama; Dry Tortugas, Florida. *Reference guide: A Birder's Guide to the Texas Coast* by Harold R. Holt (American Birding Association).

Rio Grande Valley, Texas

A verdant window into Mexico with a number of species found nowhere else in the United States. Key sites include Santa Ana National Wildlife Refuge and Bentsen–Rio Grande Valley State Park. *Some species to see:* Muskovy, Hook-billed Kite, Ringed Kingfisher, Mexican Crow, Brown Jay, Tropical Parula. *Period:* December through April. *Contact:* Santa Ana National Wildlife Refuge. *Reference guide: A Birder's Guide to the Rio Grande Valley of Texas* by Mark Lockwood, James Patton, Barry R. Zimmer, and William B. McKinney (American Birding Association).

Churchill, Manitoba, provides easy access to an array of Arctic nesting species and is a popular tour destination. *Linda Dunne.*

Churchill, Manitoba

Churchill offers northern and tundra species with a measure of traveler conveniences. Linked by air and rail (no highway), a trip itinerary can include visits to Riding Mountain National Park to savor northern forest birds (Connecticut Warbler, Great Gray Owl). *Some species to see:* Willow Ptarmigan, Ross's Gull, Arctic Tern, Northern Hawk Owl, Smith's Longspur. *Period:* June and July. *Contact:* Churchill Chamber of Commerce, Churchill, Manitoba, R0B 0E0. *Reference guide: A Birder's Guide to Churchill* by Bonnie Chartier (American Birding Association).

Rocky Mountain National Park/Pawnee National Grasslands

A geographic package offering alpine and western forest birds (White-tailed Ptarmigan, Brown-capped Rosy Finch, Hammond's Flycatcher, Western Tanager) and prairie species (Mountain Plover, Chestnut-collared Longspur), as well as a number and variety of nesting raptors. Fort Collins offers midpoint proximity to both locations, but campers have a geographic and experiential edge. *Period:* Memorial Day through July. *Contact:* Rocky Mountain National Park, Estes Park, CO 80517, 303-586-2371; Bureau of Land Management, 2850 Youngfield St., Lakewood, CO 80125, 303-236-1700; and Colorado Bird Observatory, 13401 Piccadilly Rd., Brighton, CO 80601, 303-659-4348.

Rocky Mountain National Park and the nearby Pawnee National Grasslands are a birding two-fer. Only one hundred miles (and many different species) separate the two. Pictured, obviously: the grasslands. *Pete Dunne.*

Reference guide: A Birder's Guide to Colorado by Harold R. Holt (American Birding Association).

Southeastern Arizona

This is one of the United States' most bird-rich regions. Summer (not winter) is the best time to view twelve hummingbird species and other species whose nesting range breaches the Mexican border at this point. *Some species to see:* Elegant Trogon, Violet-crowned Hummingbird, Sulphur-bellied Flycatcher, Rose-throated Becard, Mexican Chickadee, Olive Warbler, Five-striped Sparrow. *Period:* May through August. *Contact:* Southeastern Arizona Bird Observatory, PO Box 5521, Bisbee, AZ 85603-5521, 520-432-1388, sabo@SABO.org (e-mail) and www.sabo.org (Web Site); and Big Bend National Park, Texas. *Reference guide: A Birder's Guide to Southeastern Arizona* by Richard Taylor (American Birding Association).

Salton Sea, Southern California

A salty "inland sea" known for its great number of wintering waterfowl, shorebirds, and water birds as well as the periodic waif from the Sea of Cortez. Southern California is exclusive host to several species, including Yellow-footed Gull and California Gnatcatcher (coastal slopes only). *Period:* November through March. *Contact:* Los Angeles Audubon Society, 7377 Santa Monica Blvd., Los Angeles, CA 90046, 213-876-0202. *Reference Guide: A Birder's Guide to Southern California* by Brad Schram (American Birding Association).

Monterey Bay, California, teems with bird life, and a pelagic birding trip is a must for any serious birder. This Laysan Albatross entertained tripgoers on an all-day boat trip in August. *Linda Dunne.*

Monterey, California

The deep-water currents just off Monterey support a pyramid of life whose visible tip is occupied by the millions of sea birds who gather there. Prominent among them are assorted tubenoses (albatross, shearwaters, petrels), alcids, jaegers, and assorted other coastal, pelagic species. Marine mammals are also part of the marine pyramid. While birds can be seen from shore, the best technique for intercepting great numbers and diversity is to take a daylong boat trip. *Period:* August through September is best for shearwater species; October and November are better for petrels. *Contact:* Shearwater Journeys, PO Box 190, Hollister, CA 95024, 408-637-8527.

Alaska

Hardly a hotspot (the boundaries encompass 586,000 square miles and span two time zones), but undeniably worth any birder's visit. The birding opportunities are varied and exhaustive. Within any birder's reach is a trip to Denali National Park, Chugach State Park, or Homer, backed up with a coastal ferry trip to Kodiak and Seward for the bounty of sea birds. Birders can piggyback trips to the Pribilof Islands, Nome, or Gambell (for Asian species that overshoot). *Period:* June through August. *Contact:* Denali National Park, Box 9, Denali National Park, AK 99755, 907-683-2294. *Reference guide: A Birder's Guide to Alaska* by George West (American Birding Association).

The Perfect Fallout

In the perfect birding world, every morning would bring a fallout when songbirds (and other migrants) come to earth in great concentrations — not just a few birds, but gobs of birds. Catching a monster fallout, whether it is in New York's Central Park, along the Texas Gulf Coast, or in your favorite birding place near your home, can be unforgettable.

The best places for a fallout are places that are known as **migrant traps.** They are located along the coastlines of large bodies of water or in places where there are small islands of suitable habitat.

In cities and suburbs, fallouts occur in parks or other wooded patches. Some may be only a few acres in size, and sometimes smaller is better. Because habitat acceptable to forest birds has been eliminated in most of these areas, the remnant patches become the only refuges for migrants. When dawn comes, migrants look down on a sea of asphalt and concrete. The small green patches draw them like magnets. With hundreds or thousands of songbirds descending on a few acres of woodland or brush, they become relatively abundant and easy to see.

Along coastlines or rivers, the places to look are forested strips that run parallel to the shoreline. Along the Gulf of Mexico the forests are thin strips that occupy the first sand dune. In much of the midwestern, southwestern, and western United States, the forests are thin strips of forest along rivers and streambeds surrounded by desert or farmland. Again, these small forests act as magnets for migrants, and songbirds can pack into them in large numbers.

Trying to predict a fallout is more difficult. There are two things you can do to improve the odds. First, on the night before you plan to go birding, try watching the moon with your spotting scope. If the moon is at least one-third visible, focus your scope on it about one to three hours after the sun sets and keep watching for fifteen to twenty minutes. If there is a good migration, it won't take you long to start finding birds. If you see birds moving through at a rate of one every minute or so, you have a fairly decent migration. This is a prerequisite for a fallout. The birds must be migrating.

You can also hear birds migrating overhead. Listen for the high-pitched call notes of warblers or sparrows, the burry rising or sliding calls of thrushes or the squawk of herons. This can be a particularly productive way to forecast a fallout if, as often happens, clouds are preceding the front.

The second thing you can do to help predict a fallout is watch the television weather report or listen to the weather band radio. Be attuned to weather that will block migration. A line of thunderstorms or rain that crosses your birding area during the night is an obstacle to migrants. More and more birds will "pile up" at the obstacle and in the morning can be found in the forests below. In autumn, the rain should be located right over you or to the south. In spring, **cold fronts** with accompanying showers impede migrants, as do thunderstorms. As with rain and frontal boundaries, birds that encounter adverse winds will also land.

Other conditions that create fallouts include strong winds that push birds to a coastline. In autumn, the northwest and west winds that accompany a cold front in the eastern and southern United States create fallouts along the coast. A bright, crisp morning a day or so after a cold front passes brings millions of birds to coastal woodlands. Confronted by water during the night, they fall out on the last available land. After dawn many migrants come in off the ocean and drop into the first forest they encounter.

Whereas fallouts are great for birders, they are not always good for birds. The large numbers of birds you see dripping from the trees during a fallout are not normal, and sometimes fallouts indicate a minor or major tragedy. For example, when thunderstorms or northerly winds ground millions of birds along the Gulf of Mexico between Florida and Texas during spring migration, there are usually just as many birds that did not make it to shore. The rain and adverse winds literally make these birds land in the gulf. Many die. Those that make it to shore land in phenomenal numbers in the narrow strip of forest that rings the gulf — the first safe landing after flying more than six hundred miles without rest.

Fallouts in places like Central Park in Manhattan or in the ribbon-like forests along streams and rivers in the Southwest or Plains states are not likely to be as tragic. In fact, they can be good for birds, especially if the habitat provides a safe place in which to rest and eat before taking off again the next night.

Fallouts offer some of the best birding opportunities. They offer lots of birds of many different species. Because the birds are weary or energy-taxed from a storm or a long night's migration, they are usually quite easy to see and study. When you catch a fallout, don't squander the opportunity. Use every moment. It is critical to find the right place and be there at the right time. By knowing the conditions that make for a fallout, you can maximize your chances of catching the perfect fallout. Remember, however, that no matter how much you plan for and learn about the conditions that precipitate fallouts, you will also need some luck.

— **Dr. Paul Kerlinger**

Paul Kerlinger, former director of the Cape May Bird Observatory, is a writer-consultant living in Cape May, New Jersey, whose specialties include birding economics, bird migration, and fly fishing. He is author of How Birds Migrate *and* Flight Strategies of Migrating Hawks.

Little-Known North American Birding Hotspots

Birders are creatures of habit. We tend to go to the same places other birders have visited, the ones that are written up in the popular bird-finding guides. These are valuable books, but too many birders rely too heavily on them. It is also important to be able to recognize habitats, microhabitats, habitat limits and outposts, and what makes a good migrant and vagrant trap. Armed with such knowledge, birders can discover other extremely worthwhile destinations. Many excellent birding areas remain unappreciated and have been largely ignored by observers.

The following are my top choices for the best "little-known" birding sites and regions in North America.

ATLANTIC PROVINCES OF CANADA

I know this is a big area, but various islands and peninsulas in Newfoundland, New Brunswick, and Nova Scotia have a record in spring and especially fall of turning up a good number of migrants and oddball vagrants from the West, the South, and Europe. To get a look, go to places like St. John's and the Avalon Peninsula in Newfoundland; Miscou and Grand Manan Islands in New Brunswick; and Brier, Cape Sable, and Seal Islands and the Halifax/Dartmouth area in Nova Scotia. In addition, beautiful Prince Edward Island just gets no respect. (Also, to the south, add Monhegan Island in Maine to this list.)

BLUFF POINT, CONNECTICUT — CAPE CHARLES, VIRGINIA — THE OUTER BANKS, NORTH CAROLINA

The Cape May, New Jersey, area richly deserves its well-known reputation as an autumn migratory hotspot. Other lesser-known sites along the East Coast include Bluff Point, Connecticut, and Cape Charles, Virginia, where one can witness a similar sort of early morning rush of hundreds or perhaps thousands of land-bird migrants (mostly warblers). The Outer Banks are fairly well known for water birds and offshore pelagics, but the migrant passerine potential there in fall has never been fully tapped.

GREAT LAKES PENINSULAS

As a spring migration hotspot for migrant land birds, Point Pelee, Ontario, is well known . . . perhaps too well known, since crowding in May has become a problem there for many birders. But what is not well known is that Pelee is also very good for fall migrants in late August and early September. Moreover, there are several excellent spring or fall migrant traps elsewhere around the Great Lakes. Whitefish Point on Michigan's Upper Peninsula is well known, as is Minnesota's Duluth area. Crane Creek State Park on the Lake Erie shore in Ohio was for many years a sleeping giant; during the past few years, however, it too has become fairly crowded during peak periods in May. Tawas Point in Michigan's Saginaw Bay (Lake Huron) is a rising star.

GULF COAST EAST OF TEXAS

Most everyone has heard about the splendid migrant trap at High Island, Texas, which in April may be inundated with trans-gulf migrants and by birders. Dauphin Island on the Alabama coast is also well known. But equally good birding is available in the Cameron Parish area of southwestern Louisiana (the Holleyman Bird Sanctuary is a convenient public-access destination to visit) and Fort Morgan in Alabama, just to the east of Dauphin. And how many folks actually visit High Island later in the spring — in May — or during the fall?

NEW MEXICO

Just like the Canadian maritime provinces recommendation, this one is a bit broad. But New Mexico is clearly one of the best of the most under-birded states in the Union. The southwest corner (near Silver City) supports many, but not all, of the same Mexican specialties found in adjacent southeastern Arizona. The water-birding at places like the Bosque del Apache and Bitter Lakes National Wildlife Refuge is excellent, Rattlesnake Springs near Carlsbad Caverns National Park is a great migrant oasis, and there are water-bird and land-bird traps scattered throughout the state's arid western and eastern plains. And the northern mountains are pretty good too.

WHITE MOUNTAINS, ARIZONA

Only a few hours' drive north of the fabled canyons of southeastern Arizona lie the higher, moister, conifer-covered White Mountains. This beautiful region supports a number of breeding resident species with affinities closer to those of the Rocky Mountains. Species include Three-toed Woodpecker, Gray Jay, American Dipper, and Pine Grosbeak. Next time you visit the "Sky Islands" southeast of Tucson in summer, give "the Whites" a try as well.

GREAT BASIN OASES

Far from almost any major population center, this is an area rich in water-bird and land-bird migrants and vagrants. This arid region is pockmarked with isolated stands of deciduous trees, such as willows, poplars, and cottonwoods, that are found in small towns, along streams, and at ranch yards. Isolated lakes and reservoirs beckon over-flying water birds. These oases draw in large numbers of migrant flycatchers, thrushes, vireos, warblers, tanagers, grosbeaks, buntings, and sparrows and some interesting breeding species. Some of the best sites are in

Nevada (for instance, the Corn Creek oasis at the Desert National Wildlife Range refuge headquarters north of Las Vegas, a roadside rest stop just west of Tonopah, and, east of Reno, the Stillwater National Wildlife Refuge and the Carson Lake wetlands), northern Arizona (Pipe Spring National Monument, Page, Ganado), western Utah (Beaver Dam Wash, Fish Springs National Wildlife Refuge), and southeastern Oregon (Fields, Malheur National Wildlife Refuge headquarters).

— **Paul Lehman**

Paul Lehman is a tour leader for WINGS, a consultant, a former editor of Birding, and a student of North American bird distribution and identification. He lives in Cape May, New Jersey, and his major love is exploring the continent's back roads of birding.

NO SHORTAGE OF PLACES, NO SHORTAGE OF GUIDES

The locations mentioned in this chapter represent the tip of the iceberg. Virtually every state and province has a surfeit of well-known and not-so-well-known birding spots, and most have one or more printed bird-finding guides to help you find those spots.

Most guides are independently written and published, although a number are part of the excellent Bird-Finding Guide Series pioneered by the late Jim Lane and Harold Holt and published by the American Birding Association. All guides offer directions, maps, descriptions, and tips for selected birding sites, and many also provide information relating to the geology and human history of an area, as well as other aspects of natural history.

Bird-finding guides can be found in general bookstores, nature centers, and visitor center shops or can be ordered online.

AND FOR THOSE WHO (A) CAN'T DECIDE WHERE AND (B) DON'T HAVE ROOM FOR A LIBRARY . . .

Unique in the ABA Bird-Finding Guide Series is *Birdfinder: A Birder's Guide to Planning North American Trips.* Written by Jerry Cooper, this guide features a continental scope and a utilitarian, visitor-friendly summary of nineteen birding locations — the choice and ordering predicated on the objective of finding 650 species of birds in a single year! Another thirteen locations are reviewed in less detail. All the useful information found in the regular ABA guides is included, including trip cost estimates. Whether you choose to accept the 650-bird challenge or simply to use the guide to plan a birding trip to any of the listed locations, this book is invaluable.

Pelagic Principles

Sooner or later — sooner if you are fortunate, later if you are prone to seasickness (and likewise fortunate) — you are destined to take your birding ambitions to sea. A number of highly specialized bird species, pelagic birds, spend all but a short portion of their lives at sea (and their time on land is usually confined to some remote corner of the world). As a result, pelagic birds are seldom (if ever) encountered by land-based observers. Seeing birds like alcids, shearwaters, and petrels requires going to where the birds are, and unless you own a seaworthy vessel, the easiest way to do this is to sign up for a pelagic birding trip.

A number of individuals and organizations offer such trips. These are advertised in the birding publications and on the Web. Each year one whole issue of the American Birding Association's newsletter *Winging It* is dedicated to pelagic birding trips. Chances are good that your first trip offshore will be an extraordinary experience, one filled with new and exciting species. The *possibility* exists, however, that you will have a miserable time. You can increase your chances of experiencing the former and diminish the ill affects of the latter by planning ahead and taking some prudent pre-trip precautions.

First, come to the dock well equipped. Many binoculars that work fine for everyday birding fall flat when the water gets steep. Some very accomplished pelagic birders get away with 10× instruments. Most people find that lower magnification — 7× or 8× — works better. Remember, you'll be on water, not dry, firm land. Not only will the birds be moving, but so will your world. Lower magnifications are just plain easier to use when your world is in motion.

Another problem regarding boats: not only will your world be oscillating, but when the engine is running, it will also be vibrating. High-power binoculars magnify the image-distorting effects of engine vibration too.

Make sure your instrument is waterproof. Even if it's not raining, even if high seas are not casting spray over the bow, the humidity of offshore waters is high enough to make poorly sealed binoculars fog internally. When this happens, your birding is sunk.

Two final suggestions — make that edicts — with regard to optics. First, leave the spotting scope at home. There's no room and less need for a spotting scope on a boat. Finally, when you step on deck, hook your binoculars around your neck and leave them there. On almost every pelagic trip, someone removes his or her binoculars, places them on a table or bench *for just a moment,* and fails to retrieve them before the boat pitches. One of the worst sounds in the world is the sound of expensive binoculars hitting a metal deck.

No matter what the temperature onshore, it will be much cooler offshore. Water temperatures are generally lower than onshore air temperatures (sometimes dramatically so). Wind chill can be severe. Even in summer, even if water temperatures are a tepid seventy degrees, a twenty-knot wind will make a waterproof shell jacket (and perhaps an underlying fleece jacket) very desirable.

For warm-weather pelagics, light waterproof tops and bottoms are a good idea. Even if it's not raining, one wave over the bow and you'll be glad you have bottoms and won't be spending the rest of the trip in sodden jeans.

For winter pelagics, wear the best damn rain gear you can find, several layers of heat trapping wool or synthetic pile under that, and, next to your skin, a wicking layer (underwear designed to wick moisture away from your skin). Footgear? Wear rubber-soled (slip resistant) running shoes or walking shoes in warmer temperatures and rubber boots with fresh, insulating insoles and heavy socks in winter.

Other clothing items that can make the difference between comfort and discomfort include: a brimmed cap or hat (for sun and wind protection); gloves, if temperatures dictate; and sunglasses, which are almost mandatory. They protect the eyes from UV light and make it easier to find birds against a moving mosaic whose elements include shards of sunlight.

Seasickness. Nothing can ruin a pelagic trip so thoroughly as a bout of *mal de mer,* and while some people are more resistant to motion sickness than others, everyone has a breaking point. People use a lot of different drugs and homegrown remedies to ward off motion sickness. It is very possible that the greatest contribution to health and well-being that seasickness remedies impart is confidence. People who step onto a boat believing that they are destined to be sick usually fulfill this destiny.

Two things can be said with certainty. There is no single patch or pill that works for everyone. Closely related to this, there is no single patch or pill that works every time. Ask your family physician for the latest and greatest in motion sickness remedies (and tell them you don't want something that makes you drowsy).

With or without prescription drugs (or wrist bands, or ginger root, or lucky charms), there are things you can do to protect (if not proof) yourself from getting seasick. First, never, never, never get on a boat with an empty stomach. A hungry stomach is a sensitive stomach. When the world starts moving, you'll want ballast in your gut. So *eat something!* Something bland (like oatmeal). Something you don't mind seeing again. Eat something before the trip and during the trip at the first sign of queasiness. Many experienced pelagic birders stow ordinary saltine crackers in their kit.

Get a good night's sleep before the trip. Sleeping dockside in your car, instead of taking a motel room, may save a few bucks but if it leads to a long séance at the rail it's going to cost you birds (and maybe the day). Also, go easy on the alcohol. Hangovers and high seas are a marriage made in hell.

If you start to feel queasy, *do not go below.* Get up on deck. Get some fresh air into your lungs. Pin your eyes to the horizon, which will be more stable than the world close at hand. Try to distract yourself with conversation or, better yet, the birds that are hopefully all around you. (Nothing cures seasickness faster than someone shouting: "*Albatross!*")

And when all else fails, just go to the rail and barf. You'll feel better immediately and support the birding effort by making a personal contribution to the chum. You might even know the visceral pleasure of seeing some life pelagic bird coming in to your own personal chum slick.

What could be more satisfying than this?

A few more tips. Get to the boat early so that you can find a place to stow your gear and grab a strategic spot at the rail. When birds are being seen, you don't want to be in the back ranks. If seas are even a little rough, you'll want to stand where your hand can find the rail.

Generally the bow and the stern are the most strategic spots on a boat. When the boat is moving, birders stationed at the bow usually get the best looks at birds pushed off the water. Birders in the stern are better situated to see sea birds habituated to following ships. Bows and sterns have another strategic advantage: if a bird is seen on the port and you are on the starboard, there isn't a whole superstructure blocking your view. Birders at the bow and stern are only a step (or two or three) from a vantage point.

If it's a rough sea, the bow is going to take more water. If there is an upper deck and the captain allows, you'll be above most of the spray — and you'll care about spray, no matter how impervious to water your binoculars may be. Salt encrustation from spray can turn the finest optics on the planet into the image-gathering equivalent of paired Coke bottles. Bring lots of cotton handkerchiefs. Keep them in every pocket. When your instrument gets coated, lick the lenses, then dry.

No, it's not hygienic. But it's quick and it works.

One last tip. Vibration can make your binoculars dance, destroying image quality. The vibration starts in the engine, travels through the hull, runs up your legs . . . hips . . . spine . . . arms . . . hands . . . bone to bone, vibration finds an easy conduit. Buffer the transfer of energy with a little muscle and tissue and you'll dampen the effect.

How do you do this? Bend your knees slightly, putting a little elastic play in the articulation of your knee joint. You won't be able to do this all day. Your leg muscles will wear out. But when the engine is revving and there is a life bird in the balance, keeping your knees loose might make the difference between a look that's good and one that's not good enough.

All the difference in the world.

THE WORLD AT YOUR FINGERTIPS

Only about 750 species of birds regularly occur in North America, but there are about 10,000 species found on earth. With the exception of the extreme polar regions, there is not a location on the planet where birds do not regularly occur, and many countries, particularly those in the rich equatorial region, have more than twice the number of species found in North America.

Unfortunately, not all of these bird-rich areas are book-rich. In fact, some countries celebrated for their bird diversity still lack a basic field guide.

Nevertheless, many field guides and bird-finding guides are available for such celebrated locations as Kenya, Costa Rica, South Africa, Australia, and New Guinea, and guides that will fill key geographic gaps are in the works.

Those interested in visiting Northern European countries, which have a long birding tradition, will find many excellent field guides and no shortage of exceptional birders.

Mastering Difficult Identifications

Travel is not the only way to expand your birding horizons. Challenge and discovery lie no farther than your front yard. Familiar birds can look like entirely different species after molting from alternate to basic plumage (for example, male American Goldfinch) or from immature to adult plumage.

Some birds, like gulls, go through three or more distinctly different plumages on their way to full adult plumage, and many species viewed during the process of molting can look like nothing you will find in a basic field guide. Which explains why there are guides that specialize in the subtleties of bird identification — and why birders can spend their entire lives perfecting their field identification skills and never stray far from home.

The only way to become a better birder is to go birding *with the objective of discovering new things and improving your present skills.* It takes time. It takes study. It takes focus. When you see a bird you cannot identify, *study it.* When you see a bird that you *can* identify, *study it even more closely.* The best way to recognize an uncommon species is to be intimate with those you see commonly.

Whenever the opportunity for study presents itself — a seasonal gathering of shorebirds, for instance, or two very similar waterfowl species wintering together — don't hurry off. Use the time for study. Note the differences that distinguish species while they are manifest, and bank them for that solo encounter that is bound to occur somewhere in the future.

The bad news is that birds don't always look the same. Many species change plumages in response to the season or maturation. The good news is that birds don't always look the same, and birders are always being confronted by new challenges. The Dunlin in breeding plumage (top) is distinctive enough. But the one in basic plumage (bottom) is a bit more challenging. *Kevin Karlson.*

Shorebird Summer

In 1977 I was a good hawk watcher, a fair birder generally, but a failure when it came to identifying shorebirds. Oh, I had a handle on some medium-sized shorebirds. Plump and long-billed and feeding like a sewing machine? Dowitcher. Not so plump and not so long-billed but longer-legged? Yellowlegs. But that was about the extent of my knowledge.

All those small sandpipers, those **"peep."** All those different plumages. All those molting birds. It was a veritable avian chimera! But it was also July, prime time for southbound shorebirds in New Jersey, and I'd made up my mind to learn 'em or die. That might have been the end of this story had it not been for a dry summer that reduced Bunker Pond in Cape May Point State Park to a mud flat with shallows — perfect habitat for shorebirds. Visitor traffic was constant, another plus. The birds had become habituated to people, allowing long-term viewing at very close range.

Every lunch hour for several weeks, I sat at the edge of the pond, butt plastered to the sand, eye fused to the eyepiece of my spotting scope, studying the feeding masses. At first, it was all I could do to distinguish those elemental field marks that are the foundation of field guide identification. Little with yellow legs — Least Sandpiper. Bigger with yellow legs — Pectoral Sandpiper. Little and black legs — Semipalmated Sandpiper. In time I began to note more subtle distinctions. Like how Least Sandpipers were overall browner and liked to keep their feet on the mud, and Semipalmateds were grayer and stayed in the water. Like how dowitchers probed, but yellowlegs jabbed. Like how one sandpiper had a bill that drooped like a Least, but the legs were black like a Semipalmated. In fact, it looked like a Semi except for the long, drooping bill — like Western Sandpiper was supposed to have. But if it was Western, then shouldn't it have had red feathers on its shoulder?

And it did! Just one or two that hadn't molted out yet. I would have missed them before.

After a while I got to the point where I could accept the normal range of variation between birds of a species. I even reached a point where I could recognize individual birds in the flock.

So when my life Stilt Sandpiper arrived — a very worn adult that showed only a trace of barring on the breast — I realized, quickly, that it was too lean to be a dowitcher, not lanky enough to be a Lesser Yellowlegs, and so had to be . . .

"What are you seeing?" a voice inquired. The voice belonged to one of Cape May's very experienced birders, a man whose skills I admired. I'd been so intent on my study that I hadn't realized he'd joined me.

"Stilt Sandpiper," I said proudly.

"I didn't see any Stilt Sandpiper out there," he said flatly. "Where?"

"In with that group of dowitchers," I said, more pleased with one-upping one of the elders than anxious about my identification — although anxiety would have been justified.

"That's not a Stilt," he said. "That's Lesser Yellowlegs."

Stunned, I studied the bird again, trying to superimpose the image of "yellowlegs" over what I was seeing . . . but the name and the shape wouldn't match.

"But look at the curve on the bill," I said encouragingly, pointing out the single mark that most easily distinguishes Stilts from Lesser Yellowlegs. "Look how it's about the same size and shape as the dowitchers. Look at that barring." The bird was up to its belly in water. The legs, which would have been greenish, not yellow, could not be seen.

"No, that's a yellowlegs," he repeated, firmly. And then another birder showed up, who, after study and short debate, sided with the more experienced birder.

I still believed I was right. A couple of days earlier, I might have been confused, might have second-guessed my identification, but not now. In the ensuing days I'd gained more than grounding in shorebird identification; I'd gained a measure of confidence too.

No, I wasn't confused. But I was disappointed that I'd managed to find a good bird, all by myself, and couldn't share the excitement.

The next day I returned to the pond for another lesson in shorebird identification and was surprised to find the elder birder there ahead of me. Mumbling a greeting, I plopped myself down and started scanning.

"That Stilt Sandpiper is still here," he said with an offhandedness that could not mask the significance of this admission.

Twenty-one years later, I don't mind saying that whenever I think back to that moment it still feels good. Not because I was right. And certainly not because he was wrong. But because an identification problem tough enough to stump an elder had come my way, and I hadn't been found wanting.

— P.D.

SPECIALTY BOOKS FOR SPECIALTY BIRDING

Scores of specialized field guides focus on particular groups of birds, allowing an attention to detail that would be impossible in a general field guide. Some of these guides describe plumages, for example, in age classes and between closely allied species, right down to individual feathers. For some species, that is the difference between a correct identification and an incorrect one.

Here is a list of specialty guides that cover most of North America and deserve a place in your birding library (see the bibliography for complete publication information).

A Field Guide to Advanced Birding by Kenn Kaufman (1990): An exceptional, utilitarian, and easy-to-read guide that groups similar species and explains how to distinguish one from the next.

Gulls by P. J. Grant (1997): Targeting the Northern Hemisphere, *Gulls* is the definitive work on this very challenging, diversely plumaged, wander-prone group. Any gull species can turn up anywhere — and many do. Hence your need for this book.

A Field Guide to Hawks of North America by William S. Clark and Brian K. Wheeler (2001): In the Peterson Field Guide Series, this book covers North American birds of prey with an emphasis upon plumage.

Hawks in Flight by Pete Dunne, David Sibley, and Clay Sutton (1988): Differs from *A Field Guide to Hawks of North America* by placing emphasis upon North America's migratory birds of prey and identifications based upon shape and manner of flight.

Seabirds by Peter Harrison (1985): Written by the noted authority on the identification of oceanic birds, *Seabirds* is global in scope and thorough in its treatment.

Shorebirds by Peter Hayman, John Marchant, and Tony Prater (1986): An excellent treatment of an exceedingly challenging, popular, and wander-prone group.

A Field Guide to Warblers by Jon Dunn and Kimball Garrett (1997): The definitive work on these sometimes colorful, sometimes drab birds of the Americas.

Waterfowl by Steven Madge and Hilary Burn (1992): This book is thorough in its treatment of another group of birds notorious for extralimital excursions.

OTHER BOOKS BIRDERS SHOULD NOT LIVE WITHOUT
Birds are more than an identification challenge. They are animate creatures. Knowing more about them makes them more real and more alive. There are many books that delve into the natural history of birds, some extensively. Here is a basic sampling of books that will broaden your awareness and pleasure.

The Birdwatcher's Companion by Christopher Leahy (1982): Subtitled *An Encyclopedic Handbook of North American Birdlife*, the book is a handy reference for terms and topics that map the world of birds and birding.

The Birder's Handbook by Paul R. Ehrlich, David S. Dobkin, and Darryl Wheye (1988): A species-by-species natural history synopsis of North American birds interspersed with sidebar insights that focus upon the biology and behavior of birds.

A Guide to the Nests, Eggs, and Nestings of North American Birds, by Paul J. Baicich and Colin J. O. Harrison (1997): A fine treatment that summarizes much of what we know about North American bird breeding biology.

Lives of North American Birds by Kenn Kaufman (1996): A detailed one-volume encyclopedia with life histories of all regularly occurring North American birds.

Ornithology by Frank B. Gill (1995): Birding is not so removed from the parent ornithology that birders can avoid a fundamental understanding of birds and how they live. This text, written by an eminent ornithologist (and birder), is lucid and thorough.

The Sibley Guide to Bird Life and Behavior by Chris Elphick, John B. Dunning, Jr., and David Allen Sibley (2001): A thorough, informative, and readable treatment of North America's birds, using a family-by-family approach to understanding their biology and natural history.

Once birders have mastered the basics, they can expand their horizons — reaching for birds that are more challenging to identify, farther away, or not even visible and distinguishable by vocalizations alone. Spotting scopes, specialized field guides, and bird-song recordings are tools that facilitate the learning process.

Horizons are geographical too. Distant locations offer new and unfamiliar species. There are dozens of celebrated birding hotspots in North America and many more in the world. Most North American locations are described in bird-finding guides that offer detailed instructions for birding key areas. Most of the popular birding locations on the planet have at least one field guide that is specific to that country or region and its birds.

6
Applied Birding — For Fun, Purpose ...Even Profit!

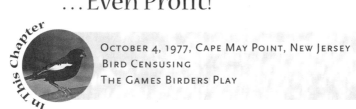

OCTOBER 4, 1977, CAPE MAY POINT, NEW JERSEY
BIRD CENSUSING
THE GAMES BIRDERS PLAY

October 4, 1977, Cape May Point, New Jersey

Stars still studded the sky over Cape May Point, New Jersey, but already hawks were on the move — shadow Sharp-shinneds weaving a course through shadow trees, Northern Harriers set like Roman crosses on a morning sky. Cradling a metal hand-counter in my pocket, I clicked off passing Sharpies as I ran.

It was the first week in October, migratory prime time. The Cape May Peninsula is a celebrated migrant trap, a geographic funnel that catches and directs birds to its terminus. As long as winds hold north, birds keep coming; and this was the fourth straight day of northerly winds. It was my second year as the official counter, and while I'd seen lots of good days at Cape May — I'd recorded over 48,000 birds of prey the previous year — I'd never seen anything like *this.*

Gaining my platform, I arranged my gear and started taking readings for the first hour of the count, noting on the data sheet the wind speed, wind direction, temperature, cloud cover, visibility — all the variables that influence both migration and a counter's ability to count. Clerical duties completed, I started a binocular sweep of the sky over the distant tree line, clicking off Sharpies at a rate of one a second, keeping a mental note of the odd Osprey, kestrel, or harrier.

A veritable *river* of birds was moving north of my site, and the sun wasn't even up yet. It wasn't incredible, it was unbelievable. A decade earlier, North American raptor populations had been on the ropes, reduced to a vestige of their former levels by the biocidal poison DDT. The decline was plainly evident in the data accumulated by Hawk Mountain Sanctuary. Systematic autumn hawk counts were initiated on this Pennsylvania ridgetop in 1934. In the 1950s and 1960s, following the widespread use of DDT, the number of raptors migrating past Hawk Mountain steadily declined.

The count I was conducting in Cape May was based on the Hawk Mountain model and funded by the U.S. Fish and Wildlife Service. Sampling primarily immature birds (adults tend to migrant more inland) — a different population than the Hawk Mountain count — it was hoped that this coastal count would also in time disclose trends in raptor populations. This proved to be so. By 1977, starting with the smaller raptor species, nest productivity was rebounding and populations were on the mend. The flight I was seeing bore witness.

By 8:00 A.M. the river of raptors had become a flood that swept across Cape May Point State Park, and by nine the flood was an ocean

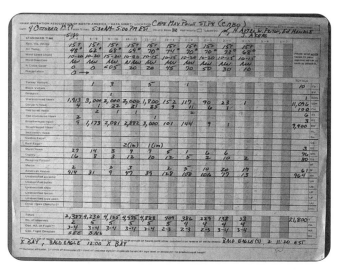

The date on the data sheet reads: October 4, 1977. The total: 21,800 birds of prey. Wish you were there? *Pete Dunne.*

of birds that filled earth and sky. A handful of Cape May stalwarts were on hand to join me.

The winds abated as the afternoon wore on. The flight diminished, and finally it stopped. By five o'clock that afternoon, the raptors in the air seemed intent on hunting, not moving. I shut down the count.

On my way back to my car I found myself keeping pace with an attractive young woman of about my age who had apparently spent the day lying on the beach. I said hello, and she said hello. I asked whether she'd had a nice day. She said she had, then asked whether I'd had a nice day too.

"Yes," I assured her. I'd had an "incredible day."

Noting that I wasn't dressed for the beach and was carrying some unusual equipment (binoculars, gun-stock-mounted spotting scope, clipboards, metal hand-counters), she asked what I'd been doing.

"Counting hawks," I replied.

"Oh, that sounds interesting," she said. "Did you see any?"

The official record that day was 21,800 birds of prey, including 11,000 Sharp-shinneds and 9,400 Broad-wingeds. The sunburn index must have been about a 2 beneath that cloud of birds in the air — but she hadn't seen any. She got in her car and drove away, never realizing that she'd been one hundred yards and one avocation away from what would have surely ranked among the greatest days of her life.

Bird Censusing

Not everyone who takes up bird watching is going to conduct season-long migration counts. But there are purposeful and less consuming ways for birders to donate their talents to the good cause (and good time) of bird conservation.

THE CHRISTMAS BIRD COUNT

Sponsored by the National Audubon Society, the annual **Christmas Bird Count (CBC)** is one of birding's most cherished traditions. Started

Some fifty thousand birders participate in the annual Christmas Bird Count conducted by the National Audubon Society. In northern regions, participants dress accordingly. *Pete Dunne.*

in 1900 as a bird-friendly alternative to the Christmas Day "side hunts" practiced by sportsmen of the day, this winter census now draws some 50,000 participants who take part in over 1,200 counts conducted across the United States, Canada, and Mexico and abroad. It stands as the largest "amateur" data-gathering effort in North America, and much of what is known about winter bird distribution and populations can be attributed to it.

The objective is simple. Participants are invited to count all the individual birds of all species found within a fifteen-mile diameter **count circle.** A compiler assigns different parties to canvass different territories within the circle, beginning at midnight. The party totals are added to get a count total.

The counts are conducted in a designated **count period,** which normally includes the two weekends before Christmas and the weekend following. Most counts are associated with a National Audubon Society chapter, local bird club, or statewide birding organization. Some local counts have been conducted ever since the ornithologist Frank Chapman instituted the tradition a century ago; some are recent additions to the CBC family.

Most of North America's avid birders lend their talents in the counts, but participation is open to all. Anyone, no matter what their skill level, is cordially invited. The compiler pairs less experienced birders with count veterans.

Much of the popularity of the CBC is attributable to the sense of purpose and the challenge of finding birds under what may be difficult conditions. But the CBC is also a social affair. Many counts include a potluck lunch in the day's activities, and most counts have a roundup at the end of the day. In keeping with the spirit of the season, these roundups are cheerful, spirited, and, when the species tally is done, capped off with a sense of communal accomplishment.

Rivalry between counts and between parties for the biggest species total is common, good-natured, and a spur to the sense of challenge inherent in the counts. Locating birds that are rare or at the limit of their seasonal range is a test of a party's ability. Finding a species that is "new for the count" is a CBC's greatest prize.

Participants are assessed a nominal fee (about five dollars), which goes to defray the costs of publishing a national summary of the count. All the CBC data from *every* count (species, count-circle descriptions, participants) are found on the Web at www.audubon.org/ bird/cbc.

Some clubs and organizations use the CBC template to conduct a summer or breeding bird count. The results are not published nationally, but the challenge and fun (and usefulness) are undiminished.

To learn how to participate in a CBC in your area, contact a local bird club or nature columnist, who will almost certainly be covering the story for the local paper. If you are traveling over the holidays and want to find the CBC in the area you'll be visiting, contact the National Audubon Society, 700 Broadway, New York, NY 10003, 212-979-3000.

My First Christmas Count

Even as a fledgling birder, I wanted to do a Christmas Bird Count. I called the regional compiler and explained that I was a novice but would like to participate if she knew of a good birder who could pick me up along a bus line. She called back later and told me to take a 5:30 A.M. bus to such and such an intersection and to look for a small car with a RUFF license plate. I was such a novice birder that I did not know that a Ruff is a bird, though I was able to find the intersection and the car.

At the first stop, an urban park with birds that even a novice could identify, I was allowed to go off on my own, but the first bird I saw stumped me and I had to call my companion. I was looking at a melanistic mockingbird. A little later we came to a waterfowl spot. My count partner asked me to stay in the car until she had done an initial count because she was concerned that I might scare the ducks and gulls away.

When the *Washington Post* reporter turned up, I knew I must be birding with someone important. Several weeks after the count, I learned that my count companion, Claudia Wilds, was a leading shorebird and tern expert. The following year, since I had learned of Claudia's stature in the birding community, I did not have the courage to call and ask whether I could join her Christmas count.

Imagine my joy when she called me!

— **Daphne Gemmill**

When she is not meeting production deadlines for Going Birding, Inc., an outdoor clothing company that specializes in birding clothes, company president Daphne Gemmill goes birding. Daphne was one of the founders of Earth Day and served for many years on the American Birding Association board of directors.

CBC Strategy

The counts are daylong affairs, conducted mostly during daylight hours. Parties hoping to maximize their species tally invest predawn hours searching for owls and, in more southerly latitudes, other night birds.

The size of the territory to be covered, weather conditions, and terrain determine the search strategy. Combined with the date, location, and severity of the weather leading up to the count, these factors largely determine the number and variety of species that will be found.

As a rule, more southerly counts record more species than northern ones. Coastal counts generally exceed interior counts in species numbers. Counts conducted early in the count period usually produce greater numbers than counts conducted later. If temperatures leading up to the count are not low, species totals tend to be higher.

In general, at dawn and dusk, parties try to position themselves to view birds coming and going from roost sites. Once the morning flights have ended, parties move from key habitat to key habitat, searching for individual species and winter flocks.

Key habitats offer birds food and shelter. Places with a surfeit of berries, fruit, or seed and shelter from cold winds attract wintering birds. Another key attraction is open water, particularly in northern regions, where standing water may be frozen during the winter months. A swift-flowing stream, a spring, or an open section of lakeshore frequently holds lingering or half-hardy species. During a bitterly cold CBC, I once found an American Woodcock foraging in the soft earth beneath a dripping outside faucet.

Feeders within a party's territory should always be checked, and opportunities like a farmer spreading manure on an open (and larkish- or longspurish-looking) field investigated. Some serious CBC practitioners scout their territories before the count to **tie down** uncommon species. Known rare or **extralimital species** are, of course, actively pursued.

THE GREAT BACKYARD BIRD COUNT

The Great Backyard Bird Count is a winter bird population monitoring program jointly sponsored by the Cornell Laboratory of Ornithology and the National Audubon Society. Thousands of individuals across North America are invited to record the number and species of birds seen in their yards (or a local site of their choosing) during a four-day count period in mid-February. Counts are entered online (www.birdsource.org). The results may be used to assess populations, bird movement, and bird distribution.

This "citizen science" project also serves to get bird enthusiasts involved with the birding community at large and imparts the understanding that the birds (and habitat) in their corner of the planet are part of a greater ecological whole.

North American Migration Count

Modeled after the CBC, the North American Migration Count, also a volunteer effort, strives to gain a better understanding of spring migration. Conducted on the second Saturday of May, the count takes a continental "snapshot" of species distribution during migration.

Counties, not count circles, are used as the organizational foundation of the migration counts, but otherwise the same standards used in the CBC apply. No fee is assessed participants. For information, contact the North American Migration Count, PO Box 71, North Beach, MD 20714.

Breeding Bird Survey

Conceived by Chandler S. Robbins and organized by the U.S. Fish and Wildlife Service, the Breeding Bird Survey (BBS) monitors changes in the number and distribution of breeding birds. Volunteers drive a twenty-five-mile route along secondary roads, stopping at half-mile intervals to watch and listen. After three minutes at a location, the volunteer tabulates all birds heard or seen, then moves on to the next stop.

The surveys are conducted between late spring and mid-summer — after most northbound migrants have passed through a region and before the vocalizations of territorial males taper off. Surveys begin at dawn, when birds begin vocalizing, and end by midmorning. Continuity is key to the project. The surveys are conducted every year by the same individuals. While the habitat and the species composition may change, the method does not.

BBS volunteers are usually experienced birders who are able to identify birds by their song. Many BBS participants have been running their routes for over thirty years. For information, contact Pautuxent Wildlife Research Center, Laurel, MD 20708-4038. Results and analysis are on the Web at www.mor-pwrc.usgs.gov/bbs/bbs.html.

Bird Atlas Projects

Breeding bird atlases use volunteers to map the distribution of breeding birds in a state or province. These surveys are usually coordinated by one or more statewide organizations, and they involve three to five years of data collection and hundreds of individuals.

To a birder, this might be "just" another Field Sparrow. But to a breeding bird atlas volunteer, this is a *confirmed breeder*— the highest and most-aspired-to level of confirmation. How can you tell? The bird is carrying prey. It's one of the things you are trained as an atlas volunteer to look for. *Frank Schleicher.*

During the breeding season, a period defined by "safe dates" that arc calibrated for the region, atlas volunteers canvass their assigned **atlas blocks,** attempting to record all the breeding species found there. An atlas is not a census. The focus is on the presence or absence of a breeding species in a block, not on how many individuals of any species occur there.

The goal in atlasing (and much of the challenge and fun) is not just to find a species but to confirm breeding. Based upon the evidence noted, a bird is recorded as "observed" (found, but not in proper breeding habitat), "possible" (recorded in good habitat during the "safe dates" but with no other evidence of breeding), "probable" (evidencing behavior that suggests breeding), or "confirmed" (evidencing behavior that certifies the existence of a nest or young).

The behavioral standards that place a bird in one of these four confidence levels were first established in England and Ireland and generally have been adopted by all atlas projects conducted in North America.

The product of all this information gathering is an atlas that maps breeding bird distribution in a state. It is a powerful tool for land-use planners and serves as a historic snapshot so that future generations can gauge changes in a state or region's avifauna.

Birders with limited skills can make a valuable contribution to an atlas effort. Even very skilled birders find that they learn a great deal about bird behavior by participating in an atlas, since atlasing forces observers to be attentive to detail and to watch individual birds for extended periods.

Atlas details are usually updated on the North American Ornithological Atlas Committee Web site: www.americanbirding.org/norac/. If your state or province is engaged or about to engage in an atlas, your local bird club officers, department of natural resources, or university ornithology department will know and be able to tell you whom to contact for information.

Hawk Counts

As predators, birds of prey are generally less common than other bird species. In summer and winter they also tend to be widely distributed. Even if an observer is in the right habitat, sightings may come few and far between.

But during migration, in many places, wind and geography conspire to concentrate birds of prey along migratory pathways called **leading lines.** These may be mountain ridges or extensive coastlines. Given the right conditions and the right dates, observers can go to these known concentration points and see hundreds, even thousands, of birds of prey in a few hours.

Hawk counts are a way of monitoring the health and stability of raptor populations in particular and bird populations in general. Hawks are nature's litmus paper. They sit at the top of the food pyramid; what happens to the prey that constitutes the base of the pyramid ultimately affects and is reflected by the birds perched at the top. By monitoring hawk populations, counters can effectively take the pulse of the whole natural world.

Usually conducted at the same strategic locations year after year, hawk counts are maintained by organizations that use paid hawk counters or a cadre of volunteers or by individuals who enlist visitors and friends. The data are often submitted to the Hawk Migration Association of North America (HMANA), an organization that caters to the interest of hawk watchers. Counts across North America are summarized in the HMANA's biannual journal.

The first systematic hawk migration counts were conducted at Hawk Mountain, Pennsylvania, and Cape May, New Jersey, in the 1930s. Beginning in the 1970s, and largely in reaction to the decline of hawk populations caused by the chemical pesticide DDT, count sites proliferated and organized data collection was codified and encouraged by the HMANA. For information, contact Hawk Migration Association of North America, c/o William J. Gallagher, PO Box 822, Boonton, NJ 07005- 0822.

The Games Birders Play

THE BIG DAY

Few events, in any avocation, match the fun, challenge, and audacity of a **Big Day**—a twenty-four-hour challenge in which practitioners attempt to record as many different species as possible between midnight and midnight. Birds may be recorded by sight or sound. Every species counts as one. The game may be played by any individual or group, using whatever standards they care to apply. But for those who

The Big Day! Midnight to midnight. How many birds can you find? Depending on where you are and how good a birder you are, your one-day total might exceed two hundred species, and your route might exceed five hundred miles driven. These Big Day birders in Cape May didn't quite reach that goal (but then, they were using bicycles). *Kevin Karlson.*

enjoy playing by the rules, the American Birding Association has established standards and maintains Big Day records for states and provinces.

Most Big Days are conducted in the spring, when birds are most vocal. Runs are timed to coincide with the period of peak bird diversity — when many wintering species are still lingering, most breeders have arrived, and more northerly breeders are migrating through. Over most of North America, this period runs from the last week in April to the end of May; earlier dates prove more productive in the South, and later dates in the far North.

Big Day Birding Strategy

The key to any Big Day is the route — one that incorporates the greatest number of habitat types (or species possibilities) in the shortest amount of time. Habitats (and species possibilities) vary greatly across North America, but some Big Day basics are universal.

1. The best route is a direct route. Plot one that incorporates the greatest number of key habitats along the shortest route and avoid the temptation to diverge from that route for one or two species.
2. Set a tight but realistic schedule that establishes how much time you will spend in each location and how much time it will take to reach the next.
3. *Stick to that schedule.* The way to add species to a list is to add habitats to a route, not minutes to a stop waiting for one reluctant species to show. The way to *really* lose species is to be forced to cut planned stops from your route because you ran out of time.
4. Go to each stop on your Big Day with a shopping list, not an open mind. *Know* what target species you need there and look for them. Scout stops before the Big Day. Don't just trust to fate.
5. Keep your list up. Update it between sites. This way you'll know if a species has been missed before you exhaust its habitat or range.

6. For especially elusive or uncommon species, have one or more backup locations.

Some other guidelines will help you get the most out of a day-long birding effort. Nocturnal species (rails, bitterns, nightjars, and owls) are naturally the focus of a team's effort before dawn. Other species vocalize at night too, however, including many migrants! Keep an ear to the sky.

Breeding birds are generally more active, more vocal, and more predictable earlier in the day than migrants are. Dawn is a good time to concentrate on residents. Migrants, because they must often search for proper habitat and are intent upon foraging after a night of flight, are often more concentrated and easier to find later in the morning.

Searching for water birds and shorebirds is best left to the afternoon (when songbirds are less vocal), but any body of water along your route is worth a stop and a look at any time.

The last hours of the day are usually reserved for mopping up — filling holes in the list or moving from spot to spot for staked-out individual species. Remember, birds that have been quiescent during the afternoon hours become active and vocal again in the evening.

The number of species you may encounter as a Big Day birder is very dependent upon where you live. Many states (and one Canadian province) have Big Day records exceeding 200 species, but counts of 130 to 160 are more common. The U.S. record of 258 species was set in Texas in 2001.

THE BIG SIT

This sedentary alternative to a Big Day is less frenetic but hardly less challenging. In a **Big Sit,** birders attempt to identify as many different species as possible from one spot. They rely upon exceptional optics and their long-range identification skills to compensate for their lack of mobility.

What route is to a Big Day, location is to a Big Sit. Key to the success of a Big Sit is finding a location that offers a variety of habitat possibilities in close proximity. Ideal locations would offer a woodland edge (for passerines), fields and pasture (for sparrows and open-country birds), marshes, and a large body of water, and they would be at some point where migrating birds concentrate. Like a Big Day, Big Sits are most productive during spring and fall when birds migrate.

The rules are simple. You must conduct your search from a circle with a fifteen-foot diameter. You can leave the circle to "ground-truth" a sighting, but you cannot add any new species encountered outside the circle.

Big Sits are naturally not as productive as Big Days in terms of species totals, but keen observers at key locations have nevertheless recorded in excess of one hundred species.

BIRDATHONS AND BIRDING COMPETITIONS

In 1972 Ontario's Long Point Bird Observatory took the idea of a Big Day and mated it to fundraising. They created a **birdathon,** an event whose key elements were a team of birders who executed a Big Day and a membership who were invited to make a pledge based on the total number of species seen by the team. It proved very successful and immensely popular. Bird observatory supporters were invited to do their own Big Days and raise money on behalf of the observatory. Other organizations quickly adopted the idea.

In 1984 the New Jersey Audubon Society took the next logical step. Relying upon the natural competitiveness of birders, and with an eye toward the publicity that competition generates, the society invited teams of birders to compete, all on the same day, using the state of New Jersey as the playing field. This event, the World Series of Birding, also proved immensely successful. Held every May, over fifty teams from North America and abroad compete and, through pledges, raise in excess of half a million dollars for the conservation cause championed by their team (or the team's organizational sponsor). The event has been emulated elsewhere with success, most notably in Texas, which in 1996 inaugurated the Texas Birding Classic, and California's Point Reyes Bird Observatory, which organizes an autumn competition.

The birdathon, pioneered by Ontario's Long Point Bird Observatory, turns a birding Big Day into a fund-raiser. A birding competition, like the World Series of Birding held in New Jersey every May, engages scores of teams that compete to see the most species of birds and to raise money for their favorite conservation cause. This 1985 photo shows the NARBA (National Rare Bird Alert) team at the finish line at midnight—(left to right) Bob Odear, Wes Biggs, Ted Parker, and Kenn Kaufman. *Brian O'Doherty/CMBO files.*

For information about the World Series of Birding, contact the Cape May Bird Observatory, PO Box 3, Cape May Point, NJ 08212, 609-884-2736.

THE BIG YEAR

As discussed in chapter 3, listing or keeping records of bird sightings is fundamental to birding. A byproduct of listing is the **Big Year** — a concerted effort to record as many different species as possible in one calendar year.

Because of budget and time constraints — and the sheer logistical challenge — most birders limit their Big Year to their home state. A Big Year not only tests identification skills and knowledge of bird distribution in a state but gives individuals an excuse to spend many hundreds of hours in the field, exonerating them from having to attend family functions and keep the yard up. Even friends and family members who don't understand birding will be sympathetic to the idea of a "challenge."

A few very keen, very knowledgeable, and usually well-funded individuals have also attempted North American Big Years. One famous odyssey, chronicled in *Wild America*, was Roger Tory Peterson's 1953 effort, during which he and his British colleague James Fisher recorded more than 550 species. Kenn Kaufman's Big Year, written up in *Kingbird Highway*, was 1973: hitchhiking across the continent and relying upon a budget that would not have sustained an anorexic cat, the sixteen-year-old Kaufman tallied 666 species. A record? No. But a personal triumph.

The Month Listing

At first look, the idea of month listing seems a contrivance. Unlike a year list, a **month list** is cumulative. Every year you try to add new species to your September list...your February List...in the same way you might add birds to your life list.

So, for every month, you try to record a robin. For every month you need a crow. The problem is that bird populations shift. Birds that may be common in your region in summer may be rare in winter. The challenge becomes finding as many marginal species as possible in as many months as possible. Not only does this birding game give even very common birds added value, but it also forces proponents to go afield at times of the year that many birders consider off-season.

If you need an excuse or motivation to get into the field during the dead of winter or the dog days of summer, month listing is the answer to your prayers.

Month Listing Strategy

A month listing strategy is simple, really. Just go birding. Find as many species as possible. Listen to the birding hotlines. Learn of rare or unusual species in the area and track them down. Invite friends to tell you when they encounter a bird that is out of season.

You will find that the first and last days in any month take on new meaning. On the last day of every month you'll be searching for birds that are pushing the temporal envelope and arriving early. On the first day of the month you'll scurry about hoping to find lingering species that may have been common the month before but constitute a prize now.

There is no organization of month listers. There is no publication catering to their interests, with the exception of journals that document the unseasonal occurrence of species. There is no prize — except for the satisfaction of being afield and meeting a challenge.

The ability to identify birds is both a talent and a skill. Birders can use their skills to support bird research and bird conservation by getting involved in organized counts and monitoring programs like the Christmas Bird Count, the Breeding Bird Survey, breeding bird atlases, and hawk counts. Birders also love the challenge inherent in finding and counting birds. Several cherished traditions cater to this competitiveness, including the Big Year and the Big Day — a one-day challenge that can also be used to raise money for conservation through pledges based upon birds tallied.

Whether you bird to support an objective or bird to master a challenge, it's all the same. No matter what the goal or the excuse, birding should always and everywhere be an activity that is done because it is fun.

7
Tips to Better Birding

AT BIRDING'S HORIZON LINE — STANDING WITH WILL
EQUIPMENT TIPS
TECHNIQUE TIPS

At Birding's Horizon Line — Standing with Will

I was standing with my World Series of Birding teammates, Pete Bacinski, Don Freiday, and Will Russell, director of WINGS, one of North America's top bird tour companies.

Around us were the midnight-darkened Vernon wetlands. Before us twenty-four hours of limit-pushing birding. Above us a sky filled with stars, clouds . . . and the nocturnal flight calls of migrating birds.

"Lincoln's Sparrow," said Will, putting a name to a single, ethereal call whose source was somewhere overhead.

If you say so, I thought. All of us had heard the sound. Only Will was skilled enough to identify it.

"Yellow-billed Cuckoo," he said a moment later.

"Got it," the three of us chanted. The nocturnal flight call of Yellow-billed Cuckoo is reminiscent of the bird's more commonly heard daytime vocalization, a sound all of us were familiar with.

"Ovenbird," he said to the stars, pinning a name to a disembodied call note.

Will Russell is on everyone's short list for finest field birder in North America, and among a handful who are pushing the limits of birding's horizons by exploring the frontier of sound. Now fifty-nine,

Will has been a birder all his life, but when asked about his birding skills, he answers simply, "I work at it."

It used to be that the audio-frontier line was the challenge of identifying birds singing rings around their territories. Birders struggled to decipher the myriad sounds, and in time their ears and minds learned to distinguish this species from that.

Most birds don't sing most of the year, however, and so the frontier moved on (because every new generation needs new challenges) to single-note utterances. Limit-pushing birders listened and learned chips and calls.

Now the frontier has shifted again, moving beyond the safety net of sight to the nocturnal flight call of migrating birds. Today's pioneers spend hours listening to and recording the flood of sounds and then more hours, in sound laboratories, decoding the disembodied noises, linking them by deduction and intuition to the names of the birds that made them.

"Dendroica," Will said, naming a genus of warbler. "Either a Yellow or a Blackpoll . . . or a Blackburnian," he added, drawing a line where even his horizon blurred.

Birding's horizon is not fixed. It moves all the time. This is not to say that experienced birders have no tips and techniques that will spced less experienced birders down the road to greater proficiency (and maybe help avoid some bumps along the way). The balance of this chapter expounds upon some of the tricks of the birding trade. To save you frustration.

And to speed your journey to the real frontier, where your talents are necded.

Equipment Tips

PROTECTING BINOCULARS WHEN IT'S WET

Inclement weather doesn't send birds indoors — and if you are prepared, it won't send you there either. Some of the best birding occurs in rainy conditions (for reasons explained later in this chapter), but some of the toughest birding happens then too.

Damn birds and English birders go out in the midday rain on the Isle of Scilly. Better cover up those binoculars. *Linda Dunne.*

Optical performance in particular is quickly compromised by rain — another way of saying: when your binoculars get wet, all you'll see is a blur. One of the easiest ways to keep rain off the ocular lens is by attaching a commercial rain guard — a loose-fitting cap, made of plastic or hard rubber, that attaches to the binocular strap and can be seated over the ocular lenses as needed.

Some rain guards, however, are too tight to slip on or off easily, and some are so poorly designed that they will not fit over the lenses when the eyecups are rolled down. Rain guards aren't necessarily specific to one binocular. Sometimes guards made by other companies, for other instruments, serve you better — or you can make your own.

Take a piece of chamois cloth approximately five-inch-square, or large enough to drape over the ocular lenses. Make two slits spaced to fit the two ends of your binocular strap. Sleeve the straps through the slits.

If you don't have a rain guard — or don't care to be bothered with one — you can help keep water droplets off the lenses by wearing your binoculars bandolier fashion, beneath an arm, where they are better protected from the elements, or you can hold your hand over the eyecups to shield them from rain.

Do not press your hands over the eyecups, sealing them. In cold weather the moisture from your hand condenses on the outside of the lens, fogging them. Leave a gap for ventilation, and your lens shouldn't fog.

Slipping binoculars inside a loose-fitting rain jacket is also common practice.

Once binoculars are raised to the eyes, objective lenses are also vulnerable to rain. The best defense is to buy binoculars whose objective lenses are recessed, so that rain falling horizontally won't spatter the glass. Homemade rain guards for objectives can be made out of three- to four-inch PVC pipe whose diameter is just wide enough to sleeve over the barrel. When dry, the tubes encircle the barrels; when it rains, the tubes can be drawn out, telescope fashion, providing the lenses with two to four inches of shielded protection.

Shifting your grip forward, so that your hands shield the objective lens, gives short-lived protection from rain.

Protecting Binoculars When It's Cold

Winter cold is tough on optics, and temperatures don't even have to fall below freezing for problems to occur.

One of the most common problems is fogging of the external lenses of binoculars. These lenses can fog when non-eyeglass-wearing birders bring cold optics up to their eyes for a prolonged scan. In cold temperatures, moisture transpires from the eyes and condenses on the lens.

To prevent this form of lens fogging, hold your eyecups slightly away from your eye sockets — perhaps just resting the top of the eyecups on your eyebrows, leaving the rest of the eyecup rim open and ventilated. If you often bird in cold climates, avoid purchasing binoculars that offer "flared eyecups," which are designed to block peripheral light. They block not only light but ventilation too.

Ocular lenses also become fogged if you breathe on them. There are two ways to avoid this. First, use your rain guard. Second, lengthen your binocular strap. The more distance between your exhaled breath and the lens, the less fogging.

The most difficult fogging problem occurs when cold binoculars are carried into a warm place, like your car. For immediate relief, try carrying a chamois cloth or a clean cotton handkerchief — something with which to wipe the lens. Or place the instrument on the dashboard, over the defroster, and turn the heater *and the air conditioner* on simultaneously.

What is the most drastic and most effective way to keep your binoculars from fogging when you get into a warm car? *Don't warm the car.* Keep your heat off and the windows open. You might not be comfortable, but at least your lenses won't fog.

What to Do When the Bird Is Too Close

There are few things more frustrating than having a bird *so* near at hand that you cannot adjust your focus close enough to see it clearly. Under normal circumstances, at distances under twenty feet, familiar or distinctly marked birds can be identified without binoculars.

But what about when it's rainy, or twilight in the deep woodlands has cast a shadow over detail? What about birds that are partially obscured by leaves and grass, showing you a wing, a cheek, or part of a breast? If only you could get your binoculars to focus two or three feet closer, you could see these disjunct parts and piece together an identification. Well, sometimes you can cut two or three (or more) feet off the minimum focus of your instrument by using the individual eyepiece adjustment and turning your binocular temporarily into a super-close-focusing *monolocular.*

> STEP 1: Focus as close as possible, using the center-focus wheel.
> STEP 2: Close one eye and peer through the barrel controlled by the individual eyepiece adjustment ring, or wheel.
> STEP 3: Turn the ring to focus down upon the bird.

Depending on make or model, you can usually gain two or three feet of focus distance — and sometimes this is enough to see the detail you need.

A Binocular in the Hand Merits a Bird in the Bush

Less experienced birders, in the company of very accomplished birders, are astonished at the rapidity with which experienced hands can bring their binoculars to bear.

In part it is a matter of quick reflexes. But often the reactive time gap between newer and more experienced birders is more a matter of anticipation and preparedness. What experienced birders know that beginners don't is *where* and *when* a bird is likely to appear — insight that allows preparation for a split-second reaction.

The ability to read a habitat is something that birders gain with experience. But beginners *can* do two things to help cut down their reaction times. Both relate to how binoculars are handled.

First, when approaching an area that looks promising — like the edge of a marsh where shorebirds teem, or that sure-fire woodland pocket that *always* holds a migrating warbler or two — *hold your binoculars at the ready,* with one or both hands wrapped around them, ready to bring them to your eyes the instant you see movement. By eliminating the need to *reach* for your binoculars and *then* bring them to bear, you can cut your reaction time in half.

Second, when approaching your chosen vantage point (some point short of flush distance), *prefocus your binoculars to fall within*

You are on the boardwalk of Corkscrew Swamp. You are looking for a Yellow-throated Warbler. You see a flicker of movement overhead. Do you know where your binoculars are? *Linda Dunne.*

the anticipated range. You don't need to bring them to your eyes to do this. Just move the wheel all the way to the closest focus setting and then focus back to a distance that accommodates the anticipated range.

Your estimated point of focus may not be perfect. You may have to make minor adjustments once your binoculars are brought to bear. But prefocusing sure beats having to go through the entire range of a binocular's focus (three full revolutions of a focus wheel on some models) to get a clear image. When split-seconds count, time spent spinning your wheel is time you can't afford.

Meet Them at the Landing Zone

Nailing flushed birds in flight is an art, one that requires practice and binoculars whose field of view and depth of field are suited to the task — and many are not, particularly many fine 10× instruments.

Rather than push your (or your binocular's) limits, here's another way to catch sight of a bird you've flushed. Try guessing where the bird is going to land and be prepared to bring your binoculars to bear on this point when it alights.

Doing this is not as improbable as it sounds. You see the bird, so you know where it is heading. You can fairly judge that if the bird is aiming for a prominent bush or stalk or wire or sign in an open landscape, then that is where it is planning to land.

Even if the bird is heading for a wall of trees or a hedgerow, anticipate that the bird is going to take *some* prominent perch in the open. If the bird disappears into the foliage, you lose. But if the bird alights in the open to see who the intruder is and you aren't prepared, you really lose.

Vibration Kills

Wind is the mortal enemy of all spotting scope users; wind makes tripods vibrate, spotting scopes dance, and images go all to hell. Heavy tripods are better at bucking the wind than light tripods, but no portable tripod is vibration-free.

There are several things that scope users can do to reduce wind-induced vibration. Placing a hand (or a couple of fingers) on the scope and pressing down marginally and temporarily improves image quality.

Retracting the tripod legs (the mechanical equivalent of trimming sail) also helps. The shortened scope can be placed on the hood of a car, which will add elevation and, at two-thousand pounds, is more stable than a five-pound tripod. Or in very windy conditions, the scope can be set close to the ground and used from a sitting position. If a car is handy, use the car as a windbreak.

One Eye on the World

Watching hawks, shorebirds, and particularly sea birds forces birders to scan the horizon for hours on end. A tripod-mounted spotting scope is not only an advantage, it is essential.

Unlike binoculars, spotting scopes are equipped with a single ocular lens. Only one eye is brought to bear on an object at a time. The ideal, and most restful, way to use a scope is to leave *both* eyes open, just as you would when using a microscope. Concentration is focused through the eye fused to the scope. That's your dominant eye. (To determine your dominant eye, point your finger to a distant object. Close one eye, then the other. The eye aligned with your finger is your dominant eye.)

Unfortunately, many people find it difficult to master this open-eyed technique. The image from the unmagnified eye keeps intruding on the magnified image, causing a visual schizophrenia and destroying concentration.

Many birders try to solve the problem by closing one eye. This technique may work for a short time, but holding one eye closed is a feat most people cannot manage indefinitely.

Others try placing one hand over their unused eye, but this too is something that most people don't care to do for extended periods. An eye patch can solve the problem, but it's an impediment if binoculars are suddenly needed.

A trick that some long-distance, long-term scanning artists use to keep their unused eye from imposing itself is to affix a cardboard buffer to the scope — one that falls in front of the unused eye. Shaped like a painter's palette, the "thumb hole" fits over the scope eyepiece. The cardboard barrier situated at nose-tip distance rests in front of the unused eye, works about as well as a cupped hand, and is more comfortable.

Technique Tips
WORKING THE CROWD
Birds are not always perched where they can be seen. Beginning birders, confronted by some skulking songbird, have two choices. One, approach for a better vantage — and chance flushing the bird. Two, wait and hope the bird eventually shows.

There is a third alternative that can often be used to good effect: mimicking the alarm or scolding calls of the bird in an effort to draw it into the open and closer. This response is called **mobbing,** the technique **pishing.** Pishing isn't foolproof, and it is not universally applicable; many European birds, for example, do not respond at all. But over much of North America, pishing, done properly, gives birders an attractive advantage. Sometimes the results can be spectacular. Birds from over a hundred yards may be drawn in, sometimes to within arm's reach.

First, realize that pishing (by which I mean *all* manners of **onomatopoeic** squeaks, squeals, *shhhh*s, and stuttering slurs) doesn't have to whip all birds within hearing into a frenzy. All pishing need do is incite one or two easily piqued species; chickadees, titmice, and nuthatches in particular are notoriously pish-prone. It is their excitement and their scolding vocalizations that draw a crowd of more pish-resistant species.

Different birders have different pishing techniques. My own standard repertoire is a three-part ensemble composed of a standard pish sequence, a predator imitation, and a squeal call.

The basic pish sequence sounds like a cross between the *psh-psh-psh* call Aunt Mable uses to call her cat and the scolding utterances of an apoplectic titmouse. Phonetically rendered, it looks like *pursss-*

EEE-pursssEEE-pursssEEE; it is usually given in a series of three. The best way to gain a sense of what you are trying to sound like is to pay attention to the scold call of a titmouse and mimic it.

The pish sequence (continued for twenty seconds or so) puts birds on notice that there is something rotten in birddom — an intruder, maybe a predator. To reinforce this idea, follow the pish sequence with a predator imitation — for example, an Eastern Screech-Owl, a Barred Owl, a Northern Pygmy-Owl, or a Northern Saw-whet (whatever owl species is common to the area).

Then I play my trump — I cut loose with a long, plaintive squeal call, the sort of sound a starling might make to protest the inopportune embrace of a Cooper's Hawk.

The squeal call is produced by placing the middle and index fingers to your lips and producing a loud, prolonged, high-pitched kissing sound. The noise is made by drawing air through tightly compressed lips. The fingers act as a resonating chamber.

Done properly, the squeal call will almost pull the fillings out of your teeth — and attract birds the way accident scenes attract onlookers. Once you have incited a mobbing action, you can keep excitement levels high by repeating the sequence or mixing the order.

Over the course of many years, I have used this sequence (or elements of this sequence) to draw all manner of birds into the open — including such notoriously reticent species as Sedge Wrens, LeConte's Sparrows, and Connecticut Warblers.

I have also lured a dozen foxes, three weasels, two bobcats, one skunk, innumerable horses, cows, pigs, one duck hunter, and one very perplexed bunch of British birders on the Scilly Islands.

"Bloody Yank didn't have any idea what he was looking at," one of the group was overheard to say later, "but he was driving the chiffchaffs *mad!*"

Pishing is not by any means guaranteed to draw birds to your side — in fact, there are times when a bout of spirited pishing will have just the opposite effect. Or as the late Dr. Harold Axtell once observed, "Pishing will do one of three things — it will attract birds, scare them away, or do nothing."

You can, however, increase your chances of success. For one thing, if you are trying to lure woodland species, it is better to step beneath the canopy than to try luring them into an open field. Birds may be gullible, but they are also bonded to habitat.

It also pays to be persistent. Once you incite a flock, give the birds five minutes to draw the attention of less pish-prone species before calling it quits.

Finally, several cautionary notes. First, pishing is intrusive. Don't overdo it, and consider not doing it at all in very heavily birded areas. Pishing intrudes not only upon the lives of birds but upon fellow birders.

Second, there are times when pishing should be avoided altogether — like at dawn on cold winter mornings. The energy reserves of birds may be sorely depleted after a cold night. Offer half-hardy species a chance to feed before tweaking them. If you draw energy-depleted birds into the open, you may be pushing them past their limit, and you are most certainly inviting their demise at the talons of some bird-eating hawk (a species, incidently, that also responds to pishing).

Be responsible. When birds begin to lose interest, or when you've gotten the look you need, stop.

SOMETIMES JUST A LITTLE *CHIP* WILL DO

Pishing is not universally effective. Many species will freeze or flee rather than approach — including many sparrow species. To attract sparrows and other pish-proof species, try imitating a *chip* note — a single, sharp call note that can bring even the most reticent sparrows to stand at attention.

To produce this sound, press your middle and index fingers to your lips and give them a short, sweet, loud, high-pitched *kiss.* As with the squeal, the fingers serve as a resonating chamber. Done properly, the sound should recall the sound of a stone skipped on ice.

Timing and position are key. Best results are had by walking up to a sparrowish-looking spot (best identified when a group of feeding birds abruptly flushes into the brush). Stop where you are. Wait thirty seconds or so for the birds to calm down. Then bring your fingers to your lips and *chip.*

One chip is usually all it takes to get skulking sparrows to pop onto perches to see what the problem is. Periodic, irregular chips may continue to keep birds in view for a short time, but keep in mind that sparrows have a very short attention span.

The chip note, produced at one-second intervals, also draws warblers into view. In fact, it seems very effective at reinciting a mobbing action after birds lose interest in pishing.

But once again, don't overdo it. Birds have their own lives to live. You are just an observer.

KNOCKDOWN PISH

How many times have you seen a small passerine zip by, just overhead, flying too fast for you to bring your binoculars (or your skills) to bear on it? Haven't you wished that there were some way to get it to land on some handy perch where you'd have a fighting chance to see it?

Well, there is. You can often get passing birds to land by making an alarm call. A single, emphatic *pewsh* (a truncated pish) or a two-note *pew-pew*. This is bird Esperanto for "Look out." Rather than be the only obvious target in an open sky, a flying bird will often react to such a call by taking evasive action, dropping like a knuckleball to get out of harm's way. Sometimes after an evasive dive the bird continues on its way. But sometimes it takes a perch to see what the problem is.

If the bird continues on, you are no worse off. If it falls for your trick and perches, so much the better for you.

TALKING OWL

Although the Eastern Screech-Owl lives only in the eastern half of North America, its whinny seems to engender pique in birds throughout the continent. Birders can imitate this call all by itself or as part of a pishing sequence to incite a mobbing reaction — on two conditions: you can whistle, and you are not dissuaded by what you are about to read.

Screech-owls have two classic vocalizations. A tremolo, the characteristic communication call, and a descending whinny, a defensive territorial call. To make either call, first listen to a recording of a screech-owl. It's always best to know what you are trying to imitate before you attempt it.

Next, work up a gob of saliva, the more viscous the better. Locate it on the back of your tongue. Tilt your head back slightly. Whistle. The force of the whistle passing over the saliva sets up a mini-wave action that breaks against the roof of your mouth, in turn breaking the flow of air into a tremolo whistle. Yes, it sounds disgusting, but that's how you do it. The tremolo is simply a matter of keeping the whistle's pitch low and even. The whinny requires changing the whistle's pitch.

If getting a passable screech-owl call is beyond your vocal capacity, you can try substituting the call of a Northern Saw-whet Owl (in the East) or a Northern Pygmy-Owl (in the West). Both calls are short, regular, whistled toots. Saw-whets use single notes; pygmy-owls often double them.

THE POWER OF PAUSE

More than sound, more than color, birds react to *motion*. Under many circumstances, a cautious or stationary observer is more likely to see birds and get better looks than a carelessly mobile one.

People who maintain window feeders know this to be true. Sit quietly and birds ignore your presence. Rise to leave or make any sudden motion and birds flee. The difference between feeding stations and field situations is that birders commonly do not see the birds that flush as they are advancing. The reaction time of birds is so much faster than our own that all birders see is an empty trail.

Try pausing for a minute (or two or three) whenever you turn a corner. Give flushed birds a chance to return to normal behavior patterns.

Better yet, pinpoint locations that habitually hold birds — sunny woodland edges on cool mornings, bottlenecks or junctions between adjacent woodlots, water sources on hot afternoons, bushy borders that *always* hold sparrows. Walk quietly to that strategic spot. Make yourself comfortable. Watch the show.

Bring a blanket, a chair, or a folding stool. Bring lunch and a beverage. Not only will birds quickly acclimate to your presence, but *their*

Sometimes the best way to find birds is to sit at a strategic spot and let them find you. *Kevin Karlson.*

subtle movements will not be masked by your own. It is far easier to detect movement in vegetation when your own locomotion hasn't put the world in motion.

If you use the power of pause, you'll increase the number of birds you see in the field. Only your physician, who may have instructed you to get more exercise, might gainsay the technique.

DIRECTIONS, PLEASE

Often more difficult than finding birds is pointing them out to other birders. "It's right there" doesn't offer much guidance, and all too often the accuracy of this assertion becomes apparent only after the bird flies.

If the bird is stationary, try to find some orienting feature in close proximity — a bunch of leaves that are darker than the rest, a patch of flowers, a boulder (if the bird is on the ground). Tell fellow birders how far above, below, left, or right the bird lies from the orienting mark. At close range, estimate the distance in standard linear feet. If the bird is in flight, say which direction it's going.

If the bird is too far away for you to estimate accurately the distance in feet or yards from an orienting point, use fields of view (the view offered through your binocular). A bird sitting on a hillside might be "half a [binocular] field left of the red barn." A bird flying overhead might be "two fields above the horizon."

As directions go, "It's right in front of us" might be accurate, but it still encompasses about half the known universe and it's not going to win you any friends. Getting other birders on a bird can be more challenging than finding and identifying birds yourself, but it's an integral part of birding. *Kevin Karlson.*

Objects on the horizon may also be used to orient hopeful observers to birds closer at hand. "The bird is going to be in line with that ship . . . *now*" is a phrase often heard on a sea-bird watch or a pelagic birding trip. In the absence of ships or navigational markers, pelagic birders often use the hands of a dial clock to direct fellow birders. Using the bow (front) of the ship for twelve o'clock, a bird slightly right of the bow might be at one o'clock. A bird directly astern lies at six o'clock.

Birds flying high overhead present their own peculiar problems of orientation. Clouds are a hawk watcher's best friend. They offer not only a silhouetting backdrop but a reference point.

HAWKS — PUTTING YOURSELF IN FORTUNE'S WAY
Identifying hawks in flight is a tricky pursuit — but it is only the second half of a challenging two-step process. Before distant birds of prey can be identified, they must be found!

The first step is placing yourself in opportunity's way. During migration, birds of prey move on a broad front, but their movements are directed and their numbers concentrated by what are called leading lines. These include mountain ridges — like the one straddled by Hawk Mountain, Pennsylvania, where birds of prey are drawn to energy-conserving updrafts — and shorelines, which cause the concentrations seen over such famous locations as Duluth, Minnesota, and Cape May, New Jersey. All birds of prey use **thermals** (rising columns of warm air) to gain easy lift. Oceans and large lakes represent thermal-poor habitat, so many birds of prey avoid them, electing instead to follow the contours of the coast.

Weather conditions also affect hawk movement and the numbers that may be seen at a certain place. In the spring (as early as February in some locations), birds of prey pulse north in waves pushed by warm southerly breezes. If these **broad-front movements** intercept an approaching cold front, the wall of stormy weather moving ahead of the front concentrates migrants along its edge. Hawks will run up along the edge of the squall line the same way they skirt the edge of an ocean or lake.

In the fall (beginning as early as late July in some places), cold fronts trigger the migratory urge, propelling hawks and other migrants south. For some thermal-dependent species, like the Broad-winged Hawk, these cold fronts not only drive them south but carry them. Northwest winds associated with the passage of a front sweep migrating birds with them in the same way that a person swimming across a river is propelled downstream. This is another reason why coastlines act as migration corridors. Like chips in a flood, birds are ferried to the coast, where they pile up, sometimes in vast numbers.

Finding Hawks

At most hawk-watching locations, migrating hawks fly established routes that are affected daily by geography, wind, weather, time of day, and, of course, season. Once you've located one bird and plotted the pattern of its movement, chances are good that more will follow.

Scanning with binoculars is the important first step. A good technique is to pan the horizon in the general direction from which you anticipate hawks to come. The full scan should approach 120 to 140 degrees. Now raise your binoculars a full binocular field above the horizon and backtrack, covering the sky above the initial sweep; then repeat the process one more time. Three sweeps is generally enough

The first step in watching hawks is to go to a known hawk migration junction where birds may be seen in numbers. From late August through November, Hawk Mountain, Pennsylvania, ranks among North America's finest. *Pete Dunne.*

to map the sky — unless your binoculars have a critically small field of view (in which case you should buy new binoculars).

From midmorning to midafternoon, particularly on days marked by excellent soaring conditions, hawks soar higher at many locations, and the effectiveness of scanning the horizon diminishes. When birds are high, try scanning directly overhead with binoculars and the unaided eye. Not only are approaching birds closest at this point, but the angle of view offers a full ventral profile (that is, more surface area), making the birds easier to see.

Blue skies — disparagingly called "broad-winged blue" by some hawk watchers — swallow birds of prey. With little contrast and little to focus upon, eyes peering into the blue go numb and birds get missed. If there are clouds or jet contrails, scan these. Your eyes will have something to focus upon, and hawk silhouettes stand out against a white backdrop. Cumulus clouds offer a special advantage. They are the visual tips of the rising columns of air that hawks ride aloft. So not only do cumulus clouds "show off" hawks to best effect, but they attract them!

Some birds of prey are easier to see than others. Large dark birds (like vultures and eagles) and birds with contrasting plumage (like Osprey) stand out. Pale or pastel-plumaged birds (like adult Cooper's Hawks) melt into the sky. Since birds of a feather do tend to migrate together, you can use obvious birds as a way to find less contrasting ones. If you find a distant or high-soaring vulture, watch it. Once your eyes have become calibrated for the proper distance and are fused to the right section of sky, you may be surprised to see other birds materialize around the vulture.

If the eye-catching raptor you've latched onto is in a glide, a good trick is to direct your binoculars along the bird's flight path to pick up any birds moving ahead of the first. Then backtrack, pick up the bellwether bird, and scan back along the bird's wake. There may be birds coming up behind as well.

Being Where the Birds Are

In the breeding season, woodland songbirds are fairly evenly distributed throughout appropriate habitat, their distribution and location dictated by the territorial prerogative. An attentive birder should be able to find nesting species at fairly regular intervals just by strolling along and listening.

But in the spring and fall, when birds migrate, and in winter, when many species stop defending territories, woodland birds may be very irregularly distributed. There can be long stretches with nothing, then suddenly . . . *wham!* you are into birds. Woodland birding in fall and winter therefore is often a matter of finding and working flocks.

In migration, search for nomadic bands of warblers and vireos moving through the canopy in search of insect prey. Brightly plumaged species like American Redstart or hyperactive birds like Golden-crowned Kinglet will draw your eye and tip you off to the presence of a mixed flock. Be alert too for the subdued chatter of a flock — the call notes of warblers, the monotonous rantings of nuthatches, the ethereal incantations of Golden-crowned Kinglets.

In winter, mixed flocks of hardy and half-hardy species move like a hungry cloud through woodlands. Their presence is usually heralded by the telltale notes of chickadees and titmice, but be alert for braying jays or a nuthatch whose rantings are pointed and incessant. It may indicate the presence of a predator and an ad hoc flock-to-be.

There is, of course, rhyme and reason to the distribution and movement of birds. Birders can increase their chances of running into flocks by using their heads as well as their feet. On cool mornings, seek out woodland edges that are exposed to the sun. Insect (and bird) activity will be greatest there. In winter, birds like warmth too. A thicket with a southern exposure protected from the wind is nearly perfect. Add a trickle of open water and it is ideal.

Birds are not evenly apportioned across the planet. As just discussed, sometimes you can travel great distances and not encounter anything that rates a raised binocular.

But the flip side of paucity is bounty. *Sometimes* birders encounter great concentrations of birds. These don't happen by accident. Be assured that if large numbers of birds are all sitting or flying in one place at one time, there is cause. At the heart of many, perhaps most, bird concentrations is food. Sometimes these banquets are predictable, such as the concentration of horseshoe crabs and shorebirds

Massed concentrations of birds are often associated with migration, and almost always associated with some opportune food source. Breeding horseshoe crabs, which deposit their eggs on the beaches of Delaware Bay each May, are responsible for this celebrated migratory shorebird concentration. *Pete Dunne.*

on the beaches of Delaware Bay every May. The crabs emerge to deposit their eggs on the beaches — and one million energy-taxed, migrating shorebirds gather to feast.

Sometimes the banquets are more impromptu. A coastal storm, one large enough to stir the bottom and deposit large numbers of mollusks onto beaches, is certain to draw a host of hungry gulls. An interior reservoir drawn down by summer drought is a magnet for southbound shorebirds, which will pause in their migration to forage along the muddy banks.

Birds move as their needs and conditions dictate. When conditions change — that is, when all the food is consumed — birds move on. If an opportune condition exists one year (perhaps a high rodent population is attracting raptors) and fails to materialize the next (the rodent population crashes), birds go someplace else. No food, no concentration.

But when you do find a concentration of birds, play it for all it's worth. A condition that attracts birds will attract *more* birds, and the chances of finding species that are new and uncommon to the region are heightened.

When the condition changes and the birds move on, take the hint. It's time to move along yourself — and look for another auspicious opportunity to cash in on.

Playing the Conditions

Many birders follow the calendar — hawk watching in October, searching for owls in December, scanning for rare gulls in January, looking for early migrants in April — and this practice is *good*. It keeps birding diverse and plays the temporal card to a birder's best advantage, maximizing success.

But while a familiarity with the natural calendar is important, often it is meteorological conditions as much or more than the calendar that determine where a birder should spend the day.

Say it's November and blowing a northwest gale. You'd planned to search your local patch for lingering passerines or irruptive northern species, but wind and woodland birding are an unproductive combination. Give up? No. Change plans. Head for the lee side of a lake or reservoir, where water birds will be seeking shelter from the wind. If rain preceded the front, it might well have knocked late migrating water birds (loons, grebes, scoters) out of the sky and onto inland lakes.

Or consider going to a hawk watch site. The peak of the migration may be over across much of North America, but birds of prey continue to migrate (or at least relocate) through December and even into January. A day on the ridge or the coast may garner treasured looks at eagles, cold-weather buteos, or maybe that Arctic raptor you've been looking for all your life.

Or say it's February. You'd planned on heading for the local winter gull hotspot, but the winds are southerly and unseasonably warm. Maybe you should head for a migrant trap instead. Winter **warm fronts** can ferry waves of early migrants (crows and raptors) and other birds that would ordinarily appear much later in the season. The gulls will still be there tomorrow. But a Purple Martin in February is a red-letter addition to anyone's ledger.

WORKING FLOCKS — FINDING THE ODD BIRD OUT

The flocking tendencies of birds can be used to a birder's advantage. Rare and uncommon species are often found among more common ones with which they can be directly compared and thus more easily distinguished.

The first thing to do when coming upon a flock of gulls (or shorebirds . . . or waterfowl . . . or blackbirds . . .) is to identify the familiar birds that constitute the bulk of the flock. Next, look at any individuals that do not fit the norm. For instance, you may see a bird that stands slightly taller or is noticeably stockier or whose color differs by a shade. *These differences don't necessarily require concerted study.* They naturally draw your eye. So relax. Let your eye be drawn to them. The study comes later.

Even beginning birders can see manifest differences — a snowy-colored, second-winter Glaucous Gull standing among an assortment of mocha-colored, first-winter-plumage Herring Gulls; the Great

Sometimes finding the odd bird out in a flock is painless, but if you having trouble finding the Ross's Goose among these Canada, maybe birding is not the activity for you. On the other hand, the Arctic Tern seen with these Forster's Terns might easily be overlooked unless an observer were being attentive to size and spacing in the ranks. *Pete Dunne.*

Cormorant whose proportions dwarf the Double-cresteds around it.

The odd bird out may also betray itself by being slightly off to one side, away from the body of the flock, or the other birds in the flock may be avoiding it, causing a slight gap in the ranks.

But sifting out birds that differ only slightly from the balance of the flock — finding, for instance, the slightly larger Black-headed Gull or the more petite Little Gull hidden among a resting flock of Bonaparte's Gulls — requires more than a glance. A birder must be aware of the possibility that these two uncommon species *may* sometimes be found among flocks of Bonaparte's Gulls and then search accordingly.

It's anyone's guess how many rare birds have been passed over because an observer didn't think to look. For that matter, it's anybody's guess how many vagrants you are destined to find because you do think to look.

All living things need water, and birds are no exception. They use it to drink, bathe, and cool off, and some rely upon aquatic habitats to provide prey. For birders, finding birds is often a simple matter of finding water.

This is particularly true in desert climates wherever a parched landscape gives way to a lush oasis. The number and diversity of resident species increase along watercourse edges. Migrating birds, searching for habitat that meets their needs, home in on these green retreats — and they are not terribly particular about the water's source.

Well-watered desert golf courses and highway rest areas maintained by sprinkler systems are magnets for migrating birds. Some of the finest birding on the planet can be had along the edges of the sewage facilities that serve desert communities.

In the prairie plains of the American West — where desiccating winds and the summer sun take the song right out of the mouths of grassland birds — one of the best ways to find endemic species is to stake out a water trough or tank in the late afternoon. When the worst of the day's heat is done, sparrows, longspurs, and other grassland species gather to drink. A quiet and strategically placed observer can get wonderful views.

Even birds in lush regions are drawn to water. Extraordinary looks at treetop warblers, tanagers, and grosbeaks can be had by staking out trickling streams on wooded slopes — particularly streams splashed with sunlight. When temperatures climb, birds come down to bathe. One bird bathing often inspires others to leave their arboreal retreats and let their feathers down.

Water is important to birds in winter too. In areas of deep cold, birds concentrate wherever open water can be found. Sometimes when temperatures plunge below freezing, open water survives in pockets on inland lakes and in swift-flowing rivers and streams.

Ducks, grebes, loons, and other water-dependent birds, frozen out of one area, seek out and crowd into those that remain. Often open pockets are kept ice-free by the action of the birds themselves. A community lake or golf course pond populated by geese or swans (the ice-breakers of the Anatidae family) may draw unusual species after other bodies of water freeze.

Even water in lesser amounts can be highly attractive to winter birds. Hardy birds like sparrows, finches, and juncos and even half-hardy species like American Robin and towhees seek out and concentrate in the habitat bordering tiny springs and trickle-sized streams. A seep or irrigation ditch in a snow-covered field may harbor a snipe or Killdeer.

The ultimate open-water mechanism is the waterfall — whether the man-made kind associated with hydroelectric dams or the natural kind like Niagara Falls. In northern areas, the combination of open water and winter-killed fish that characterizes the base of hydroelectric dams may attract hundreds, even thousands, of gulls, along with birders scanning the flocks for unusual species. It's cold birding, but the possibility of finding something truly rare — a Slaty-backed Gull or a Ross's Gull — warms the heart.

WATCHING BIRDS WATCHING BIRDS

You might own the best optics on the market. You might have thirty years' experience, be able to pick Thayer's Gull out of a flock half a mile away, and know the flight call of every eastern warbler. But next to the detection skills of the creatures you seek, you are strictly junior varsity.

If you train yourself to be attentive to the behavior patterns of birds, you can use their bird-finding skills to lead you to some great encounters.

One of the most obvious and productive examples of birds finding birds is the penchant that woodland birds, especially chickadees, titmice, and jays, have for mobbing roosting owls. Any scolding harangue is worth investigating and may lead you to . . . a Northern Pygmy-Owl . . . a Northern Saw-whet Owl . . . a Long-eared Owl . . .

Yes, their angst could be focused instead on a hunting rat snake, but you're going to tell me that the possibility of a pygmy-owl isn't worth a little sleuthing?

Birds mob in flight too. Icterids and starlings will **ball up** over a soaring raptor. The tight-packed, wheeling flock appears and disappears like a smoke cloud on the horizon, but the signal it sends is clear: look here for a bird of prey that may be too distant to be picked up by casual scanning alone.

In coastal areas, where vast numbers of tree swallows are common in the fall, kestrels signal their approach by drawing an angry entourage — the thickened clot of birds in the otherwise uniform distribution shows where the kestrel is. A raspy snarl from a swallow or martin says the same thing.

Approaching Merlins announce their arrival (and their identity) by boring little bird-free holes through the avian flocks. Swallows

No matter how good you get at spotting birds, birds are better. The photographer followed the gaze of these two Lesser Yellowlegs to discover a Peregrine Falcon soaring overhead. *Frank Schleicher.*

treat Merlins differently from the way they treat the lighter, smaller, and less dangerous American Kestrel.

If you are watching a flock of shorebirds and the birds slowly (or suddenly) crouch and freeze, look up. There's a raptor up there somewhere — count on it. If the frenetic activity around your bird feeder suddenly stops, or if your usually busy trays are empty on a cold morning, start scanning the trees. You've got another hungry bird coming to your feeders — one that doesn't eat seed.

And if you do find that perched raptor, and the bird cocks his head and looks up, do likewise. In the past, falconers intent on capturing **passage birds** relied upon tethered shrikes to warn of approaching hawks. The detection technique is even called **shriking**, and it is possible that the very name, *shrike,* is traceable to the vocalizations emitted by a raptor-piqued shrike.

Not all the bird-seeking bird interactions are antagonistic. Soaring birds will seek out, and lead attuned observers to, other thermal-dependent birds. By focusing on large soaring birds (pelicans, storks, vultures), observers often discover smaller and less obvious birds with them, such as Anhingas or small soaring raptors.

It might just be me, but it seems that once I find one woodland bird, I find more. Even birds I do not think of as flocking birds seem to like company.

If, for example, I find a wintering catbird, suddenly I note a Hermit Thrush in close proximity. If I see a Pied-billed Grebe, after navigating a bird-free stretch of marsh, I often find moorhen, Least Bittern, and maybe a rail too. Is it that I'm now focused? Or is it that birds derive security and comfort from having other birds around?

A flip side to this grouping tendency can be used to great effect when searching for Snowy Owls. In many places, these northern wanderers are habitually found on beaches, and beaches, at most access points, run two ways. Choosing the wrong direction can add hours to a search.

My technique, founded upon the bird-finding skills of other birds, is this. I scan the beach for gulls, which tend to distribute themselves fairly evenly along the shoreline. What I'm looking for, however, is not a concentration of gulls but the *absence* of gulls. That will be the stretch of beach distinguished by the presence of a large, white owl — and no gull wants to share it.

Summary There is no shortcut to becoming a better birder. There are, however, tricks that experienced birders use that make it easier to find, see, and identify birds. Some help them get the most out of equipment: keeping lenses unfogged in wet or cold weather; keeping spotting scopes steady in the wind; using the individual eyepiece adjustment knob to cut the minimum focus distance; cutting reaction time by keeping optics in hand or anticipating where a bird will land. Other techniques include: pishing to attract birds; pausing as a means of locating birds; offering bird-locating directions to other birders; using the vocalizations of resident birds to find migrant flocks; using weather conditions to predict where concentrations of birds will occur; using the magnetic quality of water to lead you to birds in summer and winter; and using the bird-finding skills of birds to lead you to other birds.

8
Ethics and Responsibilities

LOOKING FOR BAIRD'S SPARROW, WALKING ON EGGS
KEEPING BIRDING SAFE FOR BIRDS
THE ETIQUETTE OF BIRDING
COURTESY TO NONBIRDERS
CONSERVATION

Looking for Baird's Sparrow, Walking on Eggs

We were twenty abreast and three deep and moving through bird-rich grasslands. From lions hunting gazelle to Broad-winged Hawks hunting thermals, fanning out in an interception line is a time-tested technique by which predatory animals, acting in concert, find whatever it is they seek.

What we were seeking was Baird's Sparrow — a handsome prairie species distinguished by an array of streaks on the back, a beaded necklace on its breast, chestnut-touched scapulars, and a rich buff about the head and nape.

The bird is also distinguished by its very restricted range — limited, in the breeding season, to the northern prairie states and the southern portions of the prairie provinces of Canada. This bird was one of the reasons more than five hundred members of the American Birding Association had converged on Minot, North Dakota, for their 1994 convention.

In pursuit of a bird that we had heard but not sighted, all of us had eyes focused well ahead. Suddenly I felt a tug beneath my left foot. Looking down, I found a female Sharp-tailed Grouse flailing on the ground, the tips of three outer **flight feathers** of one wing pinned beneath the heel of my boot. Horrified, I lifted my foot, releasing the bird, which tried to fly but could not. The wing was broken.

To make matters worse, in the spot where the grouse had been, a ground nest containing nearly a dozen eggs was exposed. Several of the eggs were broken.

The commotion had drawn the eyes of the group. Only those closest to me had any sense of what had happened. I offered an explanation. Assumed responsibility. Urged caution.

"Okay," one of the leaders intoned. "Let's keep going, but let's be careful. There're lots of nesting birds out here."

And we were careful — as careful as people walking through tall grass filled with cryptically colored birds can be. We saw the sparrow, finally, without further incident. At least, that's what we hope and think.

Keeping Birding Safe for Birds

Harming birds is the very antithesis of what motivates birders — yet birds are sometimes injured, and their lives are often disrupted, by the efforts of those eager to appreciate them. Shorebirds feeding to fuel their long flight to the Arctic are forced to relocate when approached too closely — a waste of their time and energy. Adult birds, trying to distract birders away from nestlings, may attract a hawk that truly puts their young at risk.

And while many more ground-nesting birds have been injured by grazing buffalo and harvest combines than by birders, that doesn't mean that birders shouldn't make every effort to minimize their impact on these and other creatures that are the object of our attention.

COMMON SENSE

The first step to not causing harm to birds is a step backward. If your proximity to a bird seems to be causing stress, if birds are acting ner-

You can't hear the distress call from a photo, but the body language, the open bill, and the clutch of eggs beneath the bird all say one thing: "You are too close. Back off!" *N. J. Audubon files.*

vous and backing away, they are telling you that you have stepped over a line that responsible birders don't cross. Back off.

If you are pursuing a bird whose identity puzzles you, once you've gotten the look you need, stop.

If you are adept at pishing, don't overdo it, and don't do it at all in very cold temperatures, or in places where large numbers of bird-eating hawks are concentrated.

It is, of course, unusual for a bird to be stressed by a birder's attention. Birds vote with their wings. In most cases, when pressed too hard, birds simply leave.

Tape-recorded Playback

When birds on territory hear recordings of their song, they will approach what they assume to be a rival. They may give you a good look at them, but while defending their territory and trying to confront their phantom rival, birds become highly agitated and are not able to apply their energy more productively — to attracting a mate, foraging for a mate and young, or being vigilant for real threats to themselves and the genetic dowry. The repeated use of tapes, by multiple individ-

This immature Peregrine Falcon, by its body language, is saying, "Close enough." Falcons perch upright. They lean forward to leave the perch. Presumably the photographer was the source of the bird's unease. While approach to flush distance is no great source of stress to a healthy bird under normal field conditions, prolonged harassment is to be avoided. *Frank Schleicher.*

uals, targeted at individual birds, compounds these deleterious effects. In some cases in which birds have abandoned established territories and nesting attempts have ended in apparent failure, the zealous use of tapes is believed to have been at least a contributing factor.

Abuses notwithstanding, there are times when tapes are less intrusive, and less disruptive, than other means that birders might employ to gain a glimpse of a bird. In particular, in the hands of a skilled leader whose objective is to offer a group of birders a look at shy forest species, recorded playbacks, judiciously employed, are less intrusive than pishing (which is not species-specific) or marching a group through a sensitive area.

The ethics of using taped playback is, and will continue to be, an issue of debate. Until more is known about its effect, birders are best advised to avoid the use of tapes. For most species, patience and diligence will reward you with the satisfying look you seek.

The Etiquette of Birding

Birders are a society, and in any society there are standards of behavior and etiquette. If you want to benefit from the wisdom of the tribe, it is important not to alienate the tribe or its leaders.

COURTESY

One of birding's most fundamental ethics is the ethic of sharing. The classic greeting between birders is: "What are you seeing?" or, "Have you seen anything good?"

If you find a bird that excites you, chances are good that it will excite someone else. Let others know. Share. Most popular birding locations have **bird sighting sheets** or books to report your sighting.

In the event of something truly unusual, report the sighting to those maintaining the region's birding hotline.

Sharing is fundamental to birding. Here the late Louis Banker shows an incipient birder the field guide description of the bird that she's been watching. *Linda Dunne.*

In front of the Porthcressa Pub on England's Scilly Islands, British "Twitchers" post notice of rare and unusual birds on the blackboard. Note the Veery! A hot bird in the United Kingdom. *Linda Dunne.*

The Birder's "Walkie-Talkie": FRS Radios

You've seen them: those brightly colored radios in the fists of children running ahead of their beleaguered parents. It was only a matter of time before birders figured out that these short-range communication devices could be used to communicate the whereabouts of birds in the field.

FRS stands for "Family Radio Service." In 1997 the Federal Communications Commission (FCC) allocated the 462–267-megahertz portion of the UHF spectrum for personal, noncommercial use. To access this high-frequency, high-quality set of airwaves, FRS radios must be designed according to strict FCC standards; hence the small, permanently affixed antennae and limited power.

No license is required to operate these .5 watt radios, which purport to have a range of half a mile to one mile, *depending on terrain.* Terrain is key: the maximum range is possible only in flat, line-of-sight conditions. Between cars or in hilly areas, range can decrease. Still, these radios can be enormously helpful in many birding situations. Groups of birders use them between cars, not only to plan stops but to point out birds that might be missed by those traveling in another car. As long as everyone is set on the same channel and within range, there is no limit to the number of radios a group can utilize.

For locating a particular bird, these FRS radios are superb. Birders fan out until the target bird is found, then everyone reconnoiters. If a locale has different viewing sites within radio range, a group can split up and keep each other abreast as to what they are seeing.

Wisely, the American Birding Association (ABA) quickly had a panel make recommendations about the channels and subchannels that birders should use: 11/22, or Channel 11, subchannel 22. (Most FRS radios offer fourteen channels; birders should not get the one-channel versions.) Older FRS radios may not offer subchannels; in that case, use Channel 11. The beauty of standardizing is that a birder can travel across the United States monitoring 11/22 and by "eavesdropping" or simply asking on-air birders, stumble upon some great birds.

A new type of radio called FRS/GMRS (General Mobile Radio Service) has two watts of power and claims to have a range of up to five miles. An FCC license (but no exam) is required, as well as a fee ($50 application fee plus $35 for five years). These hybrids offer the FRS frequencies for short range and the GMRS frequencies for longer distances, so birders can still utilize the 11/22 ABA protocol. The higher power consumes more batteries and these radios cost more than FRS-only radios. Although the license and fee requirement may be waived in the future, the present hassle and cost may not be worth it; most birders report that the FRS radios are adequate for their needs.

A few notes on etiquette and features that birders may want to consider. Different models offer different "call" signals — that is, the way one caller contacts another. Unfortunately for birders in the field, many have a beep, which, if the radio is turned up high, can be loud enough to startle a bird (or the birders, who then jump and startle the bird). Try to find a model that offers a vibrating option, or at the very least develop the habit of turning the volume down when you finish speaking so that the next beep is relatively quiet. Birders tend to be rough on equipment, so choose a durable model, paying attention to how the antenna is attached.

As a birder as well as a hiker, I'm annoyed by unnecessary — particularly *loud* and unnecessary — radio chatter. It is bad enough to overhear gossip about Jackie's nasty divorce from the stranger on her cell phone shopping in the same aisle at the grocery store; ditto, on the trail to Madera Canyon.

Trust birders to latch on to whatever technology helps them "get the bird." And if you fall down and sprain an ankle while searching for your life Eared Quetzal, it's kind of nice to know that chances are there is someone within half a mile who can come to your aid.

— **Peggy Wang**

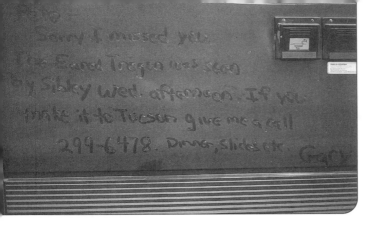

No paper? Got an update on a hot bird? A bird tour leader left this message on our van, parked in a motel lot after we'd turned in for the night. *Linda Dunne.*

DOCUMENTING RARITIES — COURTESY'S NEXT LEVEL

Birds that are *very* unusual, or *very* desirable, should be reported to the regional hotline. Those that have been designated a **review list species** by a state or region's rare bird or bird records committee invite a detailed description — a "species write-up" — that can be kept on file.

HOW DO I KNOW IF A BIRD IS RARE? HOW DO I REPORT IT?

If a bird is designated "rare," "accidental," or "hypothetical" on local or regional checklists (or is not found on the checklist at all!), it deserves reporting.

States and provinces have records or rarity committees that compile these reports. Your description should include:

1. The location, date, and time of your observation
2. A complete description of the birds, including key field marks noted (including any vocalizations)
3. A description of the habitat and the bird's behavior
4. The duration of your study, proximity to the bird, and viewing conditions
5. Your previous experience with the species and/or similar species
6. Your name, address, and telephone number so that you can be contacted if there are any questions

7. Any other information that you feel is pertinent and supports your identification

Often checklists tell you how and where to report unusual sightings. Those who operate a birding hotline will also be in touch with the records committee and can tell you where to send your report.

Do I Have to Report a Rare Bird?

No, you don't have to report your sightings. Birders are a community, not a totalitarian state. But rare birds are, by definition, *rare*. The occasions on which you may be called upon to offer details of a sighting will be few. For the sake of those who share their interest, and as a way of offering compensation for knowledge that they have drawn from the birding community at large, documenting rare birds is just something that all birders should do.

You say you haven't tapped the resources of the birding community? Think again. Do you think the elements of this book were spun from air?

Courtesy to Nonbirders

You would be hard-pressed to find a community of people more genial and more considerate than birders. Ironically, it is the benign nature of birders and their activity that sometimes leads them to inconvenience nonbirders. Since they harbor no thoughts of troubling anyone with their activity, they are frequently oblivious when they do.

The American Birding Association has established a code of ethics (see appendix 4) for birders. As someone whose birding is conducted in a place where the activities of thousands of birders and nonbirders overlap, I recommend the following additional rules:

1. Private property means just that. Benign intent is not a license to trespass.

2. Being quiet is simple courtesy. In residential areas, before 9:00 A.M., keep voices low and vehicle noises to a minimum.

3. Never, never, *never* stop your vehicle in a traffic lane to view birds. Always pull completely onto the shoulder.

4. Be careful not to point optics toward people or houses. It is intrusive, and your intentions may be misconstrued.

5. Be courteous and deferential to people engaged in other wildlife-related pursuits. They are allies, not rivals.

6. Express gratitude to individuals, institutions, and businesses that go out of their way to accommodate your interest or needs.

7. Share your excitement with nonbirders. Let them know how important open space and the natural environment are to you and to wildlife.

Conservation

You cannot be interested in birds and not concern yourself with their protection or welfare. Similarly, you cannot be concerned about birds and not be protective of the environment that sustains them.

Whatever your political leanings, however much your opinions are molded by other salient social, philosophical, and economic concerns, one thing is certain: the environment is *not* just one more interest competing among many. The environment is the playing field upon which all interests compete.

Over much of the planet, even in our own back yards, many bird species are playing a losing game. For them to have a viable place in this world, it is incumbent on birders to take their side of the field and support efforts that will ensure their well-being.

There are many organizations with a conservation mission that take a primary interest in birds and are actively courting your membership. They differ in their geographic scope, their species orientation, and their approach to meeting the needs of birds (research, habitat protection, legislative action, environmental education). All were engendered by some manifest need that defined their original goals. Some have roots that go back over a century — tapping the

The Honored Badge of Our Order

Bird watching and bird conservation are irrevocably bound. One of bird conservation's most effective tools is economic persuasion. Birders spend hundreds of millions of dollars every year in the pursuit of birds — much of it on travel-related expenses.

Communities that enjoy proximity to birding areas reap the economic benefits of visiting birders. The beneficiaries range from restaurant and motel owners to gas station attendants and muffler shop managers, to the drug store proprietors and counter clerks who dish out ice cream on hot days.

These people are also the ones who affect regional land use decisions via the voting box and by word of mouth. When they recognize how much of their trade comes from birders, they naturally become more interested in maintaining natural areas. The problem is that when birders remove their binoculars, they look pretty much like everyone else. Their interest in a region's natural attractions goes unnoticed.

The solution is simple. *Wherever you go, wear your binoculars!* Bring them into the restaurant. Sling them under an arm when you saunter into the convenience store. Birding and binoculars are synonymous. And never miss an opportunity to tell the person serving you what you are doing in his or her area and why.

Some birders and birding organizations have even gone to the trouble of printing up "business" cards to leave on lunch counters or in hotel rooms. While wording varies, the message is the same: "Hi. I'm a birder attracted to your area because of its natural resources. Protect the area, and the birds who live here, and I'll be back."

—**P.D.**

wellspring of concern and need that was the foundation of the conservation movement (and birding).

As explained in the first chapter, birders are hybrids, the product of a marriage between ornithologists and nature lovers (a.k.a. conservationists). While much has changed in the one hundred years since this union was formed, one thing has not: the need to protect birds and their habitat. We are fortunate to live in this age, when we can be the beneficiaries of one hundred years of conservation-mindedness. But unless this thinking and this initiative continue, all the victories of the past will become Pyrrhic.

You cannot be interested in birds and not be concerned for their welfare. You cannot be concerned for their welfare and not want to protect their habitat. These signs at Point Pelee National Park in Ontario were posted to keep overzealous birders on the trails. *Linda Dunne.*

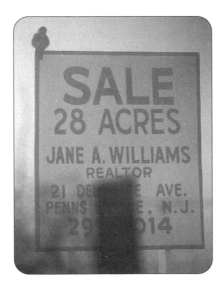

By the signs, it seems that another American Kestrel is about to be evicted. *Pete Dunne.*

Choosing Your Allies

While many organizations have my sympathy, only a few enjoy my support. My resources are limited, and I have to be selective. I find it most effective to choose organizations that support my specific interests. Here are the qualities I look for when deciding which organizations to support.

"Environment" is a broad-brush term, used in promotional literature to cover everything from water quality to habitat protection to lawn care. Determine exactly what an organization's mission is and whether it is in accord with your own.

Personally, I'm drawn to organizations that dedicate funds and effort toward habitat acquisition and those that engage in primary research. I also like organizations that have a global awareness but a defining focus — on this group of birds or that critical habitat. Some organizations with a global perspective, however, have internal bureaucracies to match. Unless a large conservation organization is *very focused* and *very specific* in its mission, a lot of funds are going to get eaten up by its bureaucracy.

This is also why I favor small, medium-sized, or relatively young organizations — those whose original focus has not been diluted, and those that have their infrastructure in place but still maintain a fire in their belly.

How can you tell whether an organization is performing? Read its published material. Check its Web site. If the focus is on what the organization has accomplished in the past, or the material is big on "threats" but vague on real action, be cautious. If the focus is on specific projects that the group is currently engaged in, and these projects are in accord with your conservation interests, give the organization your support.

I also want to hear about the organization I support. If the only time I learn about an organization's "good work" is through its literature, I'm suspicious. If I see its name in print — in newspapers, in magazines, as a witness at a hearing or as the organizer of an event that fosters environmental awareness — I know I've picked a winner.

There is one more thing I look for, something that is easy to define and not hard to perceive: *attitude*. I want the environmental organizations I support to be positive about the future and to believe that their efforts will make a better world. An organization that is all doom and gloom is already admitting defeat. That is not how I regard the future or the future of birds and birding. That is not an attitude I care to foster or support.

— P.D.

PASSING THE GLASS

If you have reached this point in the book, one thing is certain: you are a birder in fact and in spirit, and that is one of the best things a person can ever hope to be. There is one more thing you can do that will make your birding more satisfying: pass your enthusiasm and knowledge on to others.

Like who? Like the in-law who recently moved to the suburbs . . . the parent who just retired and is casting about for something to enliven her life . . . that cute new employee over in International Sales whom you have been trying to maneuver into conversation . . . the niece or nephew who "really likes nature" but doesn't have the latitude to wander woodlands and fields alone.

Even more than adults, young birders benefit from the guidance of mentors. Even if your birding skills are not superbly refined, your enthusiasm alone might be the catalyst that sparks someone else's life-long interest.

So share your skills. While birding has a great deal to do with birds, it has everything to do with people.

One of them is you.

Birders should always make the welfare of birds their first concern. Common sense and a sensitivity to the stress levels of birds are usually all that is required. Using recorded calls to attract birds is effective but not encouraged; however, in certain circumstances it may be less intrusive than other actions taken to gain a glimpse of a bird. Reporting interesting or uncommon species to other birders is common courtesy, and offering detailed descriptions of rare birds is standard practice. Birders should maintain high ethical standards and not use their avocation as an excuse to infringe upon the rights of others. Conservation of birds and their habitat is every birder's concern, and supporting organizations that work toward these ends is in every birder's interest. It is every birder's privilege to pass on his or her enthusiasm and knowledge to others.

American Birding Association
Checklist for the Birds of North America

(ALL OF NORTH AMERICA NORTH OF MEXICO AND ADJACENT WATERS TO A DISTANCE OF TWO HUNDRED MILES)

KEY:

N   Native (breeding) species
V   Visitor (nonbreeding)
I   Introduced
E   Extinct

Code 1: Birds that occur routinely
Code 2: Birds that occur regularly but are secretive or occur in low densities
Code 3: Birds that occur annually, are rare, but may occur in low numbers
Code 4: Birds that occur irregularly but with six or more total records, including at least three in the past 30 years
Code 5: Accidentals recorded five or fewer times, wih fewer than three times in the past 30 years
Code 6: Birds presumed extinct or extirpated from ABA Area, or survivors held in captivity

Order: Gaviiformes
FAMILY: GAVIIDAE (LOONS)

__ Red-throated Loon	*Gavia stellata*	N	1
__ Arctic Loon	*Gavia arctica*	N	2
__ Pacific Loon	*Gavia pacifica*	N	1
__ Common Loon	*Gavia immer*	N	1
__ Yellow-billed Loon	*Gavia adamsii*	N	2

Order: Podicipediformes
FAMILY: PODICIPEDIDAE (GREBES)

__ Least Grebe	*Tachybaptus dominicus*	N	2

_ Pied-billed Grebe	*Podilymbus podiceps*	N	1
_ Horned Grebe	*Podiceps auritus*	N	1
_ Red-necked Grebe	*Podiceps grisegena*	N	1
_ Eared Grebe	*Podiceps nigricollis*	N	1
_ Western Grebe	*Aechmophorus occidentalis*	N	1
_ Clark's Grebe	*Aechmophorus clarkii*	N	1

Order: Procellariiformes

FAMILY: DIOMEDEIDAE (ALBATROSSES)

_ Yellow-nosed Albatross	*Thalassarche chlororhynchos*	V	4
_ Shy Albatross	*Thalassarche cauta*	V	4
_ Black-browed Albatross	*Thalassarche melanophris*	V	5
_ Wandering Albatross	*Diomedea exulans*	V	5
_ Laysan Albatross	*Phoebastria immutabilis*	V	2
_ Black-footed Albatross	*Phoebastria nigripes*	V	1
_ Short-tailed Albatross	*Phoebastria albatrus*	V	3

FAMILY: PROCELLARIIDAE (SHEARWATERS AND PETRELS)

_ Northern Fulmar	*Fulmarus glacialis*	N	1
_ Herald Petrel	*Pterodroma arminjoniana*	V	3
_ Murphy's Petrel	*Pterodroma ultima*	V	3
_ Mottled Petrel	*Pterodroma inexpectata*	V	3
_ Bermuda Petrel	*Pterodroma cahow*	V	4
_ Black-capped Petrel	*Pterodroma hasitata*	V	2
_ Fea's Petrel	*Pterodroma feae*	V	3
_ Cook's Petrel	*Pterodroma cookii*	V	2
_ Stejneger's Petrel	*Pterodroma longirostris*	V	4
_ Bulwer's Petrel	*Pterodroma bulwerii*	V	5
_ Streaked Shearwater	*Calonectris leucomelas*	V	4
_ Cory's Shearwater	*Calonectris diomedea*	V	1
_ Pink-footed Shearwater	*Puffinus creatopus*	V	1
_ Flesh-footed Shearwater	*Puffinus carneipes*	V	3
_ Greater Shearwater	*Puffinus gravis*	V	1
_ Wedge-tailed Shearwater	*Puffinus pacificus*	V	4
_ Buller's Shearwater	*Puffinus bulleri*	V	2
_ Sooty Shearwater	*Puffinus griseus*	V	1
_ Short-tailed Shearwater	*Puffinus tenuirostris*	V	2
_ Manx Shearwater	*Puffinus puffinus*	N	2
_ Black-vented Shearwater	*Puffinus opisthomelas*	V	2
_ Audubon's Shearwater	*Puffinus lherminieri*	V	1
_ Little Shearwater	*Puffinus assimilis*	V	5

FAMILY: HYDROBATIDAE (STORM-PETRELS)

__ Wilson's Storm-Petrel	*Oceanites oceanicus*	V	1
__ White-faced Storm-Petrel	*Pelagodroma marina*	V	4
__ European Storm-Petrel	*Hydrobates pelagicus*	V	5
__ Fork-tailed Storm-Petrel	*Oceanodroma furcata*	N	2
__ Leach's Storm-Petrel	*Oceanodroma leucorhoa*	N	1
__ Ashy Storm-Petrel	*Oceanodroma homochroa*	N	2
__ Band-rumped Storm-Petrel	*Oceanodroma castro*	V	2
__ Wedge-rumped Storm-Petrel	*Oceanodroma tethys*	V	5
__ Black Storm-Petrel	*Oceanodroma melania*	N	2
__ Least Storm-Petrel	*Oceanodroma microsoma*	V	2

Order: Pelecaniformes

FAMILY: PHAETHONTIDAE (TROPICBIRDS)

__ White-tailed Tropicbird	*Phaethon lepturus*	V	3
__ Red-billed Tropicbird	*Phaethon aethereus*	V	3
__ Red-tailed Tropicbird	*Phaethon rubricauda*	V	4

FAMILY: SULIDAE (BOOBIES AND GANNETS)

__ Masked Booby	*Sula dactylatra*	N	3
__ Blue footed Booby	*Sula nebouxii*	V	4
__ Brown Booby	*Sula leucogaster*	V	3
__ Red-footed Booby	*Sula sula*	V	4
__ Northern Gannet	*Morus bassanus*	N	1

FAMILY: PELECANIDAE (PELICANS)

__ American White Pelican	*Pelecanus erythrorhynchos*	N	1
__ Brown Pelican	*Pelecanus occidentalis*	N	1

FAMILY: PHALACROCORACIDAE (CORMORANTS)

__ Brandt's Cormorant	*Phalacrocorax penicillatus*	N	1
__ Neotropic Cormorant	*Phalacrocorax brasilianus*	N	1
__ Double-crested Cormorant	*Phalacrocorax auritus*	N	1
__ Great Cormorant	*Phalacrocorax carbo*	N	1
__ Red-faced Cormorant	*Phalacrocorax urile*	N	2
__ Pelagic Cormorant	*Phalacrocorax pelagicus*	N	1

FAMILY: ANHINGIDAE (DARTERS)

__ Anhinga	*Anhinga anhinga*	N	1

FAMILY: FREGATIDAE (FRIGATEBIRDS)

__ Magnificent Frigatebird	*Fregata magnificens*	N	1
__ Great Frigatebird	*Fregata minor*	V	4
__ Lesser Frigatebird	*Fregata ariel*	V	5

Order: Ciconiiformes

__ American Bittern	Botaurus lentiginosus	N	1
__ Yellow Bittern	Ixobrychus sinensis	V	5
__ Least Bittern	Ixobrychus exilis	N	1
__ Great Blue Heron	Ardea herodias	N	1
__ Great Egret	Ardea alba	N	1
__ Chinese Egret	Egretta eulophotes	V	5
__ Little Egret	Egretta garzetta	V	4
__ Western Reef-Heron	Egretta gularis	V	5
__ Snowy Egret	Egretta thula	N	1
__ Little Blue Heron	Egretta caerulea	N	1
__ Tricolored Heron	Egretta tricolor	N	1
__ Reddish Egret	Egretta rufescens	N	1
__ Cattle Egret	Bubulcus ibis	N	1
__ Chinese Pond-Heron	Ardeola bacchus	V	5
__ Green Heron	Butorides virescens	N	1
__ Black-crowned Night-Heron	Nycticorax nycticorax	N	1
__ Yellow-crowned Night-Heron	Nyctanassa violacea	N	1

FAMILY: THRESKIORNITHIDAE (IBISES AND SPOONBILLS)

__ White Ibis	Eudocimus albus	N	1
__ Scarlet Ibis	Eudocimus ruber	V	5
__ Glossy Ibis	Plegadis falcinellus	N	1
__ White-faced Ibis	Plegadis chihi	N	1
__ Roseate Spoonbill	Ajaia ajaja	N	1

FAMILY: CICONIIDAE (STORKS)

__ Jabiru	Jabiru mycteria	V	5
__ Wood Stork	Mycteria americana	N	1

FAMILY: CATHARTIDAE (NEW WORLD VULTURES)

__ Black Vulture	Coragyps atratus	N	1
__ Turkey Vulture	Cathartes aura	N	1
__ California Condor	Gymnogyps californianus	N	6

Order: Phoenicopteriformes

FAMILY: PHOENICOPTERIDAE (FLAMINGOES)

__ Greater Flamingo	Phoenicopterus ruber	V	3

Order: Anseriformes

FAMILY: ANATIDAE (DUCKS, GEESE, AND SWANS)

__ Black-bellied Whistling-Duck	Dendrocygna autumnalis	N	1
__ Fulvous Whistling-Duck	Dendrocygna bicolor	N	1

__ Bean Goose	*Anser fabalis*	V	3
__ Pink-footed Goose	*Anser brachyrhynchus*	V	4
__ Greater White-fronted Goose	*Anser albifrons*	N	1
__ Lesser White-fronted Goose	*Anser erythropus*	V	5
__ Emperor Goose	*Chen canagica*	N	2
__ Snow Goose	*Chen caerulescens*	N	1
__ Ross's Goose	*Chen rossii*	N	1
__ Canada Goose	*Branta canadensis*	N	1
__ Brant	*Branta bernicla*	N	1
__ Barnacle Goose	*Branta leucopsis*	V	5
__ Mute Swan	*Cygnus olor*	I	1
__ Trumpeter Swan	*Cygnus buccinator*	N	1
__ Tundra Swan	*Cygnus columbianus*	N	1
__ Whooper Swan	*Cygnus cygnus*	N	3
__ Muscovy Duck	*Cairina moschata*	V	3
__ Wood Duck	*Aix sponsa*	N	1
__ Gadwall	*Anas strepera*	N	1
__ Falcated Duck	*Anas falcata*	V	4
__ Eurasian Wigeon	*Anas penelope*	V	3
__ American Wigeon	*Anas americana*	N	1
__ American Black Duck	*Anas rubripes*	N	1
__ Mallard	*Anas platyrhynchos*	N	1
__ Mottled Duck	*Anas fulvigula*	N	1
__ Spot-billed Duck	*Anas poecilorhyncha*	V	5
__ Blue-winged Teal	*Anas discors*	N	1
__ Cinnamon Teal	*Anas cyanoptera*	N	1
__ Northern Shoveler	*Anas clypeata*	N	1
__ White-cheeked Pintail	*Anas bahamensis*	V	4
__ Northern Pintail	*Anas acuta*	N	1
__ Garganey	*Anas querquedula*	V	3
__ Baikal Teal	*Anas formosa*	V	4
__ Green-winged Teal	*Anas crecca*	N	1
__ Canvasback	*Aythya valisineria*	N	1
__ Redhead	*Aythya americana*	N	1
__ Common Pochard	*Aythya ferina*	V	3
__ Ring-necked Duck	*Aythya collaris*	N	1
__ Tufted Duck	*Aythya fuligula*	V	3
__ Greater Scaup	*Aythya marila*	N	1
__ Lesser Scaup	*Aythya affinis*	N	1
__ Steller's Eider	*Polysticta stelleri*	N	2
__ Spectacled Eider	*Somateria fischeri*	N	2

_ King Eider	*Somateria spectabilis*	N	1
_ Common Eider	*Somateria mollissima*	N	1
_ Harlequin Duck	*Histrionicus histrionicus*	N	1
_ Labrador Duck	*Camptorhynchus labradorius*	E	6
_ Surf Scoter	*Melanitta perspicillata*	N	1
_ White-winged Scoter	*Melanitta fusca*	N	1
_ Black Scoter	*Melanitta nigra*	N	1
_ Long-tailed Duck	*Clangula hyemalis*	N	1
_ Bufflehead	*Bucephala albeola*	N	1
_ Common Goldeneye	*Bucephala clangula*	N	1
_ Barrow's Goldeneye	*Bucephala islandica*	N	1
_ Smew	*Mergellus albellus*	V	3
_ Hooded Merganser	*Lophodytes cucullatus*	N	1
_ Common Merganser	*Mergus merganser*	N	1
_ Red-breasted Merganser	*Mergus serrator*	N	1
_ Masked Duck	*Nomonyx dominicus*	N	3
_ Ruddy Duck	*Oxyura jamaicensis*	N	1

Order: Falconiformes
FAMILY: ACCIPITRIDAE (HAWKS, KITES, EAGLES, AND ALLIES)

_ Osprey	*Pandion haliaetus*	N	1
_ Hook-billed Kite	*Chondrohierax uncinatus*	N	3
_ Swallow-tailed Kite	*Elanoides forficatus*	N	1
_ White-tailed Kite	*Elanus leucurus*	N	1
_ Snail Kite	*Rostrhamus sociabilis*	N	2
_ Mississippi Kite	*Ictinia mississippiensis*	N	1
_ Bald Eagle	*Haliaeetus leucocephalus*	N	1
_ White-tailed Eagle	*Haliaeetus albicilla*	N	4
_ Steller's Sea-Eagle	*Haliaeetus pelagicus*	V	4
_ Northern Harrier	*Circus cyaneus*	N	1
_ Sharp-shinned Hawk	*Accipiter striatus*	N	1
_ Cooper's Hawk	*Accipiter cooperii*	N	1
_ Northern Goshawk	*Accipiter gentilis*	N	1
_ Crane Hawk	*Geranospiza caerulescens*	V	5
_ Gray Hawk	*Asturina nitida*	N	2
_ Common Black-Hawk	*Buteogallus anthracinus*	N	2
_ Harris's Hawk	*Parabuteo unicinctus*	N	1
_ Roadside Hawk	*Buteo magnirostris*	V	4
_ Red-shouldered Hawk	*Buteo lineatus*	N	1
_ Broad-winged Hawk	*Buteo platypterus*	N	1
_ Short-tailed Hawk	*Buteo brachyurus*	N	2

_ Swainson's Hawk	*Buteo swainsoni*	N	1
_ White-tailed Hawk	*Buteo albicaudatus*	N	2
_ Zone-tailed Hawk	*Buteo albonotatus*	N	2
_ Red-tailed Hawk	*Buteo jamaicensis*	N	1
_ Ferruginous Hawk	*Buteo regalis*	N	1
_ Rough-legged Hawk	*Buteo lagopus*	N	1
_ Golden Eagle	*Aquila chrysaetos*	N	1

FAMILY: FALCONIDAE (CARACARAS AND FALCONS)

_ Collared Forest-Falcon	*Micrastur semitorquatus*	V	5
_ Crested Caracara	*Caracara plancus*	N	1
_ Eurasian Kestrel	*Falco tinnunculus*	V	4
_ American Kestrel	*Falco sparverius*	N	1
_ Merlin	*Falco columbarius*	N	1
_ Eurasian Hobby	*Falco subbuteo*	V	4
_ Aplomado Falcon	*Falco femoralis*	N	4
_ Gyrfalcon	*Falco rusticolus*	N	2
_ Peregrine Falcon	*Falco peregrinus*	N	1
_ Prairie Falcon	*Falco mexicanus*	N	1

Order: Galliformes

FAMILY: CRACIDAE (CURASSOWS AND GUANS)

| _ Plain Chachalaca | *Ortalis vetula* | N | 2 |

FAMILY: PHASIANIDAE (PARTRIDGES, GROUSE, TURKEYS, AND OLD WORLD QUAIL)

_ Chukar	*Alectoris chukar*	I	2
_ Himalayan Snowcock	*Tetraogallus himalayensis*	I	2
_ Gray Partridge	*Perdix perdix*	I	2
_ Ring-necked Pheasant	*Phasianus colchicus*	I	1
_ Ruffed Grouse	*Bonasa umbellus*	N	1
_ Gunnison Sage-Grouse	*Centrocercus minimus*	N	1
_ Greater Sage-Grouse	*Centrocerus urophasianus*	N	2
_ Spruce Grouse	*Falcipennis canadensis*	N	2
_ Willow Ptarmigan	*Lagopus lagopus*	N	1
_ Rock Ptarmigan	*Lagopus mutus*	N	1
_ White-tailed Ptarmigan	*Lagopus leucurus*	N	2
_ Blue Grouse	*Dendragapus obscurus*	N	2
_ Sharp-tailed Grouse	*Tympanuchus phasianellus*	N	2
_ Greater Prairie-Chicken	*Tympanuchus cupido*	N	2
_ Lesser Prairie-Chicken	*Tympanuchus pallidicinctus*	N	2
_ Wild Turkey	*Meleagris gallopavo*	N	1

FAMILY: ODONTOPHORIDAE (NEW WORLD QUAIL)

_ Mountain Quail	*Oreortyx pictus*	N	1
_ Scaled Quail	*Callipepla squamata*	N	1
_ California Quail	*Callipepla californica*	N	1
_ Gambel's Quail	*Callipepla gambelii*	N	1
_ Northern Bobwhite	*Colinus virginianus*	N	1
_ Montezuma Quail	*Cyrtonyx montezumae*	N	2

Order: Gruiformes

FAMILY: RALLIDAE (RAILS, GALLINULES, AND COOTS)

_ Yellow Rail	*Coturnicops noveboracensis*	N	2
_ Black Rail	*Laterallus jamaicensis*	N	2
_ Corn Crake	*Crex crex*	V	5
_ Clapper Rail	*Rallus longirostris*	N	1
_ King Rail	*Rallus elegans*	N	1
_ Virginia Rail	*Rallus limicola*	N	1
_ Sora	*Porzana carolina*	N	1
_ Paint-billed Crake	*Neocrex erythrops*	V	5
_ Spotted Rail	*Pardirallus maculatus*	V	5
_ Purple Gallinule	*Porphyrula martinica*	N	1
_ Common Moorhen	*Gallinula chloropus*	N	1
_ Eurasian Coot	*Fulica atra*	V	5
_ American Coot	*Fulica americana*	N	1

FAMILY: ARAMIDAE (LIMPKINS)

_ Limpkin	*Aramus guarauna*	N	2

FAMILY: GRUIDAE (CRANES)

_ Sandhill Crane	*Grus canadensis*	N	1
_ Common Crane	*Grus grus*	V	4
_ Whooping Crane	*Grus americana*	N	2

Order: Charadriiformes

FAMILY: BURHINIDAE (THICK-KNEES)

_ Double-striped Thick-knee	*Burhinus bistriatus*	V	5

FAMILY: CHARADRIIDAE (LAPWINGS AND PLOVERS)

_ Northern Lapwing	*Vanellus vanellus*	V	4
_ Black-bellied Plover	*Pluvialis squatarola*	N	1
_ European Golden-Plover	*Pluvialis apricaria*	V	4
_ American Golden-Plover	*Pluvialis dominica*	N	1
_ Pacific Golden-Plover	*Pluvialis fulva*	N	2
_ Mongolian Plover	*Charadrius mongolus*	N	3
_ Collared Plover	*Charadrius collaris*	V	5

_ Snowy Plover	*Charadrius alexandrinus*	N	1
_ Wilson's Plover	*Charadrius wilsonia*	N	1
_ Common Ringed Plover	*Charadrius hiaticula*	N	2
_ Semipalmated Plover	*Charadrius semipalmatus*	N	1
_ Piping Plover	*Charadrius melodus*	N	2
_ Little Ringed Plover	*Charadrius dubius*	V	4
_ Killdeer	*Charadrius vociferus*	N	1
_ Mountain Plover	*Charadrius montanus*	N	2
_ Eurasian Dotterel	*Charadrius morinellus*	N	4

FAMILY: HAEMATOPODIDAE (OYSTERCATCHERS)

_ Eurasian Oystercatcher	*Haematopus ostralegus*	V	5
_ American Oystercatcher	*Haematopus palliatus*	N	1
_ Black Oystercatcher	*Haematopus bachmani*	N	1

FAMILY: RECURVIROSTRIDAE (STILTS AND AVOCETS)

_ Black-winged Stilt	*Himantopus himantopus*	V	5
_ Black-necked Stilt	*Himantopus mexicanus*	N	1
_ American Avocet	*Recurvirostra americana*	N	1

FAMILY: JACANIDAE (JACANAS)

| _ Northern Jacana | *Jacana spinosa* | N | 4 |

FAMILY: SCOLOPACIDAE
(SANDPIPERS, PHALAROPES, AND ALLIES)

_ Common Greenshank	*Tringa nebularia*	V	3
_ Greater Yellowlegs	*Tringa melanoleuca*	N	1
_ Lesser Yellowlegs	*Tringa flavipes*	N	1
_ Marsh Sandpiper	*Tringa stagnatilis*	V	5
_ Common Redshank	*Tringa totanus*	V	4
_ Spotted Redshank	*Tringa erythropus*	V	4
_ Wood Sandpiper	*Tringa glareola*	N	2
_ Green Sandpiper	*Tringa ochropus*	V	4
_ Solitary Sandpiper	*Tringa solitaria*	N	1
_ Willet	*Catoptrophorus semipalmatus*	N	1
_ Wandering Tattler	*Heteroscelus incanus*	N	1
_ Gray-tailed Tattler	*Heteroscelus brevipes*	V	3
_ Common Sandpiper	*Actitis hypoleucos*	V	3
_ Spotted Sandpiper	*Actitis macularia*	N	1
_ Terek Sandpiper	*Xenus cinereus*	V	3
_ Upland Sandpiper	*Bartramia longicauda*	N	1
_ Little Curlew	*Numenius minutus*	V	4
_ Eskimo Curlew	*Numenius borealis*	N	6
_ Whimbrel	*Numenius phaeopus*	N	1
_ Bristle-thighed Curlew	*Numenius tahitiensis*	N	2

__ Far Eastern Curlew	*Numenius madagascariensis*	V	4
__ Slender-billed Curlew	*Numenius tenuirostris*	V	6
__ Eurasian Curlew	*Numenius arquata*	V	5
__ Long-billed Curlew	*Numenius americanus*	N	1
__ Black-tailed Godwit	*Limosa limosa*	V	3
__ Hudsonian Godwit	*Limosa haemastica*	N	1
__ Bar-tailed Godwit	*Limosa lapponica*	N	2
__ Marbled Godwit	*Limosa fedoa*	N	1
__ Ruddy Turnstone	*Arenaria interpres*	N	1
__ Black Turnstone	*Arenaria melanocephala*	N	1
__ Surfbird	*Aphriza virgata*	N	1
__ Great Knot	*Calidris tenuirostris*	V	4
__ Red Knot	*Calidris canutus*	N	1
__ Sanderling	*Calidris alba*	N	1
__ Semipalmated Sandpiper	*Calidris pusilla*	N	1
__ Western Sandpiper	*Calidris mauri*	N	1
__ Red-necked Stint	*Calidris ruficollis*	N	3
__ Little Stint	*Calidris minuta*	V	4
__ Temminck's Stint	*Calidris temminckii*	V	3
__ Long-toed Stint	*Calidris subminuta*	V	3
__ Least Sandpiper	*Calidris minutilla*	N	1
__ White-rumped Sandpiper	*Calidris fuscicollis*	N	1
__ Baird's Sandpiper	*Calidris bairdii*	N	1
__ Pectoral Sandpiper	*Calidris melanotos*	N	1
__ Sharp-tailed Sandpiper	*Calidris acuminata*	V	3
__ Purple Sandpiper	*Calidris maritima*	N	1
__ Rock Sandpiper	*Calidris ptilocnemis*	N	2
__ Dunlin	*Calidris alpina*	N	1
__ Curlew Sandpiper	*Calidris ferruginea*	N	3
__ Stilt Sandpiper	*Calidris himantopus*	N	1
__ Spoonbill Sandpiper	*Eurynorhynchus pygmeus*	V	4
__ Broad-billed Sandpiper	*Limicola falcinellus*	V	5
__ Buff-breasted Sandpiper	*Tryngites subruficollis*	N	1
__ Ruff	*Philomachus pugnax*	N	3
__ Short-billed Dowitcher	*Limnodromus griseus*	N	1
__ Long-billed Dowitcher	*Limnodromus scolopaceus*	N	1
__ Jack Snipe	*Lymnocryptes minimus*	V	5
__ Wilson's Snipe	*Gallinago delicata*	N	3
__ Common Snipe	*Gallinago gallinago*	V	5
__ Pin-tailed Snipe	*Gallinago stenura*	V	5
__ Eurasian Woodcock	*Scolopax rusticola*	V	5

__ American Woodcock	*Scolopax minor*	N	1
__ Wilson's Phalarope	*Phalaropus tricolor*	N	1
__ Red-necked Phalarope	*Phalaropus lobatus*	N	1
__ Red Phalarope	*Phalaropus fulicarius*	N	1
FAMILY: GLAREOLIDAE (PRATINCOLES)			
__ Oriental Pratincole	*Glareola maldivarum*	V	5
FAMILY: LARIDAE (SKUAS, GULLS, TERNS, AND SKIMMERS)			
__ Great Skua	*Catharacta skua*	V	3
__ South Polar Skua	*Catharacta maccormicki*	V	2
__ Pomarine Jaeger	*Stercorarius pomarinus*	N	1
__ Parasitic Jaeger	*Stercorarius parasiticus*	N	1
__ Long-tailed Jaeger	*Stercorarius longicaudus*	N	1
__ Laughing Gull	*Larus atricilla*	N	1
__ Franklin's Gull	*Larus pipixcan*	N	1
__ Little Gull	*Larus minutus*	N	3
__ Black-headed Gull	*Larus ridibundus*	N	3
__ Bonaparte's Gull	*Larus philadelphia*	N	1
__ Heermann's Gull	*Larus heermanni*	N	1
__ Black-tailed Gull	*Larus crassirostris*	V	4
__ Mew Gull	*Larus canus*	N	1
__ Ring-billed Gull	*Larus delawarensis*	N	1
__ California Gull	*Larus californicus*	N	1
__ Herring Gull	*Larus argentatus*	N	1
__ Yellow-legged Gull	*Larus cachinnans*	V	4
__ Thayer's Gull	*Larus thayeri*	N	2
__ Iceland Gull	*Larus glaucoides*	N	2
__ Lesser Black-backed Gull	*Larus fuscus*	V	3
__ Slaty-backed Gull	*Larus schistisagus*	V	3
__ Yellow-footed Gull	*Larus livens*	V	2
__ Western Gull	*Larus occidentalis*	N	1
__ Glaucous-winged Gull	*Larus glaucescens*	N	1
__ Glaucous Gull	*Larus hyperboreus*	N	1
__ Great Black-backed Gull	*Larus marinus*	N	1
__ Kelp Gull	*Larus dominicanus*	N	4
__ Sabine's Gull	*Xema sabini*	N	1
__ Black-legged Kittiwake	*Rissa tridactyla*	N	1
__ Red-legged Kittiwake	*Rissa brevirostris*	N	2
__ Ross's Gull	*Rhodostethia rosea*	N	3
__ Ivory Gull	*Pagophila eburnea*	N	3
__ Gull-billed Tern	*Sterna nilotica*	N	1
__ Caspian Tern	*Sterna caspia*	N	1

__ Royal Tern	*Sterna maxima*	N	1
__ Elegant Tern	*Sterna elegans*	N	1
__ Sandwich Tern	*Sterna sandvicensis*	N	1
__ Roseate Tern	*Sterna dougallii*	N	2
__ Common Tern	*Sterna hirundo*	N	1
__ Arctic Tern	*Sterna paradisaea*	N	1
__ Forster's Tern	*Sterna forsteri*	N	1
__ Least Tern	*Sterna antillarum*	N	1
__ Aleutian Tern	*Sterna aleutica*	N	2
__ Bridled Tern	*Sterna anaethetus*	V	2
__ Sooty Tern	*Sterna fuscata*	N	2
__ Large-billed Tern	*Phaetusa simplex*	V	5
__ White-winged Tern	*Chlidonias leucopterus*	V	4
__ Whiskered Tern	*Chlidonias hybridus*	V	5
__ Black Tern	*Chlidonias niger*	N	1
__ Brown Noddy	*Anous stolidus*	N	2
__ Black Noddy	*Anous minutus*	V	3
__ Black Skimmer	*Rynchops niger*	N	1
FAMILY: ALCIDAE (AUKS, MURRES, AND PUFFINS)			
__ Dovekie	*Alle alle*	N	2
__ Common Murre	*Uria aalge*	N	1
__ Thick-billed Murre	*Uria lomvia*	N	1
__ Razorbill	*Alca torda*	N	1
__ Great Auk	*Pinguinus impennis*	E	6
__ Black Guillemot	*Cepphus grylle*	N	1
__ Pigeon Guillemot	*Cepphus columba*	N	1
__ Long-billed Murrelet	*Brachyramphus perdix*	N	4
__ Marbled Murrelet	*Brachyramphus marmoratus*	N	1
__ Kittlitz's Murrelet	*Brachyramphus brevirostris*	N	2
__ Xantus's Murrelet	*Synthliboramphus hypoleucus*	N	2
__ Craveri's Murrelet	*Synthliboramphus craveri*	V	3
__ Ancient Murrelet	*Synthliboramphus antiquus*	N	2
__ Cassin's Auklet	*Ptychoramphus aleuticus*	N	1
__ Parakeet Auklet	*Aethia psittacula*	N	2
__ Least Auklet	*Aethia pusilla*	N	2
__ Whiskered Auklet	*Aethia pygmaea*	N	2
__ Crested Auklet	*Aethia cristatella*	N	2
__ Rhinoceros Auklet	*Cerorhinca monocerata*	N	1
__ Atlantic Puffin	*Fratercula arctica*	N	1
__ Horned Puffin	*Fratercula corniculata*	N	1
__ Tufted Puffin	*Fratercula cirrhata*	N	1

Order: Columbiformes

FAMILY: COLUMBIDAE (PIGEONS AND DOVES)

_ Rock Dove	_Columba livia_	I	1
_ Scaly-naped Pigeon	_Columba squamosa_	V	5
_ White-crowned Pigeon	_Columba leucocephala_	N	1
_ Red-billed Pigeon	_Columba flavirostris_	N	3
_ Band-tailed Pigeon	_Columba fasciata_	N	1
_ Oriental Turtle-Dove	_Streptopelia orientalis_	V	4
_ Eurasian Collared-Dove	_Streptopelia decaocto_	I	1
_ Spotted Dove	_Streptopelia chinensis_	I	1
_ White-winged Dove	_Zenaida asiatica_	N	1
_ Zenaida Dove	_Zenaida aurita_	V	5
_ Mourning Dove	_Zenaida macroura_	N	1
_ Passenger Pigeon	_Ectopistes migratorius_	E	6
_ Inca Dove	_Columbina inca_	N	1
_ Common Ground-Dove	_Columbina passerina_	N	1
_ Ruddy Ground-Dove	_Columbina talpacoti_	V	3
_ White-tipped Dove	_Leptotila verreauxi_	N	2
_ Key West Quail-Dove	_Geotrygon chrysia_	V	4
_ Ruddy Quail-Dove	_Geotrygon montana_	V	5

Order: Psittaciformes

FAMILY: PSITTACIDAE

(LORIES, PARAKEETS, MACAWS, AND PARROTS)

_ Budgerigar	_Melopsittacus undulatus_	I	3
_ Monk Parakeet	_Myiopsitta monachus_	I	2
_ Carolina Parakeet	_Conuropsis carolinensis_	E	6
_ Green Parakeet	_Aratinga holochlora_	I	2
_ Thick-billed Parrot	_Rhynchopsitta pachyrhyncha_	V	6
_ White-winged Parakeet	_Brotogeris versicolurus_	I	2
_ Red-crowned Parrot	_Amazona viridigenalis_	I	2

Order: Cuculiformes

FAMILY: CUCULIDAE (CUCKOOS, ROADRUNNERS, AND ANIS)

_ Common Cuckoo	_Cuculus canorus_	V	3
_ Oriental Cuckoo	_Cuculus saturatus_	V	4
_ Black-billed Cuckoo	_Coccyzus erythropthalmus_	N	1
_ Yellow-billed Cuckoo	_Coccyzus americanus_	N	1
_ Mangrove Cuckoo	_Coccyzus minor_	N	2
_ Greater Roadrunner	_Geococcyx californianus_	N	1
_ Smooth-billed Ani	_Crotophaga ani_	N	3
_ Groove-billed Ani	_Crotophaga sulcirostris_	N	2

Order: Strigiformes

FAMILY: TYTONIDAE (BARN OWLS)

__ Barn Owl	*Tyto alba*	N	1

FAMILY: STRIGIDAE (TYPICAL OWLS)

__ Flammulated Owl	*Otus flammeolus*	N	2
__ Oriental Scops-Owl	*Otus sunia*	V	5
__ Western Screech-Owl	*Otus kennicottii*	N	1
__ Eastern Screech-Owl	*Otus asio*	N	1
__ Whiskered Screech-Owl	*Otus trichopsis*	N	2
__ Great Horned Owl	*Bubo virginianus*	N	1
__ Snowy Owl	*Nyctea scandiaca*	N	2
__ Northern Hawk Owl	*Surnia ulula*	N	2
__ Northern Pygmy-Owl	*Glaucidium gnoma*	N	2
__ Ferruginous Pygmy-Owl	*Glaucidium brasilianum*	N	3
__ Elf Owl	*Micrathene whitneyi*	N	2
__ Burrowing Owl	*Athene cunicularia*	N	1
__ Mottled Owl	*Ciccaba virgata*	V	5
__ Spotted Owl	*Strix occidentalis*	N	2
__ Barred Owl	*Strix varia*	N	1
__ Great Gray Owl	*Strix nebulosa*	N	2
__ Long-eared Owl	*Asio otus*	N	2
__ Stygian Owl	*Asio stygius*	V	5
__ Short-eared Owl	*Asio flammeus*	N	2
__ Boreal Owl	*Aegolius funereus*	N	2
__ Northern Saw-whet Owl	*Aegolius acadicus*	N	2

Order: Caprimulgiformes

FAMILY: CAPRIMULGIDAE (GOATSUCKERS)

__ Lesser Nighthawk	*Chordeiles acutipennis*	N	1
__ Common Nighthawk	*Chordeiles minor*	N	1
__ Antillean Nighthawk	*Chordeiles gundlachii*	N	3
__ Common Pauraque	*Nyctidromus albicollis*	N	2
__ Common Poorwill	*Phalaenoptilus nuttallii*	N	1
__ Chuck-will's-widow	*Caprimulgus carolinensis*	N	1
__ Buff-collared Nightjar	*Caprimulgus ridgwayi*	N	4
__ Whip-poor-will	*Caprimulgus vociferus*	N	1
__ Jungle Nightjar	*Caprimulgus indicus*	V	5

Order: Apodiformes

__ Black Swift	*Cypseloides niger*	N	2
__ White-collared Swift	*Streptoprocne zonaris*	V	4
__ Chimney Swift	*Chaetura pelagica*	N	1
__ Vaux's Swift	*Chaetura vauxi*	N	1
__ White-throated Needletail	*Hirundapus caudacutus*	V	4
__ Common Swift	*Apus apus*	V	5
__ Fork-tailed Swift	*Apus pacificus*	V	4
__ White-throated Swift	*Aeronautes saxatalis*	N	1
__ Antillean Palm-Swift	*Tachornis phoenicobia*	V	5

FAMILY: TROCHILIDAE (HUMMINGBIRDS)

__ Green Violet-ear	*Colibri thalassinus*	V	4
__ Green-breasted Mango	*Anthracothorax prevostii*	V	4
__ Broad-billed Hummingbird	*Cynanthus latirostris*	N	2
__ White-eared Hummingbird	*Hylocharis leucotis*	V	3
__ Xantus's Hummingbird	*Hylocharis xantusii*	V	5
__ Berylline Hummingbird	*Amazilia beryllina*	N	3
__ Buff-bellied Hummingbird	*Amazilia yucatanensis*	N	2
__ Cinnamon Hummingbird	*Amazilia rutila*	V	5
__ Violet-crowned Hummingbird	*Amazilia violiceps*	N	2
__ Blue-throated Hummingbird	*Lampornis clemenciae*	N	2
__ Magnificent Hummingbird	*Eugenes fulgens*	N	2
__ Plain-capped Starthroat	*Heliomaster constantii*	V	4
__ Bahama Woodstar	*Calliphlox evelynae*	V	5
__ Lucifer Hummingbird	*Calothorax lucifer*	N	2
__ Ruby-throated Hummingbird	*Archilochus colubris*	N	1
__ Black-chinned Hummingbird	*Archilochus alexandri*	N	1
__ Anna's Hummingbird	*Calypte anna*	N	1
__ Costa's Hummingbird	*Calypte costae*	N	1
__ Calliope Hummingbird	*Stellula calliope*	N	1
__ Bumblebee Hummingbird	*Atthis heloisa*	V	5
__ Broad-tailed Hummingbird	*Selasphorus platycercus*	N	1
__ Rufous Hummingbird	*Selasphorus rufus*	N	1
__ Allen's Hummingbird	*Selasphorus sasin*	N	1

Order: Trogoniformes

__ Elegant Trogon	*Trogon elegans*	N	2
__ Eared Quetzal	*Euptilotis neoxenus*	V	4

Order: Upupiformes
FAMILY: UPUPIDAE (HOOPOES)
_ Eurasian Hoopoe   *Upupa epops*   V   5

Order: Coraciiformes
FAMILY: ALCEDINIDAE (KINGFISHERS)
_ Ringed Kingfisher   *Ceryle torquata*   N   2
_ Belted Kingfisher   *Ceryle alcyon*   N   1
_ Green Kingfisher   *Chloroceryle americana*   N   2

Order: Piciformes
FAMILY: PICIDAE (WOODPECKERS AND ALLIES)
_ Eurasian Wryneck   *Jynx torquilla*   V   5
_ Lewis's Woodpecker   *Melanerpes lewis*   N   1
_ Red-headed Woodpecker   *Melanerpes erythrocephalus*   N   1
_ Acorn Woodpecker   *Melanerpes formicivorus*   N   1
_ Gila Woodpecker   *Melanerpes uropygialis*   N   1
_ Golden-fronted Woodpecker   *Melanerpes aurifrons*   N   1
_ Red-bellied Woodpecker   *Melanerpes carolinus*   N   1
_ Williamson's Sapsucker   *Sphyrapicus thyroideus*   N   1
_ Yellow-bellied Sapsucker   *Sphyrapicus varius*   N   1
_ Red-naped Sapsucker   *Sphyrapicus nuchalis*   N   1
_ Red-breasted Sapsucker   *Sphyrapicus ruber*   N   1
_ Great Spotted Woodpecker   *Dendrocopos major*   V   4
_ Ladder-backed Woodpecker   *Picoides scalaris*   N   1
_ Nuttall's Woodpecker   *Picoides nuttallii*   N   1
_ Downy Woodpecker   *Picoides pubescens*   N   1
_ Hairy Woodpecker   *Picoides villosus*   N   1
_ Arizona Woodpecker   *Picoides arizonae*   N   2
_ Red-cockaded Woodpecker   *Picoides borealis*   N   2
_ White-headed Woodpecker   *Picoides albolarvatus*   N   1
_ Three-toed Woodpecker   *Picoides tridactylus*   N   2
_ Black-backed Woodpecker   *Picoides arcticus*   N   2
_ Northern Flicker   *Colaptes auratus*   N   1
_ Gilded Flicker   *Colaptes chrysoides*   N   2
_ Pileated Woodpecker   *Dryocopus pileatus*   N   1
_ Ivory-billed Woodpecker   *Campephilus principalis*   N   6

Order: Passeriformes
FAMILY: TYRANNIDAE (TYRANT FLYCATCHERS)
_ Northern Beardless-Tyrannulet   *Camptostoma imberbe*   N   2

___ Greenish Elaenia	*Myiopagis viridicata*	V	5
___ Caribbean Elaenia	*Elaenia martinica*	V	5
___ Tufted Flycatcher	*Mitrephanes phaeocercus*	V	5
___ Olive-sided Flycatcher	*Contopus cooperi*	N	1
___ Greater Pewee	*Contopus pertinax*	N	2
___ Western Wood-Pewee	*Contopus sordidulus*	N	1
___ Eastern Wood-Pewee	*Contopus virens*	N	1
___ Yellow-bellied Flycatcher	*Empidonax flaviventris*	N	1
___ Acadian Flycatcher	*Empidonax virescens*	N	1
___ Alder Flycatcher	*Empidonax alnorum*	N	1
___ Willow Flycatcher	*Empidonax traillii*	N	1
___ Least Flycatcher	*Empidonax minimus*	N	1
___ Hammond's Flycatcher	*Empidonax hammondii*	N	1
___ Gray Flycatcher	*Empidonax wrightii*	N	1
___ Dusky Flycatcher	*Empidonax oberholseri*	N	1
___ Pacific-slope Flycatcher	*Empidonax difficilis*	N	1
___ Cordilleran Flycatcher	*Empidonax occidentalis*	N	1
___ Buff-breasted Flycatcher	*Empidonax fulvifrons*	N	2
___ Black Phoebe	*Sayornis nigricans*	N	1
___ Eastern Phoebe	*Sayornis phoebe*	N	1
___ Say's Phoebe	*Sayornis saya*	N	1
___ Vermilion Flycatcher	*Pyrocephalus rubinus*	N	1
___ Dusky-capped Flycatcher	*Myiarchus tuberculifer*	N	2
___ Ash-throated Flycatcher	*Myiarchus cinerascens*	N	1
___ Nutting's Flycatcher	*Myiarchus nuttingi*	V	5
___ Great Crested Flycatcher	*Myiarchus crinitus*	N	1
___ Brown-crested Flycatcher	*Myiarchus tyrannulus*	N	1
___ La Sagra's Flycatcher	*Myiarchus sagrae*	V	4
___ Great Kiskadee	*Pitangus sulphuratus*	N	2
___ Sulphur-bellied Flycatcher	*Myiodynastes luteiventris*	N	2
___ Piratic Flycatcher	*Legatus leucophaius*	V	4
___ Variegated Flycatcher	*Empidonomus varius*	V	4
___ Tropical Kingbird	*Tyrannus melancholicus*	N	2
___ Couch's Kingbird	*Tyrannus couchii*	N	2
___ Cassin's Kingbird	*Tyrannus vociferans*	N	1
___ Thick-billed Kingbird	*Tyrannus crassirostris*	N	2
___ Western Kingbird	*Tyrannus verticalis*	N	1
___ Eastern Kingbird	*Tyrannus tyrannus*	N	1
___ Gray Kingbird	*Tyrannus dominicensis*	N	2
___ Scissor-tailed Flycatcher	*Tyrannus forficatus*	N	1
___ Fork-tailed Flycatcher	*Tyrannus savana*	V	4

__ Rose-throated Becard	*Pachyramphus aglaiae*	N	3
__ Masked Tityra	*Tityra semifasciata*	V	5

FAMILY: LANIIDAE (SHRIKES)

__ Brown Shrike	*Lanius cristatus*	V	4
__ Loggerhead Shrike	*Lanius ludovicianus*	N	1
__ Northern Shrike	*Lanius excubitor*	N	1

FAMILY: VIREONIDAE (VIREOS)

__ White-eyed Vireo	*Vireo griseus*	N	1
__ Thick-billed Vireo	*Vireo crassirostris*	V	4
__ Bell's Vireo	*Vireo bellii*	N	1
__ Black-capped Vireo	*Vireo atricapillus*	N	2
__ Gray Vireo	*Vireo vicinior*	N	2
__ Yellow-throated Vireo	*Vireo flavifrons*	N	1
__ Plumbeous Vireo	*Vireo plumbeus*	N	1
__ Cassin's Vireo	*Vireo cassinii*	N	1
__ Blue-headed Vireo	*Vireo solitarius*	N	1
__ Hutton's Vireo	*Vireo huttoni*	N	1
__ Warbling Vireo	*Vireo gilvus*	N	1
__ Philadelphia Vireo	*Vireo philadelphicus*	N	1
__ Red-eyed Vireo	*Vireo olivaceus*	N	1
__ Yellow-green Vireo	*Vireo flavoviridis*	N	3
__ Black-whiskered Vireo	*Vireo altiloquus*	N	2
__ Yucatan Vireo	*Vireo magister*	V	5

FAMILY: CORVIDAE (JAYS AND CROWS)

__ Gray Jay	*Perisoreus canadensis*	N	1
__ Steller's Jay	*Cyanocitta stelleri*	N	1
__ Blue Jay	*Cyanocitta cristata*	N	1
__ Green Jay	*Cyanocorax yncas*	N	2
__ Brown Jay	*Cyanocorax morio*	N	3
__ Florida Scrub-Jay	*Aphelocoma coerulescens*	N	2
__ Island Scrub-Jay	*Aphelocoma insularis*	N	2
__ Western Scrub-Jay	*Aphelocoma californica*	N	1
__ Mexican Jay	*Aphelocoma ultramarina*	N	2
__ Pinyon Jay	*Gymnorhinus cyanocephalus*	N	1
__ Clark's Nutcracker	*Nucifraga columbiana*	N	1
__ Black-billed Magpie	*Pica hudsonia*	N	1
__ Yellow-billed Magpie	*Pica nuttalli*	N	2
__ Eurasian Jackdaw	*Corvus monedula*	V	4
__ American Crow	*Corvus brachyrhynchos*	N	1
__ Northwestern Crow	*Corvus caurinus*	N	1
__ Tamaulipas Crow	*Corvus imparatus*	N	3

__ Fish Crow	*Corvus ossifragus*	N	1
__ Chihuahuan Raven	*Corvus cryptoleucus*	N	1
__ Common Raven	*Corvus corax*	N	1

FAMILY: ALAUDIDAE (LARKS)

__ Sky Lark	*Alauda arvensis*	V, I	2
__ Horned Lark	*Eremophila alpestris*	N	1

FAMILY: HIRUNDINIDAE (SWALLOWS)

__ Purple Martin	*Progne subis*	N	1
__ Cuban Martin	*Progne cryptoleuca*	V	5
__ Gray-breasted Martin	*Progne chalybea*	V	6
__ Southern Martin	*Progne elegans*	V	5
__ Brown-chested Martin	*Progne tapera*	V	5
__ Tree Swallow	*Tachycineta bicolor*	N	1
__ Violet-green Swallow	*Tachycineta thalassina*	N	1
__ Bahama Swallow	*Tachycineta cyaneoviridis*	V	4
__ Northern Rough-winged Swallow	*Stelgidopteryx serripennis*	N	1
__ Bank Swallow	*Riparia riparia*	N	1
__ Cliff Swallow	*Petrochelidon pyrrhonota*	N	1
__ Cave Swallow	*Petrochelidon fulva*	N	1
__ Barn Swallow	*Hirundo rustica*	N	1
__ Common House-Martin	*Delichon urbica*	V	4

FAMILY: PARIDAE (CHICKADEES AND TITMICE)

__ Carolina Chickadee	*Poecile carolinensis*	N	1
__ Black-capped Chickadee	*Poecile atricapilla*	N	1
__ Mountain Chickadee	*Poecile gambeli*	N	1
__ Mexican Chickadee	*Poecile sclateri*	N	2
__ Chestnut-backed Chickadee	*Poecile rufescens*	N	1
__ Boreal Chickadee	*Poecile hudsonica*	N	1
__ Gray-headed Chickadee	*Poecile cincta*	N	3
__ Bridled Titmouse	*Baeolophus wollweberi*	N	2
__ Oak Titmouse	*Baeolophus inornatus*	N	1
__ Juniper Titmouse	*Baeolophus griseus*	N	1
__ Tufted Titmouse	*Baeolophus bicolor*	N	1
__ Black-crested Titmouse	*Baeolophus atricristatus*	N	3

FAMILY: REMIZIDAE (VERDIN)

__ Verdin	*Auriparus flaviceps*	N	1

FAMILY: AEGITHALIDAE (BUSHTITS)

__ Bushtit	*Psaltriparus minimus*	N	1

FAMILY: SITTIDAE (NUTHATCHES)

__ Red-breasted Nuthatch	*Sitta canadensis*	N	1
__ White-breasted Nuthatch	*Sitta carolinensis*	N	1

_ Pygmy Nuthatch	*Sitta pygmaea*	N	1
_ Brown-headed Nuthatch	*Sitta pusilla*	N	1
FAMILY: CERTHIIDAE (CREEPERS)			
_ Brown Creeper	*Certhia americana*	N	1
FAMILY: TROGLODYTIDAE (WRENS)			
_ Cactus Wren	*Campylorhynchus brunnei-*		
	capillus	N	1
_ Rock Wren	*Salpinctes obsoletus*	N	1
_ Canyon Wren	*Catherpes mexicanus*	N	1
_ Carolina Wren	*Thryothorus ludovicianus*	N	1
_ Bewick's Wren	*Thryomanes bewickii*	N	1
_ House Wren	*Troglodytes aedon*	N	1
_ Winter Wren	*Troglodytes troglodytes*	N	1
_ Sedge Wren	*Cistothorus platensis*	N	1
_ Marsh Wren	*Cistothorus palustris*	N	1
FAMILY: CINCLIDAE (DIPPERS)			
_ American Dipper	*Cinclus mexicanus*	N	1
FAMILY: PYCNONOTIDAE (BULBULS)			
_ Red-whiskered Bulbul	*Pycnonotus jocosus*	I	2
FAMILY: REGULIDAE (KINGLETS)			
_ Golden-crowned Kinglet	*Regulus satrapa*	N	1
_ Ruby-crowned Kinglet	*Regulus calendula*	N	1
FAMILY: SYLVIIDAE (OLD WORLD WARBLERS AND GNATCATCHERS)			
_ Middendorff's Grasshopper-Warbler	*Locustella ochotensis*	V	4
_ Lanceolated Warbler	*Locustella lanceolata*	V	4
_ Wood Warbler	*Phylloscopus sibilatrix*	V	5
_ Dusky Warbler	*Phylloscopus fuscatus*	V	4
_ Yellow-browed Warbler	*Phylloscopus inornatus*	V	5
_ Arctic Warbler	*Phylloscopus borealis*	N	2
_ Blue-gray Gnatcatcher	*Polioptila caerulea*	N	1
_ California Gnatcatcher	*Polioptila californica*	N	2
_ Black-tailed Gnatcatcher	*Polioptila melanura*	N	1
_ Black-capped Gnatcatcher	*Polioptila nigriceps*	N	4
FAMILY: MUSCICAPIDAE (OLD WORLD FLYCATCHERS)			
_ Narcissus Flycatcher	*Ficedula narcissina*	V	5
_ Mugimaki Flycatcher	*Ficedula mugimaki*	V	5
_ Red-breasted Flycatcher	*Ficedula parva*	V	4
_ Siberian Flycatcher	*Muscicapa sibirica*	V	4
_ Gray-spotted Flycatcher	*Muscicapa griseisticta*	V	4
_ Asian Brown Flycatcher	*Muscicapa dauurica*	V	5

FAMILY: TURDIDAE (THRUSHES)

__ Siberian Rubythroat	*Luscinia calliope*	V	3
__ Bluethroat	*Luscinia svecica*	N	2
__ Siberian Blue Robin	*Luscinia cyane*	V	5
__ Red-flanked Bluetail	*Tarsiger cyanurus*	V	4
__ Northern Wheatear	*Oenanthe oenanthe*	N	2
__ Stonechat	*Saxicola torquata*	V	4
__ Eastern Bluebird	*Sialia sialis*	N	1
__ Western Bluebird	*Sialia mexicana*	N	1
__ Mountain Bluebird	*Sialia currucoides*	N	1
__ Townsend's Solitaire	*Myadestes townsendi*	N	1
__ Orange-billed Nightingale Thrush	*Catharus aurantiirostris*	V	5
__ Veery	*Catharus fuscescens*	N	1
__ Gray-cheeked Thrush	*Catharus minimus*	N	1
__ Bicknell's Thrush	*Catharus bicknelli*	N	2
__ Swainson's Thrush	*Catharus ustulatus*	N	1
__ Hermit Thrush	*Catharus guttatus*	N	1
__ Wood Thrush	*Hylocichla mustelina*	N	1
__ Eurasian Blackbird	*Turdus merula*	V	5
__ Eyebrowed Thrush	*Turdus obscurus*	V	3
__ Dusky Thrush	*Turdus naumanni*	V	4
__ Fieldfare	*Turdus pilaris*	V	4
__ Redwing	*Turdus iliacus*	V	4
__ Clay-colored Robin	*Turdus grayi*	N	3
__ White-throated Robin	*Turdus assimilis*	V	4
__ Rufous-backed Robin	*Turdus rufopalliatus*	V	3
__ American Robin	*Turdus migratorius*	N	1
__ Varied Thrush	*Ixoreus naevius*	N	1
__ Aztec Thrush	*Ridgwayia pinicola*	V	4

FAMILY: TIMALIIDAE (BABBLERS)

__ Wrentit	*Chamaea fasciata*	N	1

FAMILY: MIMIDAE (MOCKINGBIRDS AND THRASHERS)

__ Gray Catbird	*Dumetella carolinensis*	N	1
__ Northern Mockingbird	*Mimus polyglottos*	N	1
__ Bahama Mockingbird	*Mimus gundlachii*	V	4
__ Sage Thrasher	*Oreoscoptes montanus*	N	1
__ Brown Thrasher	*Toxostoma rufum*	N	1
__ Long-billed Thrasher	*Toxostoma longirostre*	N	2
__ Bendire's Thrasher	*Toxostoma bendirei*	N	2
__ Curve-billed Thrasher	*Toxostoma curvirostre*	N	1
__ California Thrasher	*Toxostoma redivivum*	N	1

_ Crissal Thrasher	*Toxostoma crissale*	N	2
_ Le Conte's Thrasher	*Toxostoma lecontei*	N	2
_ Blue Mockingbird	*Melanotis caerulescens*	V	4
FAMILY: STURNIDAE (STARLINGS)			
_ European Starling	*Sturnus vulgaris*	V, I	1
_ Crested Myna	*Acridotheres cristatellus*	I	3
FAMILY: PRUNELLIDAE (ACCENTORS)			
_ Siberian Accentor	*Prunella montanella*	V	4
FAMILY: MOTACILLIDAE (WAGTAILS AND PIPITS)			
_ Yellow Wagtail	*Motacilla flava*	N	2
_ Citrine Wagtail	*Motacilla citreola*	V	5
_ Gray Wagtail	*Motacilla cinerea*	V	4
_ White Wagtail	*Motacilla alba*	N	2
_ Black-backed Wagtail	*Motacilla lugens*	N	3
_ Tree Pipit	*Anthus trivialis*	V	5
_ Olive-backed Pipit	*Anthus hodgsoni*	V	3
_ Pechora Pipit	*Anthus gustavi*	V	4
_ Red-throated Pipit	*Anthus cervinus*	N	3
_ American Pipit	*Anthus rubescens*	N	1
_ Sprague's Pipit	*Anthus spragueii*	N	2
FAMILY: BOMBYCILLIDAE (WAXWINGS)			
_ Bohemian Waxwing	*Bombycilla garrulus*	N	1
_ Cedar Waxwing	*Bombycilla cedrorum*	N	1
FAMILY: PTILOGONATIDAE (SILKY-FLYCATCHERS)			
_ Gray Silky-flycatcher	*Ptilogonys cinereus*	V	5
_ Phainopepla	*Phainopepla nitens*	N	1
FAMILY: PEUCEDRAMIDAE (OLIVE WARBLER)			
_ Olive Warbler	*Peucedramus taeniatus*	N	2
FAMILY: PARULIDAE (WOOD-WARBLERS)			
_ Bachman's Warbler	*Vermivora bachmanii*	N	6
_ Blue-winged Warbler	*Vermivora pinus*	N	1
_ Golden-winged Warbler	*Vermivora chrysoptera*	N	2
_ Tennessee Warbler	*Vermivora peregrina*	N	1
_ Orange-crowned Warbler	*Vermivora celata*	N	1
_ Nashville Warbler	*Vermivora ruficapilla*	N	1
_ Virginia's Warbler	*Vermivora virginiae*	N	1
_ Colima Warbler	*Vermivora crissalis*	N	2
_ Lucy's Warbler	*Vermivora luciae*	N	1
_ Crescent-chested Warbler	*Parula superciliosa*	V	4
_ Northern Parula	*Parula americana*	N	1
_ Tropical Parula	*Parula pitiayumi*	N	3

__ Yellow Warbler	*Dendroica petechia*	N	1
__ Chestnut-sided Warbler	*Dendroica pensylvanica*	N	1
__ Magnolia Warbler	*Dendroica magnolia*	N	1
__ Cape May Warbler	*Dendroica tigrina*	N	1
__ Black-throated Blue Warbler	*Dendroica caerulescens*	N	1
__ Yellow-rumped Warbler	*Dendroica coronata*	N	1
__ Black-throated Gray Warbler	*Dendroica nigrescens*	N	1
__ Golden-cheeked Warbler	*Dendroica chrysoparia*	N	2
__ Black-throated Green Warbler	*Dendroica virens*	N	1
__ Townsend's Warbler	*Dendroica townsendi*	N	1
__ Hermit Warbler	*Dendroica occidentalis*	N	1
__ Blackburnian Warbler	*Dendroica fusca*	N	1
__ Yellow-throated Warbler	*Dendroica dominica*	N	1
__ Grace's Warbler	*Dendroica graciae*	N	1
__ Pine Warbler	*Dendroica pinus*	N	1
__ Kirtland's Warbler	*Dendroica kirtlandii*	N	3
__ Prairie Warbler	*Dendroica discolor*	N	1
__ Palm Warbler	*Dendroica palmarum*	N	1
__ Bay-breasted Warbler	*Dendroica castanea*	N	1
__ Blackpoll Warbler	*Dendroica striata*	N	1
__ Cerulean Warbler	*Dendroica cerulea*	N	1
__ Black-and-white Warbler	*Mniotilta varia*	N	1
__ American Redstart	*Setophaga ruticilla*	N	1
__ Prothonotary Warbler	*Protonotaria citrea*	N	1
__ Worm-eating Warbler	*Helmitheros vermivorus*	N	1
__ Swainson's Warbler	*Limnothlypis swainsonii*	N	2
__ Ovenbird	*Seiurus aurocapillus*	N	1
__ Northern Waterthrush	*Seiurus noveboracensis*	N	1
__ Louisiana Waterthrush	*Seiurus motacilla*	N	1
__ Kentucky Warbler	*Oporornis formosus*	N	1
__ Connecticut Warbler	*Oporornis agilis*	N	2
__ Mourning Warbler	*Oporornis philadelphia*	N	1
__ MacGillivray's Warbler	*Oporornis tolmiei*	N	1
__ Common Yellowthroat	*Geothlypis trichas*	N	1
__ Gray-crowned Yellowthroat	*Geothlypis poliocephala*	V	4
__ Hooded Warbler	*Wilsonia citrina*	N	1
__ Wilson's Warbler	*Wilsonia pusilla*	N	1
__ Canada Warbler	*Wilsonia canadensis*	N	1
__ Red-faced Warbler	*Cardellina rubrifrons*	N	2
__ Painted Redstart	*Myioborus pictus*	N	2
__ Slate-throated Redstart	*Myioborus miniatus*	V	4

__ Fan-tailed Warbler	*Euthlypis lachrymosa*	V	4
__ Golden-crowned Warbler	*Basileuterus culicivorus*	V	4
__ Rufous-capped Warbler	*Basileuterus rufifrons*	N	4
__ Yellow-breasted Chat	*Icteria virens*	N	1
FAMILY: COEREBIDAE (BANANAQUITS)			
__ Bananaquit	*Coereba flaveola*	V	4
FAMILY: THRAUPIDAE (TANAGERS)			
__ Hepatic Tanager	*Piranga flava*	N	2
__ Summer Tanager	*Piranga rubra*	N	1
__ Scarlet Tanager	*Piranga olivacea*	N	1
__ Western Tanager	*Piranga ludoviciana*	N	1
__ Flame-colored Tanager	*Piranga bidentata*	V	4
__ Western Spindalis	*Spindalis zena*	V	4
FAMILY: EMBERIZIDAE (EMBERIZIDS)			
__ White-collared Seedeater	*Sporophila torqueola*	N	3
__ Yellow-faced Grassquit	*Tiaris olivacea*	V	4
__ Black-faced Grassquit	*Tiaris bicolor*	V	5
__ Olive Sparrow	*Arremonops rufivirgatus*	N	2
__ Green-tailed Towhee	*Pipilo chlorurus*	N	1
__ Spotted Towhee	*Pipilo maculatus*	N	1
__ Eastern Towhee	*Pipilo erythrophthalmus*	N	1
__ Canyon Towhee	*Pipilo fuscus*	N	1
__ California Towhee	*Pipilo crissalis*	N	1
__ Abert's Towhee	*Pipilo aberti*	N	1
__ Rufous-winged Sparrow	*Aimophila carpalis*	N	2
__ Cassin's Sparrow	*Aimophila cassinii*	N	1
__ Bachman's Sparrow	*Aimophila aestivalis*	N	2
__ Botteri's Sparrow	*Aimophila botterii*	N	2
__ Rufous-crowned Sparrow	*Aimophila ruficeps*	N	1
__ Five-striped Sparrow	*Aimophila quinquestriata*	N	3
__ American Tree Sparrow	*Spizella arborea*	N	1
__ Chipping Sparrow	*Spizella passerina*	N	1
__ Clay-colored Sparrow	*Spizella pallida*	N	1
__ Brewer's Sparrow	*Spizella breweri*	N	1
__ Field Sparrow	*Spizella pusilla*	N	1
__ Worthen's Sparrow	*Spizella wortheni*	V	6
__ Black-chinned Sparrow	*Spizella atrogularis*	N	1
__ Vesper Sparrow	*Pooecetes gramineus*	N	1
__ Lark Sparrow	*Chondestes grammacus*	N	1
__ Black-throated Sparrow	*Amphispiza bilineata*	N	1
__ Sage Sparrow	*Amphispiza belli*	N	1

_ Lark Bunting	*Calamospiza melanocorys*	N	1
_ Savannah Sparrow	*Passerculus sandwichensis*	N	1
_ Grasshopper Sparrow	*Ammodramus savannarum*	N	1
_ Baird's Sparrow	*Ammodramus bairdii*	N	2
_ Henslow's Sparrow	*Ammodramus henslowii*	N	2
_ Le Conte's Sparrow	*Ammodramus leconteii*	N	1
_ Nelson's Sharp-tailed Sparrow	*Ammodramus nelsoni*	N	1
_ Saltmarsh Sharp-tailed Sparrow	*Ammodramus caudacutus*	N	1
_ Seaside Sparrow	*Ammodramus maritimus*	N	1
_ Fox Sparrow	*Passerella iliaca*	N	1
_ Song Sparrow	*Melospiza melodia*	N	1
_ Lincoln's Sparrow	*Melospiza lincolnii*	N	1
_ Swamp Sparrow	*Melospiza georgiana*	N	1
_ White-throated Sparrow	*Zonotrichia albicollis*	N	1
_ Harris's Sparrow	*Zonotrichia querula*	N	1
_ White-crowned Sparrow	*Zonotrichia leucophrys*	N	1
_ Golden-crowned Sparrow	*Zonotrichia atricapilla*	N	1
_ Dark-eyed Junco	*Junco hyemalis*	N	1
_ Yellow-eyed Junco	*Junco phaeonotus*	N	2
_ McCown's Longspur	*Calcarius mccownii*	N	2
_ Lapland Longspur	*Calcarius lapponicus*	N	1
_ Smith's Longspur	*Calcarius pictus*	N	2
_ Chestnut-collared Longspur	*Calcarius ornatus*	N	1
_ Pine Bunting	*Emberiza leucocephalos*	V	5
_ Little Bunting	*Emberiza pusilla*	V	4
_ Rustic Bunting	*Emberiza rustica*	V	3
_ Yellow-headed Bunting	*Emberiza elegans*	V	5
_ Yellow-breasted Bunting	*Emberiza aureola*	V	4
_ Gray Bunting	*Emberiza variabilis*	V	5
_ Pallas's Bunting	*Emberiza pallasi*	V	5
_ Reed Bunting	*Emberiza schoeniclus*	V	4
_ Snow Bunting	*Plectrophenax nivalis*	N	1
_ McKay's Bunting	*Plectrophenax hyperboreus*	N	2

FAMILY: CARDINALIDAE (CARDINALS, SALTATORS, AND ALLIES)

_ Crimson-collared Grosbeak	*Rhodothraupis celaeno*	V	4
_ Northern Cardinal	*Cardinalis cardinalis*	N	1
_ Pyrrhuloxia	*Cardinalis sinuatus*	N	1
_ Yellow Grosbeak	*Pheucticus chrysopeplus*	V	4
_ Rose-breasted Grosbeak	*Pheucticus ludovicianus*	N	1
_ Black-headed Grosbeak	*Pheucticus melanocephalus*	N	1

__ Blue Bunting	*Cyanocompsa parellina*	V	4
__ Blue Grosbeak	*Guiraca caerulea*	N	1
__ Lazuli Bunting	*Passerina amoena*	N	1
__ Indigo Bunting	*Passerina cyanea*	N	1
__ Varied Bunting	*Passerina versicolor*	N	2
__ Painted Bunting	*Passerina ciris*	N	1
__ Dickcissel	*Spiza americana*	N	1

FAMILY: ICTERIDAE (BLACKBIRDS)

__ Bobolink	*Dolichonyx oryzivorus*	N	1
__ Red-winged Blackbird	*Agelaius phoeniceus*	N	1
__ Tricolored Blackbird	*Agelaius tricolor*	N	2
__ Tawny-shouldered Blackbird	*Agelaius humeralis*	V	5
__ Eastern Meadowlark	*Sturnella magna*	N	1
__ Western Meadowlark	*Sturnella neglecta*	N	1
__ Yellow-headed Blackbird	*Xanthocephalus xantho-*		
	cephalus	N	1
__ Rusty Blackbird	*Euphagus carolinus*	N	1
__ Brewer's Blackbird	*Euphagus cyanocephalus*	N	1
__ Common Grackle	*Quiscalus quiscula*	N	1
__ Boat-tailed Grackle	*Quiscalus major*	N	1
__ Great-tailed Grackle	*Quiscalus mexicanus*	N	1
__ Shiny Cowbird	*Molothrus bonariensis*	V	2
__ Bronzed Cowbird	*Molothrus aeneus*	N	1
__ Brown-headed Cowbird	*Molothrus ater*	N	1
__ Black-vented Oriole	*Icterus wagleri*	V	5
__ Orchard Oriole	*Icterus spurius*	N	1
__ Hooded Oriole	*Icterus cucullatus*	N	1
__ Streak-backed Oriole	*Icterus pustulatus*	N	4
__ Spot-breasted Oriole	*Icterus pectoralis*	I	2
__ Altamira Oriole	*Icterus gularis*	N	2
__ Audubon's Oriole	*Icterus graduacauda*	N	2
__ Baltimore Oriole	*Icterus galbula*	N	1
__ Bullock's Oriole	*Icterus bullockii*	N	1
__ Scott's Oriole	*Icterus parisorum*	N	1

FAMILY: FRINGILLIDAE (FRINGILLINE AND CARDUELINE
FINCHES AND ALLIES)

__ Common Chaffinch	*Fringilla coelebs*	V	5
__ Brambling	*Fringilla montifringilla*	V	3
__ Gray-crowned Rosy-Finch	*Leucosticte tephrocotis*	N	1
__ Black Rosy-Finch	*Leucosticte atrata*	N	2
__ Brown-capped Rosy-Finch	*Leucosticte australis*	N	2

__ Pine Grosbeak	*Pinicola enucleator*	N	1
__ Common Rosefinch	*Carpodacus erythrinus*	V	4
__ Purple Finch	*Carpodacus purpureus*	N	1
__ Cassin's Finch	*Carpodacus cassinii*	N	1
__ House Finch	*Carpodacus mexicanus*	N	1
__ Red Crossbill	*Loxia curvirostra*	N	1
__ White-winged Crossbill	*Loxia leucoptera*	N	2
__ Common Redpoll	*Carduelis flammea*	N	1
__ Hoary Redpoll	*Carduelis hornemanni*	N	2
__ Eurasian Siskin	*Carduelis spinus*	V	5
__ Pine Siskin	*Carduelis pinus*	N	1
__ Lesser Goldfinch	*Carduelis psaltria*	N	1
__ Lawrence's Goldfinch	*Carduelis lawrencei*	N	2
__ American Goldfinch	*Carduelis tristis*	N	1
__ Oriental Greenfinch	*Carduelis sinica*	V	4
__ Eurasian Bullfinch	*Pyrrhula pyrrhula*	V	4
__ Evening Grosbeak	*Coccothraustes vespertinus*	,N	1
__ Hawfinch	*Coccothraustes cocco-*		
	thraustes	V	4

FAMILY: PASSERIDAE (OLD WORLD SPARROWS)

__ House Sparrow	*Passer domesticus*	I	1
__ Eurasian Tree Sparrow	*Passer montanus*	I	2

Name Changes to the American Ornithologists' Union (and ABA) Check-list of North American Birds Since 1957 (CURRENT NAMES ARE BOLD-FACED)

Alder Flycatcher: Split from Traill's Flycatcher in 1973
Altamira Oriole: Name changed from Lichtenstein's Oriole by 1982
American Anhinga: Name changed to Anhinga by 1982
American Black Brant: Lumped with Black Brant to form Brant in 1976
American Black Duck: Name changed from Black Duck by 1982
American Black Oystercatcher: Name changed to Black Oystercatcher in 1984
American Coot: Name changed from Coot by 1982
American Crow: Name changed from Common Crow by 1982
American Dipper: Name changed from North American Dipper by 1982
American Flamingo: Name changed to Greater Flamingo by 1982
American Golden-Plover: Split, with Pacific Golden-Plover, from Lesser Golden-Plover in 1993
American Kestrel: Name changed from Sparrow Hawk in 1973
American Pipit: Name changed from Water Pipit
American Swallow-tailed Kite: Name changed from Swallow-tailed Kite by 1982 and back to Swallow-tailed Kite in 1995
American Tree Sparrow: Name changed from Tree Sparrow by 1982
American White Pelican: Name changed from White Pelican by 1982
American Wigeon: Name changed from American Widgeon in 1973
Anhinga: Name changed from American Anhinga by 1982
Antillean Nighthawk: Split from Common Nighthawk by 1982
Arizona Woodpecker: Lumped with Strickland's Woodpecker by 1982 and split again in 2000
Asian Brown Flycatcher: Name changed from Gray-breasted Flycatcher and/or Brown Flycatcher in 1989
Audubon's Oriole: Name changed from Black-headed Oriole by 1982

Audubon's Warbler: Lumped with Myrtle Warbler into Yellow-rumped Warbler in 1973

Bahama Honeycreeper: Name changed to Bananaquit in 1973

Bahama Pintail: Name changed to White-cheeked Pintail by 1982

Baltimore Oriole: Lumped with Bullock's Oriole into Northern Oriole in 1973; then resplit, with Bullock's Oriole, from Northern Oriole in 1995

Bananaquit: Name changed from Bahama Honeycreeper in 1973

Band-rumped Storm-Petrel: Name changed from Harcourt's Storm Petrel by 1982

Barn Owl: Name changed from Common Barn-Owl in 1989

Bay-winged Hawk: Name changed to Harris's Hawk by 1982

Bewick's Swan: Lumped with Whistling Swan to form Tundra Swan in 1982

Bicknell's Thrush: Split from Gray-cheeked Thrush in 1995

Black Brant: Lumped with American Brant to form Brant in 1976

Black Duck: Name changed to American Black Duck by 1982

Black Oystercatcher: Name changed from American Black Oystercatcher in 1984

Black Rosy-Finch: Lumped into Rosy Finch in 1976 and split from Rosy Finch in 1993

Black Scoter: Name changed from Common Scoter in 1973

Black-backed Three-toed Woodpecker: Name changed to Black-backed Woodpecker by 1982

Black-backed Wagtail: Split from White Wagtail by 1982

Black-bellied Tree Duck: Name changed to Black-bellied Whistling-Duck in 1976

Black-bellied Whistling-Duck: Name changed from Black-bellied Tree Duck in 1976

Black-crested Titmouse: Lumped with Tufted Titmouse by 1982, split again in 2002

Black-eared Bushtit: Lumped with Common Bushtit to form Bushtit in 1973

Black-headed Gull: Name changed to Common Black-headed Gull by 1982 and back to Black-headed Gull in 1995

Black-headed Oriole: Name changed to Audubon's Oriole by 1982

Black-shouldered Kite: Name changed from White-tailed Kite by 1982 and back to White-tailed Kite in 1997

Black-vented Shearwater: Split from Manx Shearwater by 1982

Blue Goose: Lumped with Snow Goose by 1982

Blue-faced Booby: Name changed to Masked Booby by 1982

Blue-headed Vireo: Split, with Cassin's and Plumbeous Vireos, from Solitary Vireo in 1998

Boat-tailed Grackle: Split from Great-tailed Grackle in 1973

British Storm-Petrel: Name changed to European Storm-Petrel in 1995

Brown Noddy: Name changed from Noddy Tern by 1982

Brown Towhee: Split into California Towhee and Canyon Towhee in 1989

Brown Tree-Pipit: Name changed from Tree Pipit in 1982 and back to Tree Pipit in 1995

Brown-backed Woodpecker: Name changed to Strickland's Woodpecker by 1982

Brown-capped Rosy-Finch: Lumped into Rosy Finch in 1976 and split from Rosy Finch in 1993

Brown-crested Flycatcher: Name changed from Wied's Crested Flycatcher by 1982

Brown-throated Wren: Lumped into House Wren by 1982

Buff-collared Nightjar: Name changed from Ridgway's Whip-poor-will by 1982

Bullock's Oriole: Lumped with Baltimore Oriole to form Northern Oriole in 1973; split, with Baltimore Oriole, from Northern Oriole in 1995

Bumblebee Hummingbird: Name changed from Heloise's Hummingbird by 1982

Bushtit: Name changed from Common Bushtit in 1973

California Gnatcatcher: Split from Black-tailed Gnatcatcher in 1989

California Towhee: Split, with Canyon Towhee, from Brown Towhee in 1989

Canary-winged Parakeet: Split into White-winged Parakeet and Yellow-chevroned Parakeet in 1998

Canyon Towhee: Split, with California Towhee, from Brown Towhee in 1989

Cape Sable Sparrow: Lumped with Seaside Sparrow in 1973

Cape Verde Islands Petrel: Split from Soft-plumaged Petrel and name changed to Fea's Petrel in 1998

Cardinal: Name changed to Northern Cardinal in 1982

Cassin's Vireo: Split, with Blue-headed and Plumbeous Vireos, from Solitary Vireo in 1998

Catbird: Name changed to Gray Catbird in 1973

Chachalaca: Name changed to Plain Chachalaca by 1982

Chihuahuan Raven: Name changed from White-necked Raven by 1982

Clark's Grebe: Split from Western Grebe in 1987

Clay-colored Robin: Name changed from Clay-colored Thrush by 1982

Clay-colored Thrush: Name changed to Clay-colored Robin by 1982

Common Barn-Owl: Name changed to Barn Owl in 1989

Common Black-hawk: Name changed from Lesser Black Hawk by 1982

Common Black-headed Gull: Name changed from Black-headed Gull by 1982 and back to Black-headed Gull in 1995

Common Bobwhite: Name changed to Northern Bobwhite by 1982

Common Bushtit: Lumped with Black-eared Bushtit to form Bushtit in 1973
Common Crow: Name changed to American Crow by 1982
Common Egret: Name changed to Great Egret in 1973
Common Flicker: Lumped from Red-shafted, Yellow-shafted, and Gilded
    Flickers in 1973; name changed to Northern Flicker by 1982
Common Gallinule: Name changed to Common Moorhen by 1982
Common Greenshank: Name changed from Greenshank by 1982
Common Moorhen: Name changed from Common Gallinule by 1982
Common Murre: Name changed from Thin-billed Murre by 1982
Common Paraque: Name changed to Paraque by 1989 and back to Common
    Pauraque in 1998
Common Pintail: Name changed to Northern Pintail by 1982
Common Poorwill: Name changed from Poor-will by 1982
Common Raven: Name changed from Northern Raven by 1982
Common Reed-Bunting: Name changed to Reed Bunting in 1995
Common Ringed Plover: Name changed from Ringed Plover by 1982
Common Scoter: Name changed to Black Scoter in 1973
Common Screech Owl: Split into Eastern Screech-Owl and Western
    Screech-Owl by 1982
Common Skylark: Name changed to Eurasian Skylark by 1982
Common Turkey: Name changed to Wild Turkey by 1982
Coot: Name changed to American Coot by 1982
Coppery-tailed Trogon: Name changed to Elegant Trogon by 1982
Cordilleran Flycatcher: Split, with Pacific-slope Flycatcher, from Western Fly-
    catcher in 1989
Couch's Kingbird: Split from Tropical Kingbird by 1982
Coues' Flycatcher: Name changed to Greater Pewee by 1982
Dark-backed Goldfinch: Name changed to Lesser Goldfinch by 1982
Dark-eyed Junco: Name changed from Northern Junco by 1982
Dotterel: Name changed to Eurasian Dotterel by 1982
Dusky Seaside Sparrow: Lumped with Seaside Sparrow in 1973
Dusky-capped Flycatcher: Name changed from Olivaceous Flycatcher by
    1982
Eastern Pewee: Name changed to Eastern Wood-Pewee by 1982
Eastern Screech-Owl: Split from Common Screech Owl by 1982
Eastern Towhee: Split from Rufous-sided Towhee in 1995
Eastern Wood-Pewee: Name changed from Eastern Pewee by 1982
Elegant Trogon: Name changed from Coppery-tailed Trogon by 1982
Eurasian Coot: Name changed from European Coot by 1982
Eurasian Dotterel: Name changed from Dotterel by 1982
Eurasian Hobby: Name changed from Northern Hobby in 1995

Eurasian Skylark: Name changed from Common Skylark in 1982 and to Sky Lark in 1995

Eurasian Wigeon: Name changed from Eurasian Widgeon in 1973

Eurasian Woodcock: Name changed from European Woodcock by 1982

European Coot: Name changed to Eurasian Coot by 1982

European Golden-Plover: Name changed from Greater Golden-Plover in 1995

European Jack Snipe: Name changed to Jack Snipe by 1982

European Starling: Name changed from Starling by 1982

European Storm-Petrel: Name changed from British Storm-Petrel in 1995

European Woodcock: Name changed to Eurasian Woodcock by 1982

Everglade Kite: Name changed to Snail Kite by 1982

Eye-browed Thrush: Name changed to Eyebrowed Thrush in 1989

Eyebrowed Thrush: Name changed from Eye-browed Thrush in 1989

Falcated Duck: Name changed from Falcated Teal in 1998

Falcated Teal: Name changed to Falcated Duck in 1998

Fea's Petrel: Split from Soft-plumaged Petrel; name changed from Cape Verde Islands Petrel in 1998

Ferruginous Owl: Name changed to Ferruginous Pygmy-Owl by 1982

Ferruginous Pygmy-Owl: Name changed from Ferruginous Owl by 1982

Flammulated Owl: Name changed from Flammulated Screech Owl by 1982

Flammulated Screech Owl: Name changed to Flammulated Owl by 1982

Florida Scrub-Jay: Split from Scrub Jay in 1995

Fulvous Tree Duck: Name changed to Fulvous Whistling-Duck in 1976

Fulvous Whistling-Duck: Name changed to Fulvous Tree Duck in 1976

Galapagos Storm-Petrel: Name changed to Wedge-rumped Storm-Petrel by 1982

Gilded Flicker: Lumped into Common Flicker and split from Northern Flicker in 1995

Gray Catbird: Name changed from Catbird in 1973

Gray-breasted Flycatcher: Name changed to Asian Brown Flycatcher in 1989

Gray-breasted Jay: Name changed from Mexican Jay by 1982, then back to Mexican Jay

Gray-crowned Ground Chat: Name changed to Gray-crowned Yellowthroat by 1982

Gray-crowned Rosy-Finch: Lumped into Rosy Finch in 1976 and split from Rosy Finch in 1993

Gray-crowned Yellowthroat: Name changed from Gray-crowned Ground Chat by 1982

Gray-headed Chickadee: Name changed to Siberian Tit by 1982; changed back to Gray-headed Chickadee in 1998

Gray-headed Junco: Lumped into Dark-eyed Junco in 1976

Great Black-backed Gull: Name changed from Greater Black-backed Gull by 1982

Great Egret: Name changed from Common Egret in 1973

Great Kiskadee: Name changed from Greater Kiskadee by 1982

Great White Heron: Lumped with Great Blue Heron in 1973

Greater Black-backed Gull: Name changed to Great Black-backed Gull by 1982

Greater Flamingo: Name changed from American Flamingo by 1982

Greater Golden-Plover: Name changed to European Golden-Plover in 1995

Greater Kiskadee: Name changed to Great Kiskadee by 1982

Greater Pewee: Name changed from Coues' Flycatcher by 1982

Greater Roadrunner: Name changed from Roadrunner by 1982

Greater Sage-Grouse: Split, with Gunnison Sage Grouse, from Sage Grouse in 2000

Greater White-fronted Goose: Name changed from White-fronted Goose by 1982

Great-tailed Grackle: Split from Boat-tailed Grackle in 1973

Green Heron: Name changed from Green-backed Heron in 1995

Green-backed Heron: Name changed to Green Heron in 1976

Greenshank: Name changed to Common Greenshank by 1982

Ground Dove: Name changed to Common Ground-Dove by 1982

Gunnison Sage-Grouse: Split from Sage Grouse in 2000

Harcourt's Storm Petrel: Name changed to Band-rumped Storm-Petrel by 1982

Harlequin Quail: Name changed from Montezuma Quail by 1973

Harris's Hawk: Name changed from Bay-winged Hawk by 1982

Heloise's Hummingbird: Name changed to Bumblebee Hummingbird by 1982

Herald Petrel: Name changed from South Trinidad Petrel by 1982

Indian Tree Pipit: Name changed to Olive Tree-Pipit by 1982

Ipswich Sparrow: Lumped with Savannah Sparrow in 1973

Island Scrub-Jay: Split from Scrub Jay in 1995

Jack Snipe: Name changed from European Jack Snipe by 1982

Juan Fernandez Petrel: Split from White-necked Petrel in 1991

Juniper Titmouse: Split, with Oak Titmouse, from Plain Titmouse in 1998

Knot: Name changed to Red Knot in 1973

La Sagra's Flycatcher: Split from Stolid Flycatcher by 1982

Least Tern: Split from Little Tern by 1982

Lesser Black Hawk: Name changed to Common Black-Hawk by 1982

Lesser Golden-Plover: Split into American Golden-Plover and Pacific Golden-Plover in 1993

Lesser Goldfinch: Name changed from Dark-backed Goldfinch by 1982

Lichtenstein's Oriole: Name changed to Altamira Oriole by 1982

Little Tern: Split to form Least Tern and Little Tern by 1982

Long-billed Marsh Wren: Name changed to Marsh Wren by 1982

Long-billed Murrelet: Split from Marbled Murrelet in 1998

Long-tailed Duck: Name changed from Oldsquaw in 2000

Louisiana Heron: Name changed to Tricolored Heron by 1982

Magnificent Hummingbird: Name changed from Rivoli's Hummingbird by 1982

Marsh Hawk: Name changed to Northern Harrier by 1982

Marsh Wren: Name changed from Long-billed Marsh Wren by 1982

Masked Booby: Name changed from Blue-faced Booby by 1982

Merlin: Name changed from Pigeon Hawk in 1973

Mexican Crow: Name changed to Tamaulipas Crow in 1998

Mexican Duck: Lumped with Mallard by 1982

Mexican Jay: Name changed to Gray-breasted Jay by 1982, then back to Mexican Jay

Mexican Junco: Name changed to Yellow-eyed Junco by 1982

Montezuma Quail: Name changed from Harlequin Quail in 1973

Mottled Petrel: Name changed from Scaled Petrel by 1982

Myrtle Warbler: Lumped, with Audubon's Warbler, into Yellow-rumped Warbler in 1973

Nelson's Sharp-tailed Sparrow: Split from Sharp-tailed Sparrow in 1995

Neotropic Cormorant: Name changed from Olivaceous Cormorant in 1991

Noddy Tern: Name changed to Brown Noddy by 1982

North American Dipper: Name changed to American Dipper by 1982

North American Jacana: Name changed to Northern Jacana by 1982

Northern Beardless Flycatcher: Name changed to Northern Beardless-Tyrannulet by 1982

Northern Beardless-Tyrannulet: Name changed from Northern Beardless Flycatcher by 1982

Northern Bobwhite: Name changed from Common Bobwhite by 1982

Northern Flicker: Name changed from Common Flicker by 1982

Northern Harrier: Name changed from Marsh Hawk by 1982

Northern Hawk Owl: Name changed from Northern Hawk-Owl in 1989

Northern Hawk-Owl: Name changed to Northern Hawk Owl in 1989

Northern Hobby: Name changed to Eurasian Hobby in 1995

Northern House-Wren: Lumped into House Wren by 1982

Northern Jacana: Name changed from North American Jacana by 1982

Northern Junco: Name changed to Dark-eyed Junco by 1982

Northern Oriole: Lumped from Baltimore Oriole and Bullock's Oriole in 1973; resplit in 1995

Northern Parula: Name changed from Parula Warbler by 1982

Northern Phalarope: Name changed to Red-necked Phalarope by 1982
Northern Pintail: Name changed from Common Pintail by 1982
Northern Raven: Name changed to Common Raven by 1982
Northern Rough-winged Swallow: Split from Rough-winged Swallow by 1982
Northern Saw-whet Owl: Name changed from Saw-whet Owl by 1982
Northern Shoveler: Name changed from Shoveler in 1973
Northern Three-toed Woodpecker: Name changed to Three-toed Woodpecker by 1982
Oak Titmouse: Split, with Juniper Titmouse, from Plain Titmouse in 1998
Oldsquaw: Name changed to Long-tailed Duck in 2000
Olivaceous Cormorant: Name changed to Neotropic Cormorant in 1991
Olivaceous Flycatcher: Name changed to Dusky-capped Flycatcher by 1982
Olive Tree-Pipit: Name changed from Indian Tree Pipit by 1982 to Olivebacked Pipit in 1995
Olive-backed Pipit: Name changed from Olive Tree-Pipit in 1995
Olive-backed Warbler: Name changed to Tropical Parula in 1973
Oregon Junco: Lumped into Dark-eyed Junco in 1973
Oriental Scops-Owl: Name changed, due to split, from Scops Owl by 1982
Pacific Golden-Plover: Split, with American Golden-Plover, from Lesser Golden-Plover in 1993
Pacific Loon: Split from Arctic Loon in 1987
Pacific-slope Flycatcher: Split, with Cordilleran Flycatcher, from Western Flycatcher in 1989
Pallas's Bunting: Name changed from Pallas' Reed-Bunting in 1995
Pallas' Reed-Bunting: Name changed to Pallas' Bunting in 1995
Parula Warbler: Name changed to Northern Parula by 1982
Pauraque: Name changed from Common Pauraque by 1989 and back to Common Pauraque in 1998
Pigeon Hawk: Name changed to Merlin in 1973
Plain Chachalaca: Name changed from Chachalaca by 1982
Plain Titmouse: Split into Oak Titmouse and Juniper Titmouse in 1998
Plumbeous Vireo: Split, with Blue-headed and Cassin's Vireos, from Solitary Vireo in 1998
Poor-will: Name changed to Common Poorwill by 1982
Red Knot: Name changed from Knot in 1973
Red-breasted Sapsucker: Split from Yellow-bellied Sapsucker by 1982
Red-naped Sapsucker: Split from Yellow-bellied Sapsucker in 1987
Red-necked Phalarope: Name changed from Northern Phalarope by 1982
Red-necked Stint: Name changed from Rufous-necked Stint in 1995
Red-shafted Flicker: Lumped, with Yellow-shafted and Gilded Flickers, into Common Flicker in 1973

Reed Bunting: Name changed from Common Reed-Bunting in 1995

Ridgway's Whip-poor-will: Name changed to Buff-collared Nightjar by 1982

Ringed Plover: Name changed to Common Ringed Plover by 1982

Rivoli's Hummingbird: Name changed to Magnificent Hummingbird by 1982

Roadrunner: Name changed to Greater Roadrunner by 1982

Rosy Finch: Split into Gray-crowned Rosy-Finch, Black Rosy-Finch, and Brown-capped Rosy-Finch in 1993, reversing the 1976 lumping of same species

Rough-winged Swallow: Name changed to Northern Rough-winged Swallow due to split with Southern Rough-winged Swallow by 1982

Rufous-backed Robin: Name changed from Rufous-backed Thrush by 1982

Rufous-backed Thrush: Name changed to Rufous-backed Robin by 1982

Rufous-necked Stint: Name changed to Red-necked Stint in 1995

Rufous-sided Towhee: Split into Eastern Towhee and Spotted Towhee in 1995

Sage Grouse: Split into Gunnison Sage-Grouse and Greater Sage-Grouse in 2000

Saltmarsh Sharp-tailed Sparrow: Split from Sharp-tailed Sparrow in 1995

Saw-whet Owl: Name changed to Northern Saw-whet Owl by 1982

Scaled Petrel: Name changed to Mottled Petrel by 1982

Scarlet-headed Oriole: Name changed to Streak-backed Oriole by 1982

Scops Owl: Name changed to Oriental Scops-Owl by 1982

Scrub Jay: Split into Florida Scrub-Jay, Island Scrub-Jay, and Western Scrub-Jay in 1995

Sedge Wren: Name changed from Short-billed Marsh Wren by 1982

Sharp-tailed Sparrow: Split into Saltmarsh Sharp-tailed Sparrow and Nelson's Sharp-tailed Sparrow in 1995

Short-billed Marsh Wren: Name changed to Sedge Wren by 1982

Shoveler: Name changed to Northern Shoveler by 1982

Siberian Chickadee: Name changed to Siberian Tit by 1982, changed to Gray-headed Chickadee in 1998

Siberian Flycatcher: Name changed from Sooty Flycatcher by 1982

Siberian Tit: Name changed to Gray-headed Chickadee in 1998

Sky Lark: Name changed from Eurasian Skylark in 1995

Slate-colored Junco: Lumped into Dark-eyed Junco in 1973

Snail Kite: Name changed from Everglade Kite by 1982

Solitary Vireo: Split into Plumbeous Vireo, Cassin's Vireo, and Blue-headed Vireo in 1998

Sooty Flycatcher: Name changed to Siberian Flycatcher by 1982

South Trinidad Petrel: Name changed to Herald Petrel by 1982

Sparrow Hawk: Name changed to American Kestrel in 1973

Spotted Towhee: Split, with Eastern Towhee, from Rufous-sided Towhee in 1995

Starling: Name changed to European Starling by 1982

Stolid Flycatcher: Name changed to La Sagra's Flycatcher by 1982

Streak-backed Oriole: Name changed from Scarlet-headed Oriole by 1982

Strickland's Woodpecker: Name changed from Arizona or Brown-backed Woodpecker by 1982, back to Arizona Woodpecker in 2000

Stripe-headed Tanager: Name changed to Western Spindalis in 2000

Swallow-tailed Kite: Name changed to American Swallow-tailed Kite by 1982 and back to Swallow-tailed Kite in 1995

Tamaulipas Crow: Name changed from Mexican Crow in 1998

Thin-billed Murre: Name changed to Common Murre by 1982

Three-toed Woodpecker: Name changed from Northern Three-toed Woodpecker by 1982

Traill's Flycatcher: Split into Willow Flycatcher and Alder Flycatcher in 1973

Tree Pipit: Name changed to Brown Tree-Pipit by 1982 and back to Tree Pipit in 1995

Tree Sparrow: Name changed to American Tree Sparrow by 1982

Tricolored Heron: Name changed from Louisiana Heron by 1982

Tropical Parula: Name changed from Olive-backed Warbler in 1973

Tundra Swan: Lumped from Bewick's Swan and Whistling Swan by 1982

Upland Plover: Name changed to Upland Sandpiper in 1973

Upland Sandpiper: Name changed from Upland Plover in 1973

Water Pipit: Name changed to American Pipit

Wedge-rumped Storm-Petrel: Name changed from Galapagos Storm-Petrel by 1982

Western Flycatcher: Split into Pacific-slope Flycatcher and Cordilleran Flycatcher in 1989

Western Pewee: Name changed to Western Wood-Pewee by 1982

Western Screech-Owl: Split, with Eastern Screech-Owl, from Common Screech Owl by 1982

Western Scrub-Jay: Split, with Florida Scrub-Jay and Island Scrub-Jay, from Scrub Jay in 1995

Western Spindalis: Name changed from Stripe-headed Tanager in 2000

Western Wood-Pewee: Name changed from Western Pewee by 1982

Whiskered Screech Owl: Name changed to Whiskered Screech-Owl by 1982

Whiskered Screech-Owl: Name changed from Whiskered Screech Owl by 1982

Whistling Swan: Lumped with Bewick's Swan to form Tundra Swan by 1982

White Pelican: Name changed to American White Pelican by 1982

White-cheeked Pintail: Name changed from Bahama Pintail by 1982

White-fronted Dove: Name changed to White-tipped Dove by 1982

White-fronted Goose: Name changed to Greater White-fronted Goose by 1982

White-necked Raven: Name changed to Chihuahuan Raven by 1982

White-tailed Kite: Lumped with Black-shouldered Kite by 1982 and split again to White-tailed Kite in early 1990s

White-throated Needle-tailed Swift: Name changed to White-throated Needletail by 1982

White-throated Needletail: Name changed from White-throated Needle-tailed Swift by 1982

White-tipped Dove: Name changed from White-fronted Dove by 1982

White-winged Black Tern: Name changed to White-winged Tern by 1982

White-winged Junco: Lumped into Dark-eyed Junco in 1973

White-winged Parakeet: Split from Canary-winged Parakeet in 1998

White-winged Tern: Name changed from White-winged Black Tern by 1982

Wied's Crested Flycatcher: Name changed to Brown-crested Flycatcher by 1982

Wild Turkey: Name changed from Common Turkey by 1982

Willow Flycatcher: Split from Traill's Flycatcher in 1973

Wilson's Snipe: Split from Common Snipe (of the Old World and rarely Alaska) in 2002

Yellow-chevroned Parakeet: Split from Canary-winged Parakeet in 1998

Yellow-eyed Junco: Name changed from Mexican Junco by 1982

Yellow-footed Gull: Split from Western Gull by 1982

Yellow-green Vireo: Lumped with Red-eyed Vireo by 1982 and split from Red-eyed Vireo in 1987

Yellow-rumped Warbler: Lumped from Myrtle Warbler and Audubon's Warbler in 1973

Yellow-shafted Flicker: Lumped, with Red-shafted and Gilded Flickers, into Common Flicker in 1973

State Audubon Societies
and Bird Observatories

Independent State Audubon Societies

Audubon Naturalists Society of the Central Atlantic States, 8940 Jones Mill
Rd., Chevy Chase, MD 20815; 301-652-9188;
www.audubonnaturalist.org

Audubon Society of New Hampshire, Three Silk Farm Rd., Concord, NH
03301; 603-224-9909; www.nhaudubon.org

Audubon Society of Rhode Island, 12 Sanderson Rd., Smithfield, RI 02917;
401-949-5454; www.asri.org

Connecticut Audubon Society, 2325 Burr St., Fairfield, CT 06430; 203-259-
6305; www.ctaudubon.org

Massachusetts Audubon Society, South Great Rd., Lincoln, MA 01773; 781-
259-9500; www.massaudubon.org

New Jersey Audubon Society, 9 Hardscrabble Rd., PO Box 126,
Bernardsville, NJ 07924; 908-204-8998; www.njaudubon.org

State Audubon Societies Affiliated with National Audubon

Audubon of Florida, 444 Brickell Ave., Suite 850, Miami, FL 33131; 305-371-
6399; www.audubonofflorida.org

Maine Audubon, 20 Gilsland Farm Road, Falmouth, ME 04105; 207-781-
2330; www.maineaudubon.org

Michigan Audubon Society, 6011 West St. Joseph Hwy., Suite 403, PO Box
80527, Lansing, MI 48908-0527; 517-886-9144;
www.michiganaudubon.org

North American Bird Observatories

Alaska Bird Observatory, PO Box 80505, Fairbanks, AK 99708; 907-451-7059;
e-mail: birds@alaskabird.org; www.alaskabird.org

Atlantic Bird Observatory, Acadia University, Wolfville, Nova Scotia, Canada
B0P 1X0; 902-585-1313; e-mail: ABO@acadiau.ca

Beaverhill Bird Observatory, Box 1418, Edmonton, Alberta, Canada T5J 2N5; 780-433-5790; www.ualberta.ca/~jduxbury/BBo/bbogage.htm
Big Sur Ornithological Lab, Coast Route, HC 67 Box 99, Monterey, CA 93940; e-mail: BSOLmail@aol.com; www.ventanaws.org/lab.htm
Black Swamp Bird Observatory, 119W. Water St., PO Box 228, Oak Harbor, OH 43449; 419-898-4070; http://oak-harbor.com/bsbo
Braddock Bay Bird Observatory, PO Box 12876, Rochester NY 14612; 716-234-3525; www.bbbo.org
Brier Island Bird Migration Research Station, RR 1, Box 1, Glen Robertson, Ontario, Canada K0B 1H0; 613-874-2449
Cape May Bird Observatory, 600 Route 47 North, Cape May Court House, NJ 08210; 609-861-0700; www.njaudubon.org
Chipper Woods Bird Observatory, 10329 North New Jersey St., Indianapolis, IN 46280; e-mail: chipperwoods@worldnet.att.net; www.wbu.com/chipperwoods
Coastal Virginia Wildlife Observatory, PO Box 111, Franktown, VA 23354; 757-253-6779; e-mail: williamsb@wjcc.k12.va.us; www.cvwo.org
Colorado Bird Observatory, 13401 Piccadilly Rd., Brighton, CO 80601; 303-659-4328; www.cbobirds.org
Cornell Lab of Ornithology Membership Dept., PO Box 11, Ithaca, NY 14851; 800-843-BIRD; www.ornith.cornell.edu
Delta Marsh Bird Observatory, RR 1, Box 1, Portage la Prairie, Manitoba, Canada R1N 3A1; 204-239-4287; www.dmbo.org
Fundy Bird Observatory, 62 Bancroft Point, Grand Manan, New Brunswick, Canada E5G 3C9; 506-662-8650; http://personal.nbnet.ca/gmwhalseabirds.htm
Golden Gate Raptor Observatory, Building 201, Fort Mason, San Francisco, CA 94123; 415-331-0730; e-mail: ggro@ggnpa.org; www.ggro.org
Great Basin Bird Observatory, 443 Marsh Ave., Reno, NV 89509; www.gbbo.org
Gulf Coast Bird Observatory, 103 West Hwy. 332, Lake Jackson, TX 77566; www.gcbo.org
Haldimand Bird Observatory, PO Box 449, Nanticoke, Ontario, Canada N0A 1J0; 519-587-5223; e-mail: miles@kwic.com
Hawk Mountain Sanctuary, 1700 Hawk Mountain Rd., Kempton, PA 19529-9379; 610-756-6660; e-mail: info@hawkmountain.org; www.hawkmountain.org
HawkWatch International; www.hawkwatch.org
Holiday Beach Migration Observatory, e-mail: raptor@webbernet.net; www.wincom.net
Idaho Bird Observatory, Dept. Of Biology, Boise State University, 1910 Uni-

versity Dr., Boise, ID 83709; 208-377-1440;
www.boisestate.edu/biology/ibo

Innis Point Bird Observatory, PO Box 72137, Kanata North RPO, Kanata, Ontario, Canada K2P 2P4; 613-820-8434; e-mail: wfpetrie@magi.com

Institute for Bird Populations, PO Box 1346, Point Reyes Station, CA 94956; 415-663-2052; www.birdpop.org

Kestrel Haven Farm Avian Migration Observatory, 5373 Fitzgerald Rd., Burdette, NY 14818; 607-546-2169; e-mail: khmo@att.net

Last Mountain Bird Observatory, Canadian Wildlife Service, 115 Perimeter Rd., Saskatoon, Saskatchewan, Canada S7N 0X4; 306-975-4091; www.unibase.com/~naturesk/lmbo.htm

Lesser Slave Lake Bird Observatory, PO Box 1076, Slave Lake, Alberta, Canada T0G 2A0; e-mail: birds@1slbo.org; www.1slbo.org

Long Point Bird Observatory, PO Box 160, Port Rowan, Ontario, Canada N0E 1M0; 519-586-3531; e-mail: lpbo@bsc-eco.org; www.bsc-eoc.org/Lpbo.html

Mackenzie Nature Observatory, PO Box 1598, Mackenzie, British Columbia, Canada V0J 2C0; 205-997-2634; e-mail: lambie@uniserve.com

Manomet Center for Conservation Sciences, PO Box 1770, Manomet, MA 02345; 508-224-6521; www.manomet.org

National Eagle Center, PO Box 242, Wabasha, MN 55981; 651-565-4989; e-mail: 4eagles@wabasha.net; www.eaglecenter.org

Point Lepreau Bird Observatory, c/o Saint John Naturalists' Club, 2 Neck Rd., Quispamsis, New Brunswick, Canada E2G 1L3; 506-847-4506; e-mail: jgw@nbnet.nb.ca

Point Reyes Bird Observatory, 4990 Shoreline Hwy., Stinson Beach, CA 94970; e-mail: prbo@prbo.org; www.prbo.org

Prince Edward Point Bird Observatory, PO Box 2, Helhi, Ontario, Canada N4B 2W8; 519-582-4738; http://home.interhop.net/~peptbo

Rio Grande Valley Bird Observatory, PO Box 8125, Welasco, TX 78599; 956-969-2475; e-mail: rgvbo@geocities.com; www.geocities.com/rgvbo

Rocky Point Bird Observatory, 3472 Sunheights Dr., Victoria, British Columbia, Canada V9C 3P7; 250-480-9433; e-mail: goshawk @pacificcoast.net

Rouge River Bird Observatory, Natural Areas Dept., 4901 Evergreen Rd., Dearborn, MI 48128; 313-593-5338; www.rrbo.org

San Francisco Bay Bird Observatory/Coyote Creek Riparian Station, 1290 Hope St., PO Box 247, Alviso, CA 95002-0247, 408-946-6548; e-mail: admin@sfbbo.org; www.sfbbo.org

Southeastern Arizona Bird Observatory, PO Box 5521, Bisbee, AZ 85603-5521; 520-432-1388; e-mail: sabo@SABO.org; www.SABO.org

Thunder Cape Bird Observatory 133 South Hill St., Thunder Bay, Ontario, Canada P7B 3T9; http://tbfn.baynet.net/TCBOtbfn.htm

Toronto Bird Observatory, 307-70 Heath St. W., Toronto, Ontario, Canada M4V 1T4; 416-604-8843; e-mail: nkhsin@netrover.com

George M. Sutton Avian Research Center, PO Box 2007, Bartlesville, OK 74005; 918-336-7778; e-mail: gmsarc@aol.com; www.suttoncenter.org

Whitefish Point Bird Observatory, 16914 North Whitefish Point Rd., Paradise, MI 49768; 906-492-3596; e-mail: warbler@up.net; www.wpbo.org

American Birding Association
Code of Birding Ethics

Everyone who enjoys birds and birding must always respect wildlife, its environment, and the rights of others. In any conflict of interest between birds and birders, the welfare of the birds and their environment comes first.

CODE OF BIRDING ETHICS

1. PROMOTE THE WELFARE OF BIRDS AND THEIR ENVIRONMENT.

   a. Support the protection of important bird habitat.

   b. To avoid stressing birds or exposing them to danger, exercise restraint and caution during observation, photography, sound recording, or filming.

   - Limit the use of recordings and other methods of attracting birds, and never use such methods in heavily birded areas or for attracting any species that is Threatened, Endangered, or Of Special Concern, or is rare in your local area.

   - Keep well back from nests and nesting colonies, roosts, display areas, and important feeding sites. In such sensitive areas, if there is a need for extended observation, photography, filming, or recording, try to use a blind or hide, and take advantage of natural cover.

   - Use artificial light sparingly for filming or photography, especially for close-ups.

   c. Before advertising the presence of a rare bird, evaluate the potential for disturbance to the bird, its surroundings, and other people in the area; and proceed only if access can be controlled, disturbance can be minimized, and permission has been obtained from private land-owners. The sites of rare nesting birds should be divulged only to the proper conservation authorities.

   d. Stay on roads, trails, and paths where they exist; otherwise keep habitat disturbance to a minimum.

2. RESPECT THE LAW AND THE RIGHTS OF OTHERS.
   a. Do not enter private property without the owner's explicit permission.
   b. Follow all laws, rules, and regulations governing use of roads and public areas, both at home and abroad.
   c. Practice common courtesy in contacts with other people. Your exemplary behavior will generate goodwill with birders and non-birders alike.

3. ENSURE THAT FEEDERS, NEST STRUCTURES, AND OTHER ARTIFICIAL BIRD ENVIRONMENTS ARE SAFE.
   a. Keep dispensers, water, and food clean and free of decay or disease. It is important to feed birds continually during harsh weather.
   b. Maintain and clean nest structures regularly.
   c. If you are attracting birds to an area, ensure the birds are not exposed to predation from cats and other domestic animals, or dangers posed by artificial hazards.

4. GROUP BIRDING, WHETHER ORGANIZED OR IMPROMPTU, REQUIRES SPECIAL CARE. *Each individual in the group, in addition to the obligations spelled out in Items #1 and #2, has responsibilities as a Group Member.*
   a. Respect the interests, rights, and skills of fellow birders, as well as those of people participating in other legitimate outdoor activities. Freely share your knowledge and experience, except where code 1(c) applies. Be especially helpful to beginning birders.
   b. If you witness unethical birding behavior, assess the situation and intervene if you think it prudent. When interceding, inform the person(s) of the inappropriate action and attempt, within reason, to have it stopped. If the behavior continues, document it and notify appropriate individuals or organizations.
   GROUP LEADER RESPONSIBILITIES (AMATEUR AND PROFESSIONAL TRIPS AND TOURS)
   c. Be an exemplary ethical role model for the group. Teach through word and example.
   d. Keep groups to a size that limits impact on the environment and does not interfere with others using the same area.
   e. Ensure everyone in the group knows of and practices this code.
   f. Learn and inform the group of any special circumstances applicable to the areas being visited (e.g., no tape recorders allowed).
   g. Acknowledge that professional tour companies bear a special responsibility to place the welfare of birds and the benefits of public knowledge ahead of the company's commercial interests. Ideally,

leaders should keep track of tour sightings, document unusual occurrences, and submit records to appropriate organizations.

Additional copies of the ABA Code of Birding Ethics can be obtained from:

ABA
PO Box 6599
Colorado Springs, CO 80934-6599

800-850-2473 or 719-578-1614;
fax: 800-247-3329 or 719-578-1480;
e-mail: member@aba.org

This ABA Code of Birding Ethics may be reprinted, reproduced, and distributed without restriction.

Glossary

Accidental (sighting) — A bird that is not native to a region and as a result is recorded at intervals spanning several years or more.

Accipiter — One of a group of forest-dwelling hawks that include or specifically target birds as their prey.

Achromatic — The two-element *objective lens* used in most spotted scopes.

Alignment — Refers to the point of focus of a binocular's barrels. Binoculars that are in proper alignment have barrels calibrated to fall on the same point. Binoculars that are out of alignment have barrels that fall on different points, causing a blurred, distorted, or double image.

Alternate plumage, or breeding plumage — The more colorful plumage worn by some birds during the breeding season.

American Birding Association (ABA) — The organization that caters to the information and communication needs of birders living primarily in the United States and Canada.

American Ornithologists' Union (AOU) — The official organization of and for scientists who study birds.

AOU Check-list of North American Birds — The list of all bird species that have been established as occurring in North America (including Mexico, Central America, the West Indies, and Lesser Antilles), according to the acceptance standards set by the American Ornithologists' Union. The latest edition, the seventh, was published in 1998.

Apochromatic — A lens system used in high-end spotting scopes that incorporates three glass elements, bringing all the colors of daylight to the same focus.

Atlas block — In *breeding bird atlases,* a geographic area (roughly nine square miles) that is assigned to an atlas volunteer, who surveys it for breeding birds.

Audubon Society — Originally an association of independent state organizations (beginning with the founding of Massachusetts Audubon in 1896) whose primary focus was bird protection. Since 1942 the name has been used by both the state organizations and the national organization headquartered in New York.

BAK-4 barium crown glass — The superior of the two grades of glass most commonly used in optics, BAK-4 glass features a higher density and less distortion as light passes through it.

Ball up — An expression used by hawk watchers to describe the tight-packed, flocking behavior of birds (most notably starlings and blackbirds) as they harass a bird of prey. Visible from great distances, a flock balling up indicates the presence of a distant *raptor* below.

Basic plumage, or **winter plumage** — The plumage worn by adult birds except, for some species, in the breeding season, when they are replaced by more brightly colored feathers (see *alternate plumage*).

Big Day — A twenty-four-hour challenge in which participants try to record as many different species of birds as possible within a designated geographic area (usually a state or county).

Big Sit — A twenty-four-hour challenge in which participants try to record as many different species of birds as possible from a single, strategic spot.

Big Year — A birding challenge in which participants try to see and record as many different species of birds as possible in a calendar year and within a proscribed geographic area, such as a state or province.

Bill-sweep — A feeding technique employed by many feeder-oriented birds, which use the bill to move aside less desirable seed in order to reach more favored seed types.

Binoculars — Twin-barreled optical instruments that magnify distant objects, making them appear much closer than they really are. Light and portable, binoculars are the primary tool of birding.

Birdathon — A fundraising event in which pledges are sought based on the number of species seen by teams of birders in a *Big Day* kind of competition.

Bird bath — Any vessel containing water that is placed so that birds can drink and bathe.

Bird box — See *nest box.*

Birder — A person who actively pursues birds for the pleasure and challenge.

Bird feeder — Any homemade or commercial structure that dispenses food items to wild birds.

Birdhouse — See *nest box.*

Birding hotspot — Any location that enjoys widespread public acclaim as a place to go and see rare, unusual, or superior numbers of birds. Hotspots may be local or international.

Bird of the year — Also called a *hatching year bird,* any bird born in the current calendar year. A young bird; a juvenile.

Bird sighting hotline — A pretaped and periodically updated telephone message service that notifies birders about and offers directions to uncommon or interesting birds in the region.

Bird sighting sheet, or **ledger** — A sign-in sheet displayed at popular birding areas that is used by birders to report unusual or significant sightings.

Bird watcher — Any person who enjoys watching birds.

BK-7 boro-silicate glass — Not as dense as BAK-4 *glass,* it is less expensive and inferior in quality.

Black flashes — Seen through a binocular when the interpupillary distance or eye relief is not properly adjusted.

Black-oil sunflower seed — A small, black *sunflower seed* that is favored by a diverse number of bird species.

Breeding bird atlases — A three- to five-year data collection effort to map the distribution of breeding birds in the state or province, using hundreds of volunteers.

Breeding Plumage — See *alternate plumage.*

Breeding Species — See *summer residents.*

Broad-front movement — A migration pattern in which birds are dispersed across a wide geographic area.

Brush pile — Any heaped latticework of branches that offers cover and shelter to the birds that frequent your feeders.

Buteo — A group of medium-sized to large soaring hawks. Buteos are mostly open-country birds, and most species are not bird-eating specialists.

Calls or **call note** — Not to be confused with a bird's song, calls are single-note *vocalizations* that can also be used to identify birds.

Canary seed — A small, pale seed used as a *filler* in less expensive seed mixes; it is not favored by most seed-eating birds.

Cavity nesters — Birds that choose to raise their young in the protective confines of a tree cavity. These include woodpeckers, nuthatches, and chickadees, as well as some flycatchers, swallows, wrens, waterfowl, falcons, and owls.

Center focus — A binocular focus mechanism, most often controlled by a wheel, that simultaneously adjusts the images seen in both barrels.

Checklist — A list of the bird species found in a defined geographic area. Checklists may be as large as the ABA checklist (birds of the continental United States and Canada) or as specific as one tailored to the birds found at a particular refuge or park. Most checklists follow the order sequence established by the American Ornithologists' Union.

Christmas Bird Count (CBC) — An annual winter bird survey organized by the National Audubon Society that uses volunteers to establish the number of individuals and species within an established *count circle,* whose diameter is fifteen miles.

Class — The large biological grouping that includes all living things that have in common a fundamental, unifying, and distinguishing characteristic.

In the case of birds, which are in the class Aves, this characteristic is feathers.

Close focus — The near limit at which a binocular or spotting scope can offer a sharp image.

Clutch — The total number of eggs laid by a bird in a single nesting effort.

Cold front — The leading edge of colder air associated with a high pressure weather system. Often associated with squall lines or storms, cold fronts both concentrate migrating birds ahead of areas of bad weather and, in fall, spur birds to migrate following passage of the front.

Common name — The English name that is applied to a bird species and is widely accepted by birders.

Count circle — The geographic area surveyed by volunteers during a *Christmas Bird Count*. The diameter of the circle is fifteen miles.

Count period — The three-week period bracketing December and January during which Christmas Bird Counts are conducted.

County list — A birder's cumulative list of species found in a particular county.

Cracked corn — One of the less desirable *filler* seeds often found in less expensive seed mixes. Grackles and blackbird species are nevertheless partial to it.

Degrees of arc — A unit of measure that describes the linear value of a binocular's field of view.

Depth of field — The distance, measured near to far, at which objects seen through binoculars are in focus. A generous depth of field facilitates finding birds in woodlands; a shallow depth of field makes it difficult to find and hold fast-moving birds.

Dihedral — The term used to describe the uplifted or V-shaped wing configuration characteristic of some soaring birds.

Diseases — Birds, like other creatures, are subject to diseases whose transmission may be facilitated by contact at feeding stations. Rarely do these bird diseases pose a health concern for people.

Distribution — See *normal range*.

Double (and triple) clutch — A reproductive strategy in which birds lay two or more sets of eggs in a breeding season as a way of increasing nesting success.

Drips, drippers — Any elevated container that releases water in droplet form for the purpose of attracting birds.

Drumming — A sound made by the male Ruffed Grouse to attract a mate. Made by rapidly beating the wings, the sound is reminiscent of a rubber ball bouncing to a stop.

Elements — Any of the optical components *(lenses* and *prisms)* that are housed in a binocular or a spotting scope.

Endemic species — A species confined to a specific geographic region — for example, Island Jay is like Scrub Jay but found only on Santa Cruz Island, California.

Epaulets — A shoulder adornment. Most often used to refer to the red shoulder patch of the Red-winged and Tricolored Blackbirds.

Ergonomic design — In binoculars, a shape that follows the contours of the user's hands and eyes.

Exclusionary feeder — A feeder designed to prevent less desirable birds (or animals) from reaching seed or food items.

Exit pupil — The silver dot floating in the *ocular lens* that is the diameter of the shaft of light passing through the instrument. The diameter, measured in millimeters, can be calculated by dividing the diameter of the *objective lens* by the power of the instrument.

Extra-density (ED) glass — Glass that is even heavier and denser than BAK-4 *glass,* resulting in superior light transmission. Known in Europe as *high-density (HD) glass.*

Extralimital species — A bird species found in a place outside its normal range.

Eyecups — The short rubber (sometimes plastic) tubes that lie between the ocular lens and the eye.

Eyepiece — The lens that birders peer through when using a spotting scope. Usually interchangeable, scopes can be fitted with eyepieces of greater or lesser power depending upon the need for *magnification.*

Eye point — The actual point where the image projected through a binocular is focused. Set above the *ocular lens,* a high eye point serves eyeglass-wearers whose eyes are set back behind a plate of glass.

Eye relief — The distance, measured in millimeters, between the ocular lens and the top of the *eyecup.*

Falcon — One of a group of fast, open-country birds of prey that specialize in capturing prey in flight.

Fallout — Usually meteorologically linked and coastal in nature, a phenomenon in which large numbers of migrating birds are forced to land. Fallouts last only a day or two but may involve millions of birds deposited in areas as small as offshore islands or as large as coastlines.

Family — The taxonomic grouping between order and genus that incorporates birds of similar traits.

Fast focus — A binocular focus system that permits users to move quickly from distant to near objects, but at the cost of getting a sharp image without effort. Not recommended for birding.

Field card — See *checklist.*

Field glass — An optical device that is similar to a binocular, whose barrels project two distinct images, not a single image.

Field-glass ornithology— The study of live birds through observation in the field. Made possible with the improvement of optics in the post–Civil War era.

Field guide— A light, portable book that incorporates pictures and descriptive text tailored to help birders identify the birds they encounter in the field.

Field marks— Any characteristic relating to plumage, shape, or parts that can be noted in the field and that helps to distinguish one species from another.

Field of view— That section of the world that can be seen through binoculars or a spotting scope.

Field quality— Refers to the resolving quality and consistency of a binocular image as seen across the entire field.

Filler seed— Any of the less expensive or less desirable seed types *(milo, flax, rapeseed, cracked corn,* and *canary seed)* that companies sometimes include in their mixed birdseed to reduce cost or increase profit.

Flax— One of the filler seed types.

Flight feathers— Those feathers associated with the wing and tail that facilitate a bird's flight. These include primary feathers (primaries), secondaries, tertials, and rectices (tail feathers).

Flush distance or **flush point**— That point at which a bird will no longer tolerate a birder's approach and flies away.

Focus system— The mechanism that controls how optical instruments move the point of focus and maintain a sharp image.

Focus wheel— The preferred mechanism for adjusting a binocular's focus.

Fully multicoated— The application of several thin layers of reflection-reducing coatings to all the glass *elements* of an optical instrument to allow close to 95 percent light transmission through the instrument.

Genus— The taxonomic grouping between family and species that incorporates birds of very similar characteristics.

Good bird— A common expression in birding that signifies a very unusual species or one that birders are eager to see.

Half-hardy species— A species of bird that remains in colder regions of America during the winter months but whose ability to withstand cold is frequently pushed to, and sometimes beyond, its tolerance.

Harriers— A genus of hawks that are slimmer than their hawk cousins and adept at catching small birds and mammals by employing a low, slow, cruising flight.

Hatching year bird— See *bird of the year.*

High-density (HD) glass— See *extra-density glass.*

Hopper feeder— A platform feeder that enjoys the convenience of a food reservoir.

Hummingbird feeder—A specialty feeder that dispenses a sugar-water solution to attract hummingbirds.

Image quality—What birders actually see when looking through an instrument, image quality is the product of optical quality and the stability of the image in the glass.

Important Bird Area (IBA)—An initiative originally developed by BirdLife International in Europe, whose objective is the recognition and designation of all areas deemed vital for bird nesting, migration, and wintering. In the United States the effort is now spearheaded by the National Audubon Society.

Individual eyepiece adjustment—A wheel or knob that changes the focus on just one barrel of a binocular, making it possible to customize optics for the small differences between a binocular user's eyes.

Insectivorous—A bird that eats insects almost exclusively.

Interpupillary distance—The distance between the *ocular lenses* of a binocular and the user's eyes. For the binocular to offer a single, strain-free image, the interpupillary distance must be adjustable to match the interpupillary distance of the user.

Irruptions—Irregular migrations that take place every few years and are associated with seed crop failures or crashes in prey populations.

Irruptive species—A species whose migrations or redistributions are infrequent and unpredictable.

Journal—A diary in which a birder writes detailed accounts of his birding experiences, including species and individuals seen, weather, other birders encountered, habitat, and whatever other personal impressions he wishes to record. Sketches can add detail and charm to journal accounts.

Leading lines—A geographic feature such as a coastline or a mountain ridge, along which hawks (and other birds) orient themselves during migration.

Leaf-bathing—The avian equivalent of sponge-bathing; birds use dew or water droplets on leaves as they would standing water.

Lens—Elliptically shaped piece of glass that magnifies images.

Lens coatings—Thin layers of magnesium fluoride or other chemicals that are baked onto the surface of *lenses* and *prisms* to prevent light from being reflected away as light strikes the glass.

Life bird—A species encountered by a birder for the first time; also known as a lifer.

Life list—The cumulative list of all species seen by a birder since the day he or she started birding.

Listing—Keeping a record of the birds one has seen.

Local patch—The place, usually close to home, that you frequently bird and whose nuances you are familiar with.

Lumping—A taxonomic reinterpretation in which two birds thought to be distinct species are reclassed as one (see *splitting*).

Magnification—The degree to which an object is enlarged when looking through a binocular or spotting scope. The amount of magnification is measured in "powers of magnification."

Marine binoculars—Binoculars whose primary function is aboard ship and whose primary need is the ability to withstand frequent dousing with water.

Mealworms—The larval form of the yellow mealworm beetle, these hard-shelled grubs may be set out to attract non-seed-eating birds like bluebirds and wrens.

Migrant trap—Any geographic feature or vegetative oasis that attracts or concentrates migrating birds, such as a peninsula or a wooded park in an urban setting.

Migration—A biannual redistribution across the surface of the planet, practiced by many bird species.

Millet—Either red or *white proso millet* is one of the favored seed types; it's particularly popular with sparrows and doves.

Milo (sorghum)—A seed type that appeals to doves and some sparrows.

Mini-binoculars—Small, lightweight instruments that are popular among backpackers but unsuitable for birding.

Misters—Water-dispensing devices that spray a fine mist and are particularly attractive to birds in places where water can collect on leaves.

Mixed birdseed—A seed package that combines a variety of seed types in an effort to appeal to a wide variety of birds. They range in quality and appeal.

Mixed flock—In general, any flock that contains more than one species. Usually refers to a wintering flock or a foraging migrant flock that also contains year-round residents.

Mnemonics—In birding, a word pattern rhyme that mimics or recalls the song or call of a species. For example, *teakettle, teakettle, teakettle* is one of the common songs of Carolina Wren.

Mobbing—A defensive reaction in which birds of one or more species gather to drive a predator (or presumed predator) away.

Month list—The cumulative list of all bird species that a birder has encountered in a particular month.

Multilayer coatings—The application of several very thin layers of reflection-reducing coatings to the glass *elements* of an optical instrument.

Natural plantings—A landscaping style that depends on native plant species and a certain amount of "benign neglect" to creat a habitat favorable to bird species.

Neotropical Migrants—A category of birds that nest in the United States and/or Canada but migrate to the neotropics (Latin America and the Caribbean) before the northern winter. These species are, for the most part, synonymous with our temperate woodland birds.

Nest box—An artificial structure built to replicate a natural tree cavity and sized to meet the requirements of different cavity-nesting bird species.

Niger—A tiny, caraway-shaped seed favored by goldfinches, siskins, and redpolls.

Nocturnal flight call—A *vocalization* that nocturnal migrants emit during their flight and also, infrequently, during daylight hours.

Nocturnal migrant—A bird species that migrates primarily or exclusively during hours of darkness.

Normal range—The geographic space that encompasses all of a species' breeding and wintering range.

Objective lens—The lens closest to the object being viewed.

Ocular lens—The lens closest to the user and seated close to the user's eye.

Onomatopoeic—Sounds that phonetically mimic what they describe *(buzz, chip, pish)*.

Order—The taxonomic grouping between *class* and *family* that incorporates birds that share fundamentally similar traits. For example, the family of passerines, the "perching" birds, comprises many different groups of birds, including flycatchers, larks, swallows, warblers, tanagers, and sparrows.

Ornithology—A branch of biological science that specializes in the study of birds.

Passage bird—A bird engaged in its first *migration.*

Passerines—The order of birds that incorporates all "perching" birds. More than half the species found on earth belong to this order.

Peanut feeder—A specialty feeder designed to dispense peanuts or peanut parts.

Peanut kernels—The shelled peanut, whole or halved; this "seed" type is very popular with blue jays and titmice.

Peep—An expression that collectively refers to all small sandpiper species.

Pelagic birding—Looking for any of a diverse group of birds (including shearwaters, petrels, and albatrosses) that spend most of their lives at sea.

Permanent residents—Bird species that are nonmigratory and remain in an area or a habitat type all year. Permanent residents are often common feeder birds, and some form the base of wintering or foraging flocks.

Phase coating (also **phase corrective coating**)—A chemical coating applied to the elements of *roof prism* binoculars to correct a light-wave shift that is inherent in the roof prism design.

Physiographic region — A geographic area distinguished by a common geographic characteristic, such as a coastal plain.

Pishing — An onomatopoeic term used to describe a birder's imitation of the generic alarm or scolding calls of many bird species.

Platform feeder — The simplest bird-feeding structures, platform feeders are flat, open surfaces that support seed.

Porro prism — The "classic" wide-bodied binocular design type that offers superior light transmission but marginally less stability than the *roof prism* design.

Power — See *magnification*.

Prism — One of the glass components found in binoculars and most spotting scopes. Its function is to redirect the shaft of light as it moves through the instrument.

Range — See *normal range*.

Range maps — Graphic depictions that show the summer, winter, and migratory distributions of a bird species.

Range of focus — The number of revolutions required of a focus wheel to move the point of focus from as close as possible to infinity. In binoculars, the ideal range is one full turn.

Rapeseed — One of the *filler seed* types.

Raptors — Birds of prey. These include hawks (diurnal raptors) and owls (nocturnal raptors).

Rare bird committee or **bird records committee** — A review panel, usually associated with a state or provincial organization, that reviews documentation relating to the sighting of rare and uncommon birds and administers the state's or province's species list.

Rarity — Any bird that is not commonly found in an area.

Reflecting scopes — A spotting scope type that uses mirrors to gather light. Reflecting scopes are popular among astronomers but less popular among birders.

Refracting scopes — A spotting scope type that uses prisms and lenses. Slimmer and generally more rugged than reflecting scopes, refractors are the preferred scope among birders.

Relative abundance — A comparative value that measures the prevalence of one species against another — usually as a means of establishing the probability of a bird's occurrence.

Relative brightness — A measure of an instrument's brightness determined by squaring the diameter of the exit pupil.

Relative light efficiency — A measure of instrument brightness that attempts to give numeric weight to coated lenses by taking relative brightness and adding 50 percent of this value.

Resolution — The capacity of a binocular to discern detail.

Review list species—Any species that a records committee has determined to be rare enough to warrant documentation and committee review.

Roof prism—The slim and popular binocular design that offers greater stability and a light-gathering system that can reach parity with the porro prism design, only at greater cost.

Scanning—A method of search in which binoculars are panned across a lake, horizon, or sky.

Scientific name—The Latin (sometimes Greek) binomial that is unique to every species (example: *Turdus migratorius*, the American Robin). Since *common names* are not universally accepted and are therefore open to confusion, a bird's scientific name is the preferred reference among ornithologists.

Seasonal occurrence—A measure of a species' abundance or occurrence as it relates to a particular season.

Shorebirds—Among birders, that group of mostly migratory species that include the sandpipers and plovers.

Shotgun ornithology—A branch of bird study that relies upon collecting bird specimens as a means of gaining intimacy and insight (see *field-glass ornithology*).

Shriking—An archaic term, seldom used, that relates to a bird warning of another bird's approach. Tethered shrikes were once used by falconers to warn them of a hawk's approach.

Soft parts—Inexplicably, the term used to refer to a bird's bill, feet, and legs.

Song—A simple or complex bird vocalization that usually involves two or more notes.

Sonogram—A graphic depiction of bird song that replicates the pattern sounds and pauses by using lines on paper.

Species—The most basic taxonomic grouping. At this level of differentiation, a bird is genetically distinct from all other birds except one of its own kind.

Splitting—A taxonomic reinterpretation in which two forms of a species originally thought to be genetically similar are split into two separate species (see *lumping*).

Spotting scope—A single-barreled, optical aid whose advantage is higher magnification and whose primary function is the study of very distant birds or the detailed study of birds that are difficult to separate from similar species.

Stabilized binoculars—A binocular with an internal mechanism that reduces vibration and the image-distorting effects of hand shake.

State (or provincial) bird list—A birder's cumulative list of species found in a particular state or province.

Striped sunflower seed — A type of birdseed favored by grosbeaks, as well as other species.

Subspecies — A taxonomic level *below* the species level that serves to recognize regional or genetic variation within a species. For example, among Hermit Thrushes *(Catharus guttatus)*, the subspecies common to the East is *Catharus guttatus faxoni;* the larger, grayer, paler *C. g. auduboni* is found throughout most of the West. Another distinct subspecies is *C. guttatus*, a smaller, grayer, flanked form found on the Pacific Coast.

Suet — The fat that surrounds beef kidney. Energy-rich suet is a popular food among woodpeckers and chickadees.

Suet feeder — A rubber or plastic-coated wire-mesh feeder that holds beef *suet.*

Summer residents — Bird species that are native to an area in summer (usually synonymous with *breeding species*).

Sunflower seed — A very popular seed type that is favored by the majority of seed-eating birds. Of the two types, *black-oil* or *striped,* black-oil is the most preferred.

Syrinx — The avian voice box.

Tail-wagging — A behavioral characteristic in which birds pump their tails up and down. This trait can be used to identify species at a distance where other marks cannot be seen.

Taxonomy — The science of grouping and ordering living things.

Taxonomic order of birds — The arrangement of birds according to their physical traits, beginning with the species assessed to be most primitive and concluding with those assessed to be most evolutionarily advanced.

Telescope — See *spotting scope.*

Territory — The geographic area that a bird claims and will defend.

Thermals — Rising columns of air caused by uneven heating of the earth's surface. Thermals are sought by soaring birds, who ride the columns aloft, gaining height with little energy cost.

Thistle feeder — A specialty feeder (actually a modified *tube feeder*) that effectively dispenses the tiny thistle seed.

Thistle sock — A nylon mesh dispenser for thistle seeds.

Tie down — To scout for and establish the location of key birds prior to a *CBC* or *Big Day* with the objective of recording them quickly and without search during the actual event.

Transients — Migrating birds that stop in an area for a while but then continue on their way.

Trip list — A list of species recorded during a day afield.

Tube feeder—A cylindrical feeder that dispenses seed from ports that open on the sides.

Twilight factor—A measure of binocular brightness that gives (with some justice) weight to higher magnification. To calculate, multiply power times diameter of the objective lens and determine the square root of this product.

Understory—The vegetative layer lying between the canopy and the forest floor. Many of the plants in this zone offer food and cover to birds.

Vagrants—Birds with a penchant for wandering great distances from their *normal range*.

Vignetting—Refers to the distracting *black flashes* that binocular users see most often when the *interpupillary distance* or eye relief is not properly adjusted.

Vocalizations—The characteristic sounds of birds.

Warm front—The leading edge of a warm air system moving into a region. Warm fronts promote waves of spring migrants.

Water birds—Broadly speaking, any bird species that is usually associated with ponds, estuaries, or marshes *and* actually stands or swims in water.

Whisper song—A subdued or truncated rendition of the song a bird uses on territory. Whisper songs are sometimes uttered during migration and in winter.

White proso millet—A type of birdseed favored by many sparrow species.

Window kills—The deplorable number of birds killed every year by striking glass. The best and least expensive defense is to use outside screens year-round.

Wing flicking—A behavioral trait common to some species (most notably some flycatchers and kinglets), which "flick" their wings rapidly and then return them to a folded position.

Winnowing—A sound made by snipe during their courtship.

Winter residents—Birds that are common to an area in winter.

Yard list—The cumulative list of all bird species that have occurred in your yard.

Year list—The cumulative list of all bird species that you have encountered in the calendar year.

Zoom binocular/scopes—An instrument whose magnification can be increased or decreased by moving a lever. In binoculars, this feature compromises performance and is generally regarded as the sign of an inferior product, but in some high-quality spotting scopes a zoom eyepiece can be optically precise and, in some situations, very useful.

Bibliography

American Ornithologists' Union Checklist of North American Birds, 7th ed. Lawrence, KS: Allen Press, 1998.

"Bird Observer." *A Birder's Guide to Eastern Massachusetts.* Colorado Springs, CO: American Birding Association, 1994.

Buff, Sheila. *Birding for Beginners.* New York: Lyons & Burford, 1993.

————. *The Birder's Sourcebook.* New York: Lyons & Burford, 1994.

Bull, John, and John Farrand. *The Audubon Society Field Guide to North American Birds, Eastern Region.* New York: Chanticleer Press, 1977.

Chapman, Frank M. *Birds of Eastern North America.* New York: D. Appleton, 1895.

Chartier, Bonnie. *A Birder's Guide to Churchill.* Colorado Springs, CO: American Birding Association, 1994.

Choate, Ernest A. *The Dictionary of American Bird Names.* Rev. ed. Boston: Harvard Common Press, 1985.

Clark, William S., and Brian K. Wheeler. *Hawks.* Boston: Houghton Mifflin, 1987.

Coe, James. *Eastern Birds.* New York: Golden Press, 1994.

Connor, Jack. *The Complete Birder.* Boston: Houghton Mifflin, 1988.

Cronin, Edward W. *Getting Started in Bird Watching.* Boston: Houghton Mifflin, 1986.

Dunn, Jon, et al. *A Field Guide to Warblers.* Boston: Houghton Mifflin, 1997.

Dunne, Peter, David Sibley, and Clay Sutton. *Hawks in Flight.* Boston: Houghton Mifflin, 1989.

Dunne, Peter. *Optics for Birding.* Cranston, RI: Swarovski Optik, 1992.

Ehrlich, Paul R., David S. Dobkin, and Darryl Wheye. *The Birder's Handbook.* New York: Simon & Schuster, 1988.

Farrand, John, Jr. *How to Identify Birds.* New York: McGraw-Hill, 1988.

Forshaw, Joseph, Steve Howell, Terence Lindsey, and Rich Stallcup. *Birding.* New York: Time-Life Books, 1995.

Gill, Frank B. *Ornithology,* 2nd ed. New York: W. H. Freeman and Co., 1995.

Grant, P. J. *Gulls — A Guide to Identification,* 2nd ed. San Diego: Academic Press, 1997.

Griggs, Jack. *All the Birds of North America*. New York: HarperCollins, 1997.

Hale, Alan R. *How to Choose Binoculars*. Redondo Beach, CA: C&A Publishing, 1991.

Harrison, Peter. *Seabirds—An Identification Guide*, 2nd ed. Boston: Houghton Mifflin, 1985.

Hayman, Peter, John Marchant, and Tony Prater. *Shorebirds—An Identification Guide*. Boston: Houghton Mifflin, 1986.

Holt, Harold R. *A Birder's Guide to the Texas Coast*. Colorado Springs, CO: American Birding Association, 1993.

————. *A Birder's Guide to Colorado*. Colorado Springs, CO: American Birding Association, 1997.

Kaufman, Kenn. *Advanced Birding*. Boston: Houghton Mifflin, 1990.

————. *Lives of North American Birds*. Boston: Houghton Mifflin, 1996.

————. *Birds of North America*. Boston: Houghton Mifflin, 2000.

Kerlinger, Paul. *How Birds Migrate*. Mechanicsbuurg, PA: Stackpole Books, 1995.

Leahy, Christopher. *The Birdwatcher's Companion*. New York: Gramercy Books, 1982.

Lockwood, Mark, James Patton, Barry R. Zimmer, and William B. McKinney. *A Birder's Guide to the Rio Grande Valley*. Colorado Springs, CO: American Birding Association, 1994.

Madge, Steven, and Hilary Burns (illustrator). *Waterfowl: An Identification Guide to the Ducks, Geese, and Swans of the World*. Boston: Houghton Mifflin, 1992.

Peterson, Roger T. *A Field Guide to the Birds*. Boston: Houghton Mifflin, 1936.

————. *Eastern Birds*, 4th ed. Boston: Houghton Mifflin, 1980.

————. *Western Birds*, 3rd ed. Boston: Houghton Mifflin, 1990.

Pranty, Bill. *A Birder's Guide to Florida*. Colorado Springs, CO: American Birding Association, 1996.

Reed, Chester A. *Guide to the Land Birds East of the Rockies*. New York: Doubleday, Page & Co., 1909.

Reed, Chester A., Harry F. Harvy, and R. I. Brasher. *Western Bird Guide*. New York: Doubleday, Page & Co., 1913.

Robbins, Chandler S., Bertel Bruun, and Herbert S. Zim. *Birds of North America*. New York: Golden Press, 1966.

Schram, Brad. *A Birder's Guide to Southern California*. Colorado Springs, CO: American Birding Association, 1998.

Scott, Shirley L., ed. *Field Guide to the Birds of North America*. Washington, DC: National Geographic Society, 1983.

Sibley, David. *The Birds of Cape May*, 2nd ed. Cape May, NJ: Cape May Bird Observatory, 1997.

———. *The Sibley Guide to Birds.* New York: Alfred A. Knopf, 2000.

Stokes, Donald, and Lillian Stokes. *The Complete Birdhouse Book.* Boston: Little, Brown, 1990.

———. *Field Guide to Birds, Eastern and Western Regions,* 2 vols. Boston: Little, Brown, 1996.

Taylor, Richard Cachor. *A Birder's Guide to Southeastern Arizona.* Colorado Springs, CO: American Birding Association, 1995.

Thompson, Bill, III. *Bird Watching for Dummies.* Forster City, CA: IDG Books Worldwide, 1997.

Udvardy, Miklos D. F. *The Audubon Society Field Guide to North American Birds, Western Region.* New York: Chanticleer Press, 1977.

West, George. *A Birder's Guide to Alaska.* Colorado Springs, CO: American Birding Association, 2002.

Wetmore, Alexander. *Song and Garden Birds of North America.* Washington, DC: National Geographic Society, 1964.

———. *Water, Prey, and Game Birds of North America.* Washington, DC: National Geographic Society, 1965.

Zim, Herbert S. *Birds.* New York: Simon & Schuster, 1949.

Index

binoculars (*cont.*)
importance of, 39, 43–44, 243
initial setup, 66
lens coatings, 55–57
magnification, 52–54
for pelagic birding, 178–79
prefocusing, 211
protecting against cold, 209–10
protecting against moisture, 60, 207–9
resolution, 60, 63
10×, myths about, 49
testing, 61–64
using, 99–100, 210–11
weight, 50–51
birdathons, 202–3
bird atlas projects, 196–98
bird baths, 32
"BirdChat" (e-mail list), 134–35
Birder's Handbook (Ehrlich, Dobkin, and Wheye), 187
Birder's Sourcebook (Buff), 187
Birder's World magazine, 133
bird feeders. *See* feeders
bird feed stores, as information source, 125
Birdfinder: A Birder's Guide to Planning North American Trips (Cooper), 177–78
bird-finding guides, 177–78
bird identification. *See* identifying birds
birding
and bird watching, 3
popularity of, 3, 39–40, 243
birding CD/ROMs, 85
birding clubs
field trips, 126–29
finding, 125–26, 129–31

Birding by Ear (Walton and Lawson), 163
birding locations. *See* recommended birding locations
Birding magazine, 132
birding organizations, 130–32
birding process
approaching birds properly, 98–99
birding by ear, 107–8, 154–64
choosing a location, 97–98
critical thinking and looking, 80–81, 91–92, 112–15
ethical issues/field etiquette, 233–42
field guides, 89–90
field trips, 85–89, 127–29, 219–20, 238–39
habitats, 93–94
keeping records, 115–20
scanning, 142, 221–22
sharing knowledge and skills, 242–46
what to wear and carry, 85–89
when to go, 96–97
where to go, 93–96
birding publications, 132–34
birding terms, glossary of, 298–310
birding tours, workshops, 136–39, 178–82
bird names, changes in since 1957, 278–88
bird observatories, list of, 289–91
"Bird Show, The" (Cape May, N.J.), 139
bird sighting hotlines, 131–32
bird sighting sheets, 237
Bird Watcher's Digest magazine, 133
birds, feeding. *See* feeding birds

descriptive representations of bird
sounds, 157
design of field guides, 78
Dick E. Bird News (e-mail newsletter), 134
dihedral flight pattern, 106
Diomedeidae (albatrosses), 252
dippers, 270
disease, protecting feeders from, 29
distribution of birds
climatic factors, 225–26
as identification tool, 14–15,
109–10
massed concentrations, 224–25
seasonal fluctuations, 110–11,
223–24
Dobkin, David S., 187
double-clutch breeding, 37
doves, 263
food preferences, 5
shape, 103
dowitchers, 260
vocalizations, 108
Downy Woodpecker, nesting box
requirements, 36
drippers, 32–33
drumming sound, 155
ducks, 254–56
breeding behavior, 38
flight patterns, 106
nesting box requirements, 36
Dunlin, seasonal color changes, 183
Dunn, Jon, 114, 187
Dunne, Pete, 186
dust, checking binoculars for, 65

eagles, 256–57
Eared Quetzal, 87–88
East-Central/Midwest region, bird-attracting plants for, 24–25

Eastern Bluebird, nesting box requirements, 35
Eastern Pewee
behaviors, 105
vocalization, 107
Eastern Phoebe, mannerisms, 105
Eastern Screech-Owl, mimicking
sounds of, 215, 217
ecotourism, 136
ED (extra-density) lenses, 148
Edwards, Scott, 7, 31
egrets, 254
Ehrlich, Paul R., 187
Elegant Trogon, 87
e-mail resources, 134–35
Emanuel, Victor, 138
Emberizidae (sparrows, towhees),
274–75
endemic species, 95
environmental awareness, fostering,
242–46
epaulets as field mark, 104
ergonomic binoculars, 89
ethics
code of, 241–42, 295–97
field behavior, 233–42
etiquette of birding, 98–99, 237–41
European Starling, food
preferences, 6
Evans, Bill, 163
Evening Grosbeak, irruptions, 14
Everglades, Fla., birding in, 167
exclusionary feeders, 9
exit pupil, 55–57
experience, importance of in birding, 114–15
experienced birders, sharing of
knowledge by, 121–25, 246–47
extra-density (ED) lens, 148
extralimital species, 195

Motacillidae (wagtails, pipits), 272
motion, birds' reactions to, 218
Mourning Dove
  food preferences, 5
  shape, 103
multilayer coated lenses, 56–57
murres, murrelets, 262
Muscicapidae (Old World flycatchers), 270
Myiarchus flycatchers, breeding behavior, 38

names of birds, changes in since
  1957, 278–88
National Audubon Society, 130
  Christmas Bird Count, 191–95
  Great Backyard Bird Count, 195
*National Geographic Field Guide to
  the Birds of North America,* 84
natural plantings, 23
neighbors, handling complaints
  from, 30–31
nesting boxes
  desirable qualities, 36–37
  height, 36 (table), 38
  placement, 38
  protecting, 38–39
  size (table), 35–36
  timing of placement, 37
nesting season
  cavity nesters, 34
  taking care during, 233–34
  vocalizations during, 161
networking. *See* resources, information sources; socializing
Nevada, recommended birding sites,
  176–77
New Jersey, recommended birding
  sites, 166

New Jersey Audubon Society,
  289
  World Series of Birding, 202
New Mexico, recommended birding
  sites, 176
niger (thistle) seed, 6, 10–11
nighthawks, nightjars, 264
  flight patterns, 106
nocturnal flight calls, 161, 163, 207
*Nocturnal Flight Calls of Migrating
  Thrushes* (Evans), 163
no-focus binoculars, 52
North American birds checklist,
  251–77
North American Migration Count,
  196
North Carolina, recommended
  birding sites, 175
northeast region, bird-attracting
  plants for, 23
northern border states/Canada,
  bird-attracting plants for, 25
Northern Cardinal
  crashing into glass by, 19
  food preferences, 6, 31
  tips for attracting, 31
Northern Goshawk, irruptions, 15
Northern Harrier, identifying,
  143–44
Northern Oriole, 77
Northern Pygmy-Owl, mimicking
  sounds of, 215
Northern Saw-whet Owl, mimicking sounds of, 218
Northern Shrike, irruptions, 15
northwest region, bird-attracting
  plants for, 26
notebooks for bird songs/vocaliza-
  tions, 157

Pycnonotidae (kinglets), 270

quail, 258

rails, 258
  flight patterns, 106
rain, birding in, 207–9
Rallidae (rails, gallinules, coots), 258
Ramsey Canyon Preserve, Ariz.,
  birding in, 87
range of focus in binoculars, 51–52
ranges of birds
  identification by, 109–10
  maps, 76
  seasonal fluctuations, 110–11
rapeseed, 5
raptors. *See also* hawks
  migrations, 97, 189–91
  spotting of, by other birds, 230–31
rare bird committees, 131
rare birds
  habitats that attract, 229
  identifying, 112, 227–28, 237
  reporting sightings of, 240–41
rats, protecting feeders from, 30
ravens, 269
recommended birding locations
  Alabama/Louisiana coast, 175–76
  Alaska, 171
  Arizona, 87, 170, 176
  California, 170–71
  Canada, 167, 169, 174–75
  Connecticut, 175
  Florida, 167
  Massachusetts, 166
  Michigan, 175
  Nevada, 176–77
  New Jersey, 166
  New Mexico, 176

North Carolina, 175
Texas, 168
Virginia, 175
record keeping
  checklists, 115–16
  journals, 119
  listing software, 117–19
Recurvirostridae (stilts, avocets), 259
Red-breasted Nuthatch, food preferences, 6
Red Crossbill, irruptions, 14
Red-faced Warbler, 33
redpolls
  food preferences, 6
  irruptions, 14
Red-tailed Hawk, habitat, 108
Red-winged Blackbird
  field marks, 104
  food preferences, 6
Reed, Chester, 72
reflecting versus refracting scopes,
  146–47
relative abundance
  identifying birds by, 111–12
  information about, in field
  guides, 77
relative brightness in binoculars, 55
relative light efficiency in binoculars, 55
Remizidae (Verdin), 269
resolution in binoculars, 60
  testing, 63–64
resources, information sources
  birding clubs, 125–29
  birding organizations, 130–32
  birding tours, workshops, 136–39
  experts and teachers, 121–25
  festivals, birding events, 139–40
  publications, 132–34